NARVIK

And the Norwegian Campaign of 1940

CAPTAIN DONALD MACINTYRE
DSO & 2 Bars, DSC, RN

SAPERE BOOKS

NARVIK

Published by Sapere Books.
24 Trafalgar Road, Ilkley, LS29 8HH
United Kingdom

saperebooks.com

Copyright © The Estate of Donald Macintyre, 1959.
First published by Evans Brothers Ltd, 1959.
The Estate of Donald Macintyre has asserted its right to be identified as the author of this work.
All rights reserved.

No part of this publication may be reproduced, stored in any retrieval system, or transmitted, in any form, or by any means, electronic, mechanical, photocopying, recording, or otherwise, without the prior written permission of the publishers.

ISBN: 978-0-85495-379-0.

There will always be a strong tendency to assume that any future war will start where the last one left off. We should learn our lessons from what went wrong at the beginning of the last war, and not from what went right at the end of it.

HRH the Duke of Edinburgh, addressing the cadets at RAF College, Cranwell, July 28th, 1953.

TABLE OF CONTENTS

PREFACE	9
PROLOGUE	11
CHAPTER 1	16
CHAPTER 2	27
CHAPTER 3	39
CHAPTER 4	47
CHAPTER 5	61
CHAPTER 6	72
CHAPTER 7	83
CHAPTER 8	98
CHAPTER 9	110
CHAPTER 10	131
CHAPTER 11	150
CHAPTER 12	167
CHAPTER 13	184
CHAPTER 14	199
CHAPTER 15	216
CHAPTER 16	227
CHAPTER 17	239
CHAPTER 18	258
ACKNOWLEDGMENTS	264
A NOTE TO THE READER	265

PREFACE

The brief, untidy campaign fought along the shores and in the fiords of Norway in the spring of 1940 has received little publicity and is largely forgotten by all but those who took part in it. This is perhaps not surprising as it was so overshadowed by the vaster sweep of events following on the German advance into France which began before the Norwegian episode was over.

It has, however, a special place in history. It was the first campaign in which the three arms, naval, military and air, were employed in co-operation. Lessons of far-reaching consequence for the future conduct of the war were learnt by both sides, particularly in regard to the effectiveness of aircraft.

The Allies learned in pain and sorrow that anti-aircraft guns alone were insufficient defence against the bomber and that fighter cover was essential both for ships and troops. Both sides discovered that warships free to manoeuvre were much more difficult to hit with bombs aimed from a height than had been calculated. Both sides learned that, without adequate defence against the dive bomber, neither fleets nor armies could operate.

Perhaps the most lasting lesson, however, though alas one which democracies seem incapable of absorbing, is the futility of allowing their armed forces to dwindle and wither in time of peace and then throwing them, inadequate in numbers and equipment, into tasks far beyond their capabilities. In Norway, the Royal Navy was crippled and suffered heavy losses owing to the insufficiency and inefficiency of aircraft under its own control and aircraft carriers from which to operate them. The

Army was not trained to operate in the Arctic conditions it encountered and was bereft of any defence against an enemy enjoying complete air supremacy. The Royal Air Force was unable either to provide the necessary fighter defence or effectively to scout for or strike at the enemy's ships.

Most of these shortcomings can be placed at the door of democracy's unwillingness to pay in peacetime for the sinews of war.

For this reason alone the events of that spring of 1940 with all their evidence of unpreparedness, leading to tragic losses and the abandonment of the Norwegian people, are worth while recalling. At the same time, shining out of the sombre picture, are examples of matchless gallantry, signalised by the award of three Victoria Crosses, the first of the war, to men of the Royal Navy. Such deeds can never be too often retold.

PROLOGUE

As the winter of 1939 dragged out its weary course, the menacing shadow of Hitler's Germany brooded over darkened Europe. Like a huge vulture, glutted with the flesh of Poland's carcass, it preened its feathers and pondered on the next victim.

Britain and France, goaded into a war for which neither felt any universal enthusiasm and for which neither had been prepared, seemed passively to await the blow they knew must fall but which they hoped to postpone by avoiding provocation. The French, with a false belief in the impregnability of the Maginot Line, had adopted a defensive attitude of mind which was surely corroding the morale of their fighting forces. Caught in a condition of military weakness which was the inevitable outcome of a decade during which it was still believed that the Kaiser's War had been a 'War to end Wars', followed by a decade in which the Peace Pledge campaign was the outward sign of a rooted unwillingness to pay for defence, the British were belatedly adapting their industry to armaments production.

Meanwhile, the absence of the expected air raids on Allied cities was granting a breathing space which neither of the Allies wished to jeopardise by taking the offensive. Royal Air Force aircraft flew into enemy territory armed with nothing more lethal than pamphlets which had a negligible effect on the will to fight of the German people, their powers of reasoning deadened by the brassy propaganda of their Nazi rulers.

The anticlimactic overture to Armageddon was to be known as the 'phoney war'. Except at sea, indeed, it was 'phoney'.

There, in home waters, warships and merchantmen alike were assailed by mine, torpedo and bomb; further afield merchant ships were being intercepted by disguised commerce raiders and warships, of which the best-known and most successful was the pocket battleship *Graf Spee*.

The realities of the war at sea were briefly brought home to the British people when the *Graf Spee* was at last brought to action in the South Atlantic in December, 1939, by three light cruisers, driven damaged into the neutral part of Montevideo and thereafter scuttled by her commander. The story made a nine-days' wonder in a Britain bored by the blackout, irked by rationing and wartime restrictions and expecting some evidence that the enemy was being injured.

Then events relapsed into their previous leisurely pace. It was a pace agreeable to most of the British and French political leaders. In both countries the Governments, only too conscious of their military unpreparedness, were happy to postpone the moment of combat as long as possible. Their cautious attitude, however, was not left unchallenged. In France, Paul Reynaud was advocating a more active policy, though it was not until he came to power as Premier in March, 1940, that he was able to translate his ideas into action.

In Britain, the First Lord of the Admiralty was Winston Churchill. A defensive 'wait and see' attitude was anathema to him. His questing eye roved over the map seeking points at which sea power could be applied. His combative spirit was roused by the revelation that German merchant ships were able to carry high-grade iron ore, mined in Sweden, from the Norwegian port of Narvik to Germany by a route safe from interception by reason of its being inside neutral Norwegian territorial waters.

This route ran for the greater part of its length inside the myriad offshore islands and skerries of the Norwegian coast, through channels known as The Leads. Only when ships passed south of Stavanger were they forced to head out into the open sea; but from this point they came under the protection of German shore-based aircraft.

Swedish iron ore from the mines of Gaellevare in the far north were of immense, and possibly vital, importance to Germany's armament industry. For five months of the year its normal outlet, the port of Lulea on the Gulf of Bothnia, was ice-bound. Consequently a railway had been laid to the ice-free Norwegian Ofot Fiord at the head of which the port of Narvik had been built.

In October, 1939, a month after the outbreak of war, Churchill was already pressing the Cabinet to let the Navy lay a minefield in The Leads which would force the iron ore ships to seaward where they would be liable to interception by British warships. Refused sanction, Churchill was to return again and again to the subject in the months which followed.

Such action would comprise a clear violation of Norwegian territorial waters, and raised the whole question of the possibility of Norway remaining strictly neutral. So long as she did so, it was unthinkable that the Allies should make any move which would antagonise a country whose people had shown sympathy for the Allied cause in 1914-18 and were doing so again.

So long as the war hung fire elsewhere, eyes began to turn northwards and discussion revolved around the implications of Norway's neutrality. The existence of The Leads seriously weakened the effectiveness of the blockade, the one weapon available to Britain to strike at the enemy at that stage of the war. On the other hand, only by drawing Norway into the war on the Allied side, which would entail occupation by British and French troops for her defence, could this disadvantage be overcome. After a century of unbroken peace, Norway's power to defend herself had been allowed to dwindle.

It is a measure of the complete misunderstanding by the Allied leaders, political and military, of the facts of modern war, and of the overwhelming force of armour and air power which was soon to sweep across Europe when the Germans were ready, that such an idea was seriously considered. That the Allies would have been able to spare the troops and aircraft to hold all Norway — which would probably have entailed defending Sweden also — is a laughable proposition now, but at that time the Allies had much to learn about the business of modern war.

Thus it was that when, on November 30th, Russia, with Germany's acquiescence, suddenly made an unprovoked attack on Finland, causing a wave of sympathy for the Finns to sweep through the Scandinavian people as well as the Allies, a proposal to send volunteers and equipment through Norway and Sweden to the aid of the Finns was wedded to a plan to occupy Narvik and Lulea and the railway between them which constituted the most direct route to Finland. A further small British force was to occupy three ports in Southern Norway — Trondheim, Bergen and Stavanger. All this was to be done in agreement with the Norwegians and Swedes.

A more hare-brained scheme can seldom have been solemnly concerted by the leaders of a country at war. The Swedes and Norwegians, the fate of Poland vividly before them, would have nothing to do with it. A diplomatic wrangle continued through the winter months while British and French military leaders planned hopefully, gradually convincing themselves that, if landings were made, the Norwegians would accept a *fait accompli* and would thereafter co-operate. In this they were encouraged by the advice of Admiral Sir Edward Evans who had a considerable knowledge of Norway and the Norwegians, spoke the language, had a Norwegian wife and had been selected to command the naval forces in the Narvik operation.

The brain behind the project was the same adventurous mind which had conceived the Dardanelles campaign in the First World War, but this time Churchill at least had the support of the Chiefs of Staff who judged the scheme our 'first and best chance of wresting the initiative and... shortening the war'.

CHAPTER 1

Throughout the war, Churchill's roving thoughts turned from time to time to examine the possibilities of a flank attack on Germany through Norway. Similarly, in Germany, Hitler was to develop an obsession that Churchill planned an attack in the north, a mistake which was to have a marked effect on the German conduct of naval operations.

Hitler's attention was first drawn to Norway at the very time Churchill began to urge the mining of The Leads. On October 10th, Grand-Admiral Raeder, Commander-in-Chief of the German Navy, pointed out the great advantages which would accrue from submarine bases established on the Norwegian coast. The seed thus planted in the Fuehrer's mind had fallen on fruitful ground. In his efforts to understand the principles of sea power and naval strategy, he had studied and accepted the conclusions of a well-known book by Vice-Admiral Wolfgang Wegener, *The Sea Strategy of the World War*, published in 1929.

In this book, Wegener had claimed that Germany had made a fatal mistake in not occupying Norway during the First World War. Re-stating the principle — often forgotten even by maritime nations — that the prime function of a navy in war is the defence of its own mercantile shipping on the ocean routes, he criticised the acceptance by the High Seas Fleet of its restriction to the southern half of the North Sea, allowing the British to impose an impenetrable blockade line across the short sea area between Scotland and Norway.

Thus when, on December 8th, Raeder again brought up the subject and stated categorically that Norway should be occupied, he found a willing listener in the Fuehrer. At this moment a further weapon came to strengthen Raeder's hand in the shape of a report by Rosenberg, the Nazi 'expert' on Fifth Columns, that Vidkung Quisling, leader of the tiny National Union party in Norway, was ready and able to ensure a peaceful occupation of his country. Not for the first or last time, Rosenberg proved an unreliable counsellor. Quisling's following being in reality almost negligible.

An interview with Quisling did not convince Raeder of the likelihood of a peaceful occupation with the aid of his Fifth Column; but Quisling's information as to British negotiations with Hambro, President of the Storthing, raised the possibility of the Allies forestalling the Germans, with aid to the Finns the ostensible pretext.

This could on no account be allowed. Bringing Quisling before Hitler, Raeder had no difficulty in persuading the Fuehrer that the time had come to prepare for action in Norway. Though alternative plans were to be prepared either for a peaceful occupation with the connivance of Quisling and his followers or by open assault against opposition by the Norwegians and the Allies, the former was not seriously considered, Quisling being kept in the dark until the last moment.

So, in the two opposing camps plans were begun each having the same object — the occupation of Norway to deny it to the enemy. From a preliminary study of the problems involved, German preparations were transformed on January 27th, 1940 into detailed planning. 'Weserübung' was the name given to the proposed operation but no date was as yet fixed for it. In Britain, the scheme for landing at Narvik and three other points was approved on February 5th and was timed to take place by the middle of March.

But whereas German plans and preparations were made with the meticulous detailed care which was the hall-mark of the German staff officer and were based on the sensible assumption that the assault would be opposed, the British plan, in spite of months of consideration, wore an air of amateurish improvisation. Intelligence on the coast fortifications was scanty, maps were few, knowledge of the terrain and the likely climatic conditions, very sketchy. Relying on Admiral Evans' optimistic report that the Norwegians so loathed the Germans that they would not oppose us, the force was to depend upon the Norwegians for mechanised transport and artillery support.

This sanguine view continued to be held even after the incident of the *Altmark* had shown that the Norwegian Government was more anxious to avoid offending Germany than to insist strictly on their neutral rights. Prior to the Battle of the River Plate which had brought his career to an end, the captain of the *Graf Spee* had placed aboard the *Altmark* 299 merchant navy prisoners from the ships he had sunk, for passage to Germany as prisoners-of-war.

On February 14th the supply ship, evading British patrols in storm and low visibility, arrived off Bergen and entered Norwegian territorial waters. There by international law the prisoners should have been released. Though informed by the British Government that prisoners were aboard, the Norwegians accepted the German captain's denial and failed to make any serious search of the ship. Furthermore, from that time onwards the *Altmark* was given escort by Norwegian torpedo-boats as she sailed southwards inside territorial waters.

On instructions drafted by the First Lord of the Admiralty himself, the *Altmark* was intercepted by a force of British destroyers on February 16th and, when she took refuge in a narrow fiord, the destroyer *Cossack* was taken in after her. In spite of protests by the Norwegian torpedo boats and a threat to use force to prevent her, *Cossack* was put alongside the German ship and a boarding party released the prisoners.

The inability or unwillingness of the Norwegians to maintain their neutral rights against German infringement, as compared to their armed intervention to prevent an equally plain but more justifiable infringement by the British, stiffened the British Government in their determination that such a state of affairs could not be allowed to go on indefinitely. Immediate action against the iron ore traffic was again mooted but was at the last moment shelved in favour of the more extensive landing operation timed for less than a month ahead.

The same incident was taken by the Germans as a clear warning that the British would only respect Norwegian neutrality so long as it suited them. It lent colour to Quisling's tales of an impending Allied occupation of Norway, a move which must be forestalled. Five days later, planning for a possible assault on Norway was transformed into active preparation for an approved operation by the appointment of a commander for the troops involved — General von Falkenhorst.

Yet it was at this very time that Raeder and the Naval Staff were modifying their earlier categorical advice that an occupation of Norway was essential. Further consideration had convinced them that the operation would involve them in action with the British Fleet for which they were not ready and that defence of the long Norwegian coast could not be guaranteed. At the same time the German Naval Staff with a clearer sense of reality than the British Chiefs of Staff were 'doubtful whether Britain had sufficient forces available for the occupation of Norway and for countering the ensuing German threat'.

So when Raeder attended a conference with the Fuehrer on February 23rd, he 'hedged' in his advice so far as to say that for the maintenance of the ore traffic it would be best if Norwegian neutrality could be maintained. Germany must be ready to counter any British descent on Norway, but it was not believed that such a move was likely.

In the first days of March came firmer indications that an Allied landing might be imminent. The Finnish Government was exhorting its people to stand fast as outside help was on its way. Article XVI of the Covenant of the League of Nations was being referred to by the Allies. Under this Article the right of transit might be claimed for troops to go to the aid of a victim of aggression.

On March 4th, therefore, orders went out that preparations for Weserübung were to be pressed ahead so that by March 10th only four days' notice would be required to launch it.

Raeder fell into line and, at a conference on the 9th, agreed that the occupation of Norway had become a matter of urgency to forestall the British. At the same time consideration of the risks for the German Navy led him, somewhat belatedly, to warn Hitler of them in some detail.

This was a wise precaution when in the service of an autocrat, no doubt. Raeder was 'clearing his own yardarm', in naval parlance. At the same time his warnings were well founded. Raeder was a sound strategist.

'The operation in itself,' he said, 'is contrary to all principles in the theory of naval warfare. According to this theory, it could be carried out by us only if we had naval supremacy. We do *not* have this; on the contrary we are carrying out the operation in face of the vastly superior British Fleet. In spite of this, provided surprise is complete, our troops can and will successfully be transported to Norway.'

The converse was presumably assumed to be true. If surprise was lost the British Navy could intercept and annihilate the assault forces. As we shall see, German intentions were exposed early in the proceedings but failure to interpret correctly the information gained and to act with speed and vigour lost the British their opportunity.

Raeder continued, 'The most difficult operation for the ships is the return voyage, which entails breaking through the British naval forces.' Nothing could save them from that ordeal. That there might be heavy losses was appreciated and accepted though whether on such a scale as in fact occurred is perhaps doubtful.

While the Germans were thus approaching the point of no return, in Britain all was still in doubt. Though troops for the landing operation in aid of the Finns had been gathered and made ready, with a naval commander — Admiral Evans — and a commanding general — General Mackesy — designated, no approval or instructions had been issued by the War Cabinet. On March 12th at a meeting at No 10 Downing Street, Evans expounded his views that a bold descent on the chosen landing points in Norway would be welcomed by the Norwegians or at worst would meet only token resistance.

Though the Prime Minister, Neville Chamberlain, obviously disliked the whole idea, he was sufficiently won over to authorise final preparations and the issue of instructions to the Force Commander who was told, 'It is the intention of HM Government that your force should land provided it can do so without serious fighting.'

By this time, however, it was known that the Finns had been negotiating with the Russians for the last three days for armistice terms. The Cabinet meeting at which plans for the

British operation were approved had not long ended when news was received that the Finns had surrendered. The pretext under which the Allied troops might have landed with some show of legality had evaporated.

The British Cabinet at once withdrew their approval. The troops were stood down. The only formation trained as skiers, a battalion of the Scots Guards, was disbanded. Scruples against too flagrant a violation of neutrality — which bothered Nazi Germany not at all — brought all movements to a standstill for a time.

Winston Churchill, however, at once began pressing again for his long-desired minelaying operation. When Paul Reynaud came to power in France on March 21st, support arrived from that quarter. The Supreme War Council at last decided in favour of the plan. Norway and Sweden were to be warned that their interpretation of their neutral rights operated to the advantage of Germany. The Allies could no longer tolerate this. As champions of the freedom and independence of small nations against totalitarian aggression they claimed the right to take appropriate action of which no warning would be given.

Such was the justification for mining The Leads. Though the operation was dubbed 'Wilfred' by Churchill because it was 'minor and innocent', the Allies had no doubt that it would provoke immediate retaliation by the Germans and that the unfortunate Norwegians would be their target. A military expedition was therefore once again assembled which would be ready to go to Norway's aid.

By this plan, designated 'R4', troops for Stavanger and Bergen, two battalions for each, would sail in four cruisers. A further battalion for Trondheim would arrive two days later in a transport. For Narvik there would be one battalion in a transport, accompanied by two cruisers. This force would be increased to a Brigade in the days following the initial landing and with the addition of French troops would finally total 18,000 men.

Lying ready for sea at Rosyth there was to be the Second Cruiser Squadron under Vice-Admiral Edward-Collins, its orders being 'to deal with any seaborne expedition the Germans may send against Norway'. Only when 'the Germans set foot on Norwegian soil or there is clear evidence that they intend to do so' would the military expedition sail.

This inability of the Allies to act with the ruthlessness of total war, however laudable in principle, was to prove a fatal obstacle in the way of success. Yet it might not have been so had a last-minute postponement not altered the date for 'Wilfred' from April 5th to the 8th. In the race for Norway the loss of these three days was to take the lead from the Allies and give it to the Germans — by a few hours only, but they were to be crucial.

In Germany, the ability at that time to decipher a proportion of British signals had betrayed the fact that preparations had been in train for a landing in Norway but had been postponed when the collapse of Finnish resistance removed the pretext. On March 26th, Raeder gave his opinion that the danger of a British landing was no longer acute but that the British would take steps to cut off German imports from Narvik, penetrating Norwegian territorial waters to do so and causing incidents which might give a pretext to invade Norway.

Raeder was not far out in his estimate; but he was unable to appreciate the scruples which held the Allies back from being the first to put troops into a neutral country. He went on to say, therefore, that sooner or later Germany would be faced with the necessity of carrying out Operation Weserübung.

Therefore the sooner it was done the better. Days were getting longer, increasing the dangers of interception of the assault forces by the British Navy. Dark nights of the new moon period were ideal for the operation, and some time between April 7th and 15th was recommended.

On April 1st the die was cast. Hitler signed the order, naming 5.15 am on April 9th as Zero Hour for the assault. Between the morning of the 7th and early on the following day the entire German surface fleet fit for action would sail in six separate groups from their Home Ports at times calculated to enable them to reach their allotted assault points simultaneously. Transports carrying additional troops, vehicles, horses, stores and ammunition would have sailed earlier so as to arrive on the same day. Others, innocent-seeming merchantmen, would already be lying at anchor in Narvik, Trondheim and Stavanger, with troops concealed in their holds awaiting the arrival of the warships.

The organisation of the assault groups was as follows:

> *Group I* for Narvik. — Ten destroyers under Commodore Bonte, carrying 2000 troops, supported by the battle-cruisers *Scharnhorst* and *Gneisenau* which would make a diversionary cruise in the Arctic after escorting the destroyers to Vestfiord.
>
> *Group II* for Trondheim. — Heavy cruiser *Hipper* and four destroyers carrying 1700 troops.
>
> These two groups were to sail in company, commanded by Vice-Admiral Lütjens, his flag in the *Gneisenau*.
>
> *Group III* for Bergen. — The light cruisers *Köln* and *Königsberg*, the old training cruiser *Bremse* and a number of small craft, carrying altogether 1900 troops.
>
> *Group IV* for Kristiansand and Arendal. — The light cruiser *Karlsruhe*, three torpedo boats, a flotilla of MTB.s and their parent ship *Tsingtau*.

Group V for Oslo. — The heavy cruiser *Blücher*, the pocket battleship *Lützow*, the fight cruiser *Emden* and some smaller craft, carrying 2000 troops.

Group VI for Egersund. — Four minesweepers taking 150 men to occupy the Cable Station.

The transports for the initial assaults were similarly organised in groups though they were to sail singly and inconspicuously. In the role of Trojan Horses, seven ships would leave Hamburg well in advance, joining the normal traffic to Murmansk, but remaining in wait at Narvik, Trondheim and Stavanger.

Another fifteen merchantmen would carry 3761 troops, 672 horses, 1377 vehicles and 5935 tons of Army stores, divided among the various ports. Finally there was the all-important question of oil fuel for the destroyers, particularly those at Narvik, which could not carry sufficient for the return voyage. Two tankers *Kattegat* and *Skagerrak* from Wilhelmshaven would make for Narvik and Trondheim respectively. Another, the *Jan Wellen*, would leave Murmansk for Narvik.[1]

The whole plan was a model of Teutonic thoroughness and care. As Raeder had said, provided secrecy and surprise were achieved it should succeed, at least so far as delivering the troops to their assault points.

Even as the first assault group slipped out of Wilhemshaven and steered north, British troops for Narvik and Trondheim were filing aboard transports in the Clyde where Admiral Evans had hoisted his flag in the cruiser *Aurora*. Others for Bergen and Stavanger were aboard the ships of the First Cruiser Squadron, *Devonshire*, *Berwick*, *York* and *Glasgow* at

---

[1] At the same time three Groups were to land troops at Copenhagen and two other ports for the occupation of Denmark.

Rosyth. Far to the north four destroyers were thrusting through heavy seas and snowstorms towards the Vestfiord at the entrance to which they were to lay their mines. In support of them were the battle-cruiser *Renown* and eight destroyers. Further south the minelayer *Teviot Bank* and four destroyers were heading for an area off Stadtlandet.

It might seem that the Fates were setting the stage for a head-on clash as the forces of each side converged on the same chosen areas, ignorant of the other's movements. The facts were to prove far otherwise.

CHAPTER 2

Grand-Admiral Raeder had laid it down that secrecy and surprise were an essential element if Operation Weserübung was to be successful. His sound strategic sense told him that otherwise those sections of his fleet committed to operation in the North Sea would find themselves brought to action by superior British forces. His ships would not only be outnumbered but, crowded with troops, many of them would be in no shape to fight an action.

Secrecy was not in fact ever fully maintained. During the first week of April a steady stream of reports reached the Admiralty of a concentration of shipping in Baltic ports and the Heligoland Bight. RAF bombers on leaflet raids had noted unusual activity and lights near German ports. On April 4th air reconnaissance discovered *Scharnhorst* and *Gneisenau* at anchor in Wilhemshaven Roads. On the 6th a neutral Minister in Copenhagen supplied the information that a division contained in ten ships was scheduled to land at Narvik two days later.

Unfortunately the 'war of nerves' which had been going on through the winter months had released a flood of rumours about impending German moves. A proportion of them had foretold imminent invasion of Norway. Thus even the steadily accumulating evidence of preparations for Weserübung was examined with unshaken scepticism. The report from Copenhagen received on the 6th was passed to the Commander-in-Chief, Home Fleet on the following day but its value was destroyed by the comment, 'All these reports are of doubtful value and may well be only a further move in the war of nerves'.

Taken in conjunction with a report reaching the Commander-in-Chief a few hours earlier from RAF reconnaissance aircraft which had sighted the German Groups I and II steering northwards near the Horn's Reef, it is fair to say that the secrecy Raeder had hoped for had been destroyed. Had the intelligence in possession of the British at midday on the 7th been correctly interpreted and evaluated and the fleet taken to sea at once, Group II of the German expedition at least might well have been brought to action before reaching its objective. Had the cruisers available at Rosyth been ordered to cover the important port of Bergen, Group III would similarly have been intercepted by a superior force. As it was, the news that a force of heavy bombers had taken off to attack the German Squadron and a confusing air report that three German destroyers had been sighted steering south — returning perhaps from some minor operation, it was thought — led the Commander-in-Chief to delay sailing, though he brought the fleet to one hour's notice for steam.

The bomber force failed to do any damage to the enemy. What was more important, they failed to get the vital information through, until their return to base nearly four hours later, that the enemy force had been found off the Skagerrak, still steering north, in a position seventy-eight miles further north than when last reported.

On receipt of this, at 5.27 on the evening of April 7th, Sir Charles Forbes at last gave the order to raise steam, the fleet clearing harbour at 8.15 and shaping course to the northeastward at high speed. At the same time Vice-Admiral Sir G. F. Edward-Collins' Second Cruiser Squadron, *Galatea*, *Arethusa* and eleven destroyers, were ordered to sea from Rosyth to a position some eighty miles west of Stavanger, aiming to arrive there at 5 pm on the 8th and then sweep northwards.

As through the dark night of April 7th ships of both sides steamed through a rising westerly gale to their various assigned destinations or rendezvous, let us pause briefly to list their positions and courses at midnight.

Of the German forces, Groups I and II were making northwards at high speed up the Norwegian coast and had reached the latitude of Stadtlandet. Group III was about to leave Wilhelmshaven for Bergen. Groups IV and VI were making final preparations at Cuxhaven and Group V at Kiel. All would sail for their destinations before dawn.

The transports were all on their way but their schedule was already being upset by delays which, taken in conjunction with calamities which were to befall many of them later, were to nullify the German plan for early reinforcement of their assault groups. The seven ships intended to act as Trojan Horses were particularly unfortunate. Some were considerably delayed at the entrance to The Leads where the Norwegian pilot station could not provide sufficient pilots. As a consequence none arrived off their destinations until after the first landings had raised the alarm and alerted the Norwegians. All but one, the smallest for Trondheim, were captured or sunk by British or Norwegian forces as will be related later.

Even more serious was the failure of two out of the three tankers to arrive. Only the *Jan Wellen* from Murmansk reached her destination.

So much for the German naval forces. On the British side, as we have seen, the Commander-in-Chief was to the eastward of the Shetland Islands steering north-east, his principal object being to place himself so as to prevent a breakout into the

Atlantic by the German surface ships. Besides his flagship, *Rodney*, he had with him the battleship *Valiant*, the battlecruiser *Repulse*, the cruisers *Sheffield* and *Penelope* and ten destroyers. The Second Cruiser Squadron and eleven destroyers were making for the position off Stavanger whence they were to sweep northwards.

The four cruisers of the First Cruiser Squadron under Vice-Admiral John Cunningham lay at Rosyth, their troops aboard, awaiting orders to sail with them for Stavanger and Bergen. Off the Shetlands, two ships of Vice-Admiral Layton's Eighteenth Cruiser Squadron, *Manchester* and *Southampton*, were still accompanying a convoy which had been bound for Norway but which had been turned back at the first alarm.

Far to the north, in his flagship *Renown*, Admiral Whitworth had arrived off the entrance to the Vestfiord with his force, and had detached the four minelaying destroyers of the Twentieth Flotilla under Captain Bickford who were to carry out their task at daylight on the following morning. Alone in the storm and thick weather, the destroyer *Glowworm* of Whitworth's force, which had fallen behind through searching for a man swept overboard, was to the westward of Trondheim, making what speed she could to rejoin. Unknown to Lieutenant-Commander Roope, her captain, her course was taking her to a fatal rendezvous with the German force for Narvik.

From the bridges of all the ships at sea that wild morning of April 8th, dawn revealed an empty storm-tossed sea with visibility only a few miles. In the *Glowworm* the ship's company were about to be stood down from the customary dawn action stations to get what breakfast they could in the lurching wetness of their mess decks when there came a cry from a lookout. Out of the smother to leeward the dim shape of a destroyer had loomed. A brief scrutiny identified it as German. The *Glowworm*'s ship's company swung into action at once. The first shots of the Norwegian campaign flashed out.

The enemy ship at once turned away and by the time two salvoes from the *Glowworm*'s 4.7-inch guns had been hurled at her, she had vanished in the mist. But then a second destroyer came in sight and fire was shifted on to this new target. The wild rolling of the ship, the seas tumbling along the decks and the spray flying up to blur telescopes and binoculars made shooting difficult. It was accurate enough, however, to set both ships manoeuvring at high speed to avoid being hit. The German destroyer, *Bernd von Arnim*, more heavily armed than the *Glowworm*, and for that reason less seaworthy, plunged and rolled so wildly that her superstructure was damaged and she narrowly escaped capsizing. She called for help and the *Hipper* was soon heading to intervene.

Running into sight of the *Glowworm* at short range out of the mist her 8-inch guns thundered out and were quickly scoring devastating hits on her little opponent.

The *Glowworm* turned to escape, for her first and most important duty was the transmission of reports of the enemy being sought so urgently by the whole British fleet. By the time her first message had been acknowledged, the destroyer had been heavily damaged. Escape was impossible. At bay she turned towards the *Hipper*. In spite of shell hits which were rapidly reducing her to a wreck she ran in to a close range before swinging round to bring her torpedo tubes to bear and loosing a salvo of torpedoes. It was a forlorn hope. The German cruiser was able to swerve parallel to the tracks of the torpedoes which sped harmlessly by.

Meanwhile, from the funnels of the destroyer, black, oily smoke poured, making a screen behind which she was able momentarily to escape the storm of shell. The *Hipper* plunged in only to find, as she emerged beyond it, that Roope, knowing his ship was doomed, was steering in a last desperate effort to damage his opponent by ramming her.

In the gale and heavy seas the *Hipper* answered her helm but sluggishly. She could not escape the *Glowworm*'s last, fierce rush. The destroyer's bow crashed against the cruiser's side just abaft her starboard anchor; then, grinding her way down the *Hipper*'s hull, she tore away 130 feet of the cruiser's armoured belt, and wrenched her starboard torpedo tubes from their mounting.

The dauntless destroyer had shot her bolt. She sheered off and lay burning furiously and wallowing in the rough sea, the *Hipper*'s guns silent, forbearing to torment further so gallant a foe. Shortly after 9 o'clock, the *Glowworm* blew up and sank, leaving only thirty-eight survivors to be picked up by the enemy. Lieutenant-Commander Roope was among those who reached the *Hipper*'s side, but as he was being hauled aboard and had almost reached the deck, he suddenly let go the rope and fell back exhausted to be drowned. When the details of his gallant last fight were learnt he was posthumously awarded the Victoria Cross.

The damage to the *Hipper* was not enough to put her out of action. At noon that day, April 8th, she and the destroyers for Trondheim parted company with Group I which held on northwards for Narvik. The *Glowworm*'s signals had been taken in by the Commander-in-Chief and Admiral Whitworth. The former detached the *Repulse*, *Penelope* and four destroyers to try to make contact with the enemy, while Whitworth took the *Renown* southwards to intercept him.

The chances were slim of either force finding the enemy in that weather, so that when the Admiralty took the unusual step of ordering, over the head of the senior officer on the spot, the four minelaying destroyers and their four escorts to join him, Admiral Whitworth turned back north to facilitate a rendezvous off Vestfiord. A further message from the Admiralty to the Commander-in-Chief at this time made this move doubly wise. At last some credence was being given to the accumulated evidence of the last few days as to the Germans' intentions. The previous day's report might well be true that a German expedition was heading for Narvik.

By this time, Admiral Forbes has said, he was convinced in his own mind that a German attack on Norway had started. It is strange, therefore, that instead of hauling off on a course for the entrance to the key port of Trondheim which he could have reached in good time to intercept the *Hipper* and her destroyers, he continued north-easterly, far out to seaward, where he would be unlikely to meet an invasion force. Similarly, the Second Cruiser Squadron could have been ordered to a position close in to the coast where they would have intercepted the group making for the equally important port of Bergen.

Yet even now, when conclusive evidence reached the Admiralty early in the afternoon that an invasion of Norway by the Germans was in progress, it was not passed to the Commander-in-Chief until 10.55 pm.

On patrol in the Skagerrak, the Polish submarine *Orzel* at midday had surfaced to challenge a large steamer heading northwards. Its identity as the German transport *Rio de Janeiro* was quickly established, the crew and passengers given time to take to the boats before a torpedo sent the ship to the bottom. As the *Orzel* slid below the surface again, a Norwegian destroyer and fishing boats arrived to pick up the men in the crowded lifeboats. To their astonishment and alarm, the

Norwegians discovered that many of them were German soldiers in uniform who made no bones about announcing that they were on their way, with guns and transport, to 'protect' Bergen.

Notwithstanding this clear evidence which was made public by Reuter's that evening, no appreciation of the true facts of the situation was made either by the Norwegian Government or by the British Admiralty. The former refused to believe it and took no steps for a time even to alert the coast defences. Mobilisation had not yet been considered at all.

In Whitehall, preoccupation with the possibility that the enemy naval squadron might be heading for a breakout into the Atlantic was distracting attention from this significant piece of intelligence. Thus Admiral Forbes was still not in possession of it when a brief sighting of an enemy naval formation was passed to him by a patrolling flying-boat at 2 pm. Before being driven off and damaged by anti-aircraft fire, this aircraft had seen, some 180 miles ahead of the Home Fleet flagship, a force which was thought to consist of a battle-cruiser, two cruisers and two destroyers. It was steering west.

It was a piece of singular ill-luck for Admiral Forbes that the enemy squadron, which was, in fact, the *Hipper* and her four destroyers, was sighted on this one occasion only, when, to adjust its time of arrival off Trondheim, it was heading seaward. Still with no sure information that a descent on Norway was the German objective, he not unnaturally turned north-westward on to an interception course while he awaited further news from a second flying boat and the *Rodney*'s aircraft, catapulted off to search — news which never came.

The absence of aircraft carriers with the fleet was a crucial handicap, not for the last time during the war. Of the handful of these vitally important elements of a fleet with which the

British had begun the war, the *Courageous* had been sunk, the *Ark Royal* and *Glorious* were in the Mediterranean for essential training. The *Furious*, the only one in Home waters, was in the Clyde not yet fully operationally fit.

It would seem that the Commander-in-Chief feared to back his own judgment at this stage, for so certain was he that an invasion had started that he personally briefed the pilot of the *Rodney*'s aircraft, the weather being too rough for it to be recovered at sea, that he was to break off his reconnaissance with enough fuel remaining to land in Norwegian waters. There he was to give himself up, but would undoubtedly be free the next day as Germany was going to war with Norway.

Yet Admiral Forbes kept the fleet on a course to the northwest to intercept the enemy squadron, assuming it to be steering west as reported. While this fruitless search proceeded, news was pouring in to the fleet flagship. Early in the afternoon, the Admiralty gave the Commander-in-Chief information which showed that Plan R4 had been incontinently abandoned. The First Cruiser Squadron had been ordered to disembark their troops and get to sea as soon as possible. They would leave Rosyth at 2 pm and head north.

The *Aurora* would haul down the flag of Admiral Sir Edward Evans and, with the destroyers in the Clyde, go north to Scapa. The minelayer *Teviot Bank* had been recalled. Her escort of four destroyers was put at the Commander-in-Chief's disposal, together with the Eighteenth Cruiser Squadron.

The abandonment of R4 was a great surprise to Admiral Forbes. The very situation had arisen for which it had been devised. Had Cunningham's cruisers been sent at once on their mission, they could have got to Stavanger before the Germans and their troops could have seized the airfield, which was to prove of vital importance in the coming campaign.

Soon after 3 pm a report of great significance from the Naval Attaché at Copenhagen was passed by the Admiralty to Admiral Forbes. The *Gneisenau* or *Blücher* with two cruisers and three destroyers had passed northwards through the Belt into the Kattegat. At 6 pm the same force was reported off the Skaw by the submarine *Triton*, which unsuccessfully attacked it, and the *Sunfish*. This was Group V for Oslo. Raeder's hopes for secrecy and surprise were thus further shattered.

With these reports in his hands the British Commander-in-Chief, the hoped-for encounter with the enemy still eluding him, reviewed the situation. To the northward there was at least one big enemy ship, perhaps a battle-cruiser. Its destination could not be known, but Narvik suggested itself. The *Repulse*, *Penelope* and a screen of destroyers were therefore detached to join Admiral Whitworth in support.

In the Kattegat or Skagerrak a powerful force including a battle-cruiser or perhaps two pocket-battleships had been located. If it was coming north it might fall in with Admiral Edward-Collins' weak force of two light cruisers and destroyers who were unsupported by any heavy ships. With the remainder of the Fleet, therefore, Forbes turned south at 8 pm. This course kept his ships some eighty miles off the Norwegian coast although by now it was certain that a German invasion of Norway was taking place.

Soon after this turn to the south, the Admiralty took a hand in directing Admiral Forbes' forces. So long as both the Admiralty and the Commander-in-Chief allowed themselves to be diverted from the Norwegian problem by the expectation of meeting the German surface fleet out at sea, it would make little difference what variations they made in the disposition of their forces. Off the key ports of Norway was where they should have been.

In a signal dispatched to the Commander-in-Chief at 6.42 that evening the Admiralty informed him that they had two objectives in view — to prevent the German force known to be in the north from returning, and to deal with the German forces reported passing north through the Great Belt at 2 pm if they were going to Stavanger or Bergen.

They were worthy objectives, though in fact it was other forces which were making for Bergen and Stavanger, forces which had so far escaped detection. The dispositions ordered by the Admiralty to fulfil them were unfortunate. The four separate forces available were given patrol areas for the night of which three were more than eighty miles from the Norwegian coast. Cunningham's First Cruiser Squadron to which had been added the French cruiser *Emile Berlin*, flying the flag of Admiral Derrien, was to sweep northwards far out in the middle of the North Sea. The Second and Eighteenth Cruiser Squadrons were to be held waiting in the same area. Only the main body of the fleet, under the Commander-in-Chief himself, was left free to sweep to the eastward of the longitude 2° 35' E. Falling in with the Admiralty's evident expectation of meeting the enemy forces well out to sea, he steered south during the night never less titan sixty miles from the coast.

When the Commander-in-Chief, apparently more clearly appreciating the course of events than the Admiralty, directed the First and Second Cruiser Squadrons to be in position by 5 am the next day, to sweep northwards from a latitude between that of Stavanger and Bergen with the most easterly pair of ships within sight of land, the Admiralty intervened to annul the order. They objected that such a patrol line would expose a dispersed and weaker force to being trapped between two enemy forces while the British battle fleet was still 135 miles away. Instead, the cruisers were now to rendezvous some hundred miles to seaward at dawn and then steer to meet the fleet.

By this time, however, the confused and contradictory orders reaching the cruiser squadrons could no longer affect the issue. As daylight approached, the German assault forces were nearing their several objectives, dead on time. A sleeping Norway, on terms of friendship with all the world, was to wake to the sound of guns as coast defences and guardships, caught unwarned and unawares, opened fire on the invaders in brief and gallant defiance before being overwhelmed.[2]

At the same time, beyond the Arctic Circle, in snow and gale, the 15-inch guns of the *Renown* were about to thunder out. Other warships were manoeuvring in the preliminary movements which would lead to a dramatic clash in which Hitler's navy would pay heavily for the strategic advantage it had so boldly seized. Let us look first, however, at events in the south.

---

[2] Meanwhile, Denmark had fallen almost without a shot being fired.

CHAPTER 3

While the ships of the British Home Fleet were pitching and rolling through the night of April 8th in vain pursuit of a phantom enemy, the German assault forces were making their way undetected and unopposed to their several objectives. In the north, the *Scharnhorst* and *Gneisenau* with the ten destroyers for Narvik had reached the entrance to the Vestfiord at 8 pm. The destroyers, under Commodore Bonte, his pennant in the *Heidkamp*, had thereupon been detached to make their way up the long fiords to arrive off Narvik before daybreak. The two battle-cruisers then turned north-westwards and into the ever-increasing gale and swirling snowstorms to carry out their instructions to cruise in the Arctic until it was time for them to bring support to the other naval units returning to their bases in the south.

So great were the seas that speed had soon to be reduced to seven knots to avoid damage; and by dawn they were still to the westward of the Skomvaer Light at the southern tip of the Lofoten Islands. Thus, as the first grey streaks of daylight revealed a wild, storm-tossed sea swept at intervals by scudding squalls of snow, out of the still dark horizon to the westward came the flash of big guns. They had encountered Admiral Whitworth's force, the battle-cruiser *Renown* and nine destroyers, an event which was no part of their plans.

Similarly it was only through force of weather that Whitworth found himself in that position just as daylight was growing sufficiently for the German battle-cruisers to be sighted as they were passing at a range of ten miles. It will be recalled that during the previous day when the Admiralty had directed the four destroyers of the minelaying force and their four escorts to leave the Vestfiord and join him, Whitworth had turned back from the southerly course which he had been pursuing in the hope of meeting the force which had sunk the *Glowworm*. With only one destroyer in company he had felt there was small hope of intercepting an enemy force in the misty smother of the gale. Furthermore, the Admiralty message received at midday giving their opinion that it might well be true that a German force was making for Narvik, made the entrance to Vestfiord a key position to occupy.

At 5.15 that evening *Renown* duly made rendezvous with the destroyers off the Skomvaer Light; but in the meantime the unfortunate sighting report had come in of the *Hipper*'s force off Trondheim on a westerly course. Admiral Whitworth had reviewed the possible courses of action open to the enemy. They might return to their base at once — in which case the Commander-in-Chief's forces to the southward were well placed to intercept them. Or they might be heading for Iceland for a descent on the Atlantic convoy routes, or for Murmansk, where a tanker might be waiting to refuel them. Finally, they could be part of a force for Narvik.

Like the Admiralty and his Commander-in-Chief, Whitworth conceded prior claim, in his own movements, to barring the way against a breakout into the Atlantic. He decided to stand out to sea where he might hope to intercept them.

It is hard to say whether there was sufficient evidence in Whitworth's hands at this time to suggest that an invasion of Norway was in progress. Probably not, owing to the Admiralty's delay in passing the vital information gleaned from the sinking of the *Rio de Janeiro*. Furthermore, though the Commander-in-Chief himself had reached this conclusion by midday, he, too, had stood to seaward with his fleet, where he hoped to bring the enemy's warships to action.

The fact remains that, just as the Commander-in-Chief's seaward cast left open the approaches to Trondheim, so Whitworth opened the entrance to Vestfiord — the gate to Narvik. Once committed, Whitworth found himself seized in the grip of the Arctic gale. When a signal from the Admiralty reached him soon after dark — *Most immediate. Concentrate on preventing any German force proceeding to Narvik*, he could not immediately comply. It was indeed already too late. Though neither the Admiralty nor the Admiral knew it as yet, Commodore Bonte's ten ships, thankfully running from the fury of the seas into the shelter of the Vestfiord, were threading their way up the fiords towards Narvik.

At the same time, Whitworth, his destroyers severely limited in what courses they could safely steer through the great seas, had decided that his immediate duty was to keep his ships concentrated and in a condition of sea-going and fighting efficiency for whatever encounters the morrow might bring. Hearing from the Commander-in-Chief that *Repulse*, *Penelope* and four destroyers were coming to him he gave them his intentions 'to patrol the entrance to Vestfiord when weather moderates'.

Meanwhile, having told his destroyers that the objective was to prevent German forces reaching Narvik, he ordered a westerly course until midnight, after which the squadron would turn southerly to reach Vestfiord at daylight. The westerly course proved impossible for his destroyers which were unmanageable in the quartering sea. The squadron was forced to turn north-west to ride out the worst of the storm. At midnight the force of the gale moderated somewhat, but it was not until 2.30 on the morning of the 9th that the first streaks of dawn gave enough light for the Admiral to feel confident that he could reverse course without his destroyers losing touch in the widespread snow squalls.

Thus the squadron was still some fifty miles west of Skomvaer at 3.37 making to the south-eastward at twelve knots, the destroyers strung out astern of the *Renown*, when to the eastward the black storm clouds parted like the curtains of a gigantic stage, to reveal the dark shape of a large warship. As the silhouette was scrutinised and identified as the *Gneisenau*, a second ship was seen to be following her. It was the *Scharnhorst*, but a similarity of outline of the various classes of German heavy ships led to her being mistaken for a heavy cruiser of the *Hipper* class.

The German ships were steering to the north-westward, on an opposite course to that of the *Renown*. At a disadvantage with regard to light, they were unaware as yet that they had company. In the half light of early dawn the range was still too great for the layer in the *Renown*'s gun director to distinguish the target through his telescope. Captain Simeon swung his ship round to an easterly course to close the range and increased speed to twenty knots. The range-takers could soon see the *Gneisenau* in their lenses at 19,000 yards. The *Renown* turned again on to a course parallel to the enemy's; her six 15-inch guns in their turrets swivelled smoothly round and steadied on the target. A few last-moment adjustments of range and deflection, the clang of the fire gongs, and the ship lurched and shuddered as the guns erupted in flame and blast at five minutes past four.

In the German flagship, the *Renown* had been dimly sighted fifteen minutes earlier but it had been impossible to make out whether she was friend or foe. Not until six minutes after the first British shells had been sent on their way did the *Gneisenau* reply.

In the *Scharnhorst*, surprise was complete, no warning having been passed to her from the flagship. The first alarm came from her navigating officer who, taking advantage of the brief clearance of the sky, his sextant steadied on the western horizon for a star sight, suddenly saw, instead of the expected star, the ripple of orange flashes as the *Renown* opened fire. As the huge 15-inch shells came tearing out of the darkness to raise tall splashes round the *Gneisenau*, the German crews leapt into action. With the two forces running on parallel courses into the heavy seas, plunging their bows deep into the tall rollers, a fierce duel developed. The enemy were able to concentrate their eighteen 11-inch guns on the *Renown* and her position might have been unenviable had the enemy stayed to fight. But from the still gloomy twilight to the westward Admiral Lütjens could see a line of gun-flashes where the British destroyers, faced for the first time by ships of Hitler's fleet, had been unable to resist joining in the fight with their 4.7-inch guns — quite ineffective at such a range in heavy weather. It had the effect of giving Lütjens the impression that he was facing more than one British capital ship. And it was no part of the German plan to get their only two capital ships involved with such a force at this stage.

Though the *Renown* was twice hit by heavy shells, they failed to penetrate deeply and did little damage. In return she put a shell into the foretop of the *Gneisenau*, destroying the main fire control equipment. While control was being shifted to an auxiliary system in the German ship, only her secondary armament of 5.9-inch guns remained in action. Admiral Lütjens turned away to the north-eastward and increased speed while the *Scharnhorst* steamed across her sister ship's wake, screening her with smoke.

Renown turned in chase, bringing all her guns to bear on the *Scharnhorst* for a time. The gale had been slowly veering since midnight and by now was blowing from the north-north-east. It was thus dead into the teeth of it that the three ships were plunging. The Germans increased speed to twenty-eight knots and began to take solid water over their bows. Hundreds of tons of foaming sea smashed again and again against their forward turrets. When another shellburst sent a splinter through the range-finder hood of the *Gneisenau*'s fore-turret, the water poured in, flooding the gun house. A third hit was taken among her anti-aircraft battery.

Lütjens had only one desire now — to get clear away from the enemy at his heels. At the cost of the forward turrets in both ships being put out of action by the seas, he held on at high speed. The *Renown* strove to keep up with him, but Admiral Whitworth could not afford to have his only big ship damaged in the same way. The full speed with which the *Renown* had begun the action had had to be successively reduced until it was down to twenty knots. The enemy steadily drew away. When they disappeared into a snow squall, bringing the duel temporarily to a halt, the *Renown* was altered to a more easterly course, putting the seas on her port bow. She could now steam at a higher speed, though not so directly in chase, but when the enemy came in sight again they were further off than before, still running north at high speed.

The gun duel opened again, but, with both sides jinking to avoid being hit, the fire was ineffective at the ever-increasing range. Though the *Renown* strained herself to the utmost to gain on the enemy, doing twenty-nine knots for a time, it was of no avail. The last view of the German battle-cruisers came at 6.15, far ahead and out of range. Whitworth held on until 8 o'clock and then turned westward to head the enemy off should they have tried to break back to the southward. Soon after nine, however, he intercepted a message from the Admiralty telling the Commander-in-Chief to prepare plans for attacking Bergen and Trondheim, adding, 'Narvik must be watched to prevent Germans landing, as we shall probably want to land a force there.'

Whitworth had already told his destroyers, left behind in the chase after the *Gneisenau* and *Scharnhorst*, to patrol the mouth of the Vestfiord and had directed the *Repulse*'s detachment to do the same. He now made a rendezvous to concentrate all his forces in that area at 6 pm that day, the 9th.

At last the full scope of the German invasion was beginning to be suspected. During the forenoon the Commander-in-Chief signalled to Captain Warburton-Lee of the *Hardy*, senior officer of Whitworth's destroyers, to *'send some destroyers up to Narvik to make certain that no enemy troops land'*. Then at midday the Admiralty intervened by signalling directly to Warburton-Lee, *Press reports state one German ship has arrived Narvik and landed a small force. Proceed Narvik and sink or capture enemy ship. It is at your discretion to land forces if you think you can recapture Narvik from number of enemy present.*

With only this scanty and, of course, very erroneous intelligence to go upon, Warburton-Lee was left to decide with what proportion of his destroyer force he should act. Previous orders had called for a patrol to be maintained in the vicinity of the newly-laid minefield and, furthermore, Admiral Whitworth would need destroyers to screen his two battle-cruisers, *Renown* and *Repulse*, when they joined company that evening. Warburton-Lee therefore left Captain Bickford with the ships of the Twentieth Flotilla, while he himself set off with the four of his own flotilla, the Second — *Hardy*, *Hotspur*, *Havock* and *Hunter*.

There we must leave him for the time being, feeling his way through snow flurries and mist up the fiord, intending to arrive off Narvik at 8 o'clock that evening, while we consider the momentous happenings which had been taking place elsewhere since before dawn.

CHAPTER 4

During the night of April 8th-9th while the British Government, the Admiralty and the Commander-in-Chief were all belatedly reaching the firm conclusion that an invasion of Norway was under way, the Norwegian Government, at last similarly convinced, was taking halting, reluctant and quite inadequate steps to meet it.

On April 5th the Norwegian Legation in Berlin had sent a warning — 'Rumours of an occupation of points on the south coast of Norway.' Though rumours had been daily fare throughout that first winter of the war, the Government took this one seriously enough to begin desultory consultations among Ministers as to the advisability of mobilising the Army. Then, on the morning of the 8th came reports from Sweden and Denmark of strong German naval forces moving northwards into the Kattegat.

At this time greater political interest was being devoted to the dispatch of an urgent protest at the breach of neutrality by Britain in laying minefields in territorial waters. At 5.15 from the Divisional General at Kristiansand, came the startling news of the character and destination of the *Rio de Janeiro*, From London came a warning from the British Admiralty that a German attack on Narvik was imminent.

The Norwegian Parliament was in session; ministers gathered for consultation; but except for an alert dispatched to the harbour defence fortresses, no action was taken. The Army was not mobilised nor were naval and military commanders authorised to open fire on foreign warships. German forecasts were well founded that the Norwegian Government would be too slow in their reactions to resist an assault carried out with speed and surprise simultaneously on all key points of the coast. Fortunately for Norway's honour, there were devoted men in their warships and fortresses ready and willing to take the responsibility of firing the first shot though it was to cost most of them their lives. Not only was it to cost the German Navy dear, but it gave the Norwegian King and Government a brief breathing space to get away intact from the capital, taking the treasury bullion with them, to carry on the fight for a time and eventually to escape to form a government in exile to which loyal Norwegians could rally.

The first of these heroes was Wielding Olsen, an officer of the naval reserve and captain of the little patrol-boat *Pol III*, a whaler of 214 tons stationed in the entrance to Oslo Fiord. Sighting darkened warships making up the fiord soon after 11 pm on the 8th, he challenged and, on getting no reply, signalled an alarm as he boldly went into action with his solitary gun. His little ship was quickly overwhelmed and set on fire and he himself mortally wounded, but not before he had rammed and damaged the torpedo boat *Albatross*.

Thus the first assault group to encounter the light defences of an innocent, neutral state, Group V under Admiral Kummetz, acted in accordance with Raeder's directive — 'Resistance is to be broken ruthlessly.' Passing on up the fiord, Kummetz's Flagship *Blücher* led the *Lützow* and *Emden* to the first shore defences on the islands of Rauoy and Bolaerne, facing each other across the fiord. Here the battery commanders had not the confidence of the captain of the *Pol III*. No orders had come from Oslo. Illuminating the German ships with their searchlights, they contented themselves with putting warning shots across their bows. A fortunate mist then shrouded the German formation which was able to slip by without further interference.

Even now Kummetz's ships could have met disaster if the defences had been put in order in good time, for between Rauoy and Bolaerne a controlled minefield had been projected. But vainly hoping to avoid involvement, the government had delayed ordering it to be laid. Now it was too late.

The first major obstacle to passage to Oslo safely passed, the German ships stopped to transfer assault troops into the smaller craft which were to attack Rauoy and Bolaerne from the rear. Other torpedo boats and minesweepers were detached with troops to occupy the undefended naval base of Horten on the western shore of the fiord. At Horten there lay only one warship, the minelayer *Olav Tryggvason*, with an armament of four 4.7-inch guns. On the approach of the German flotilla, Captain Briseid at once opened fire, sinking the minesweeper and forcing the torpedo boat *Albatross* to withdraw. Horten itself, however, could offer no resistance to the assault troops landed further down the fiord and surrendered without fighting.

Bolaerne, on the other hand, proved a tougher nut to crack, and it was not until the evening of the 10th that its commander capitulated after inflicting casualties on the enemy.

Meanwhile, at twelve knots in gradually clearing weather and growing daylight the German heavy ships had steamed on towards the crucial point of the Oslo fiord, the Drobak Narrows.

Here, where the channel narrows to less than 600 yards, was the fortress of Oscarsborg. Though now nearly a hundred years old and equipped with guns installed at the turn of the century, it was still by reason of its strategic position a formidable obstacle.

On the starboard side of a ship approaching from the sea was a battery of 8-inch guns at Drobak. To port were not only 11-inch guns at Kaholm but torpedo tubes also. It was thus foolhardy of Admiral Kummetz, relying upon a similar hesitancy from the garrison as he had experienced at Rauoy, to approach the narrows at slow speed, his flagship, the brand-new heavy cruiser *Blücher*, leading.

Commanding these defences were men who had no doubt where their duty lay. Holding their fire until the leading German ship was well into the narrows, they opened fire at point blank range with devastating effect; 11-inch and 8-inch shells smashed into the *Blücher*. A hit in her aircraft hangar set both aircraft on fire and started an uncontrollable petrol blaze. Another damaged the steering gear, sending the ship swerving towards the shore at Kaholm.

As the starboard engine was reversed to turn her clear of this danger the *Blücher* was almost at a standstill. More shells hit her from both sides. Then suddenly two heavy underwater explosions shook the cruiser.

The torpedo tubes at Kaholm were in the care of a few elderly reservists. For year after year they had tended them and their torpedoes, never seriously believing they would ever have an opportunity to use them. The brasswork and the paint on the tubes gleamed. The compartment was maintained in the state of spotless cleanliness that only Scandinavians seem able to achieve. The unthinkable possibility of war coming to the peace-loving Norwegians might have excused a less meticulous care of the deadly machines which lay hidden in the tubes.

Now, as the alarm came in from Rauoy, the fascinated tubes' crews saw the huge cruiser, dead in their sights, moving slowly past. The firing levers were jerked down. A hiss, a smooth rush and the torpedoes were on their way.

The two which hit wrecked the main engines of the *Blücher* and started further fires. She still had a little headway, however. Listing and burning, this at last took her out of the arc of fire of the guns. Her captain ordered the anchors to be dropped while valiant efforts were made to repair the engines and master the fires. There were some hopes of the former, though the ship listed further and further until she was lying over at an angle of near twenty degrees. But the blaze spread to a magazine for the 4-inch guns; the flood valves could not be reached. At 6.30 it blew up, wreaking further damage which sealed the ship's fate. The crew and troops were ordered to abandon ship and swim to the nearby shore before she capsized and sank. But more than a thousand men had lost their lives, including most of the staff of General Engelbrecht, who was to command the troops occupying the capital.

Meanwhile, Captain Thiele of the *Lützow*, seeing the fate of the flagship, turned back, though not before his ship had also suffered three hits from 11-inch guns, one of which put her foremost turret out of action. With the *Emden* he retired down the fiord for what would have been a more sensible proceeding from the start. The troops in the warships were landed on the eastern shore of the fiord, some to bypass the defences of the Narrows and attack them from the rear, others to press on by road to the capital.

It was not until the afternoon, however, that a combined attack by troops, warships and aircraft secured the surrender of Drobak, while Kaholm held out until the morning of April 10th. This spirited defence of Oscarsborg against hopeless odds might seem to have been a sacrifice of Norwegian lives for the sake of honour alone. But it was to have important material results also. Though a simultaneous airborne assault on Oslo was part of the German plan, the paratroops who were to have been dropped on the airfields of Fornebu were delayed by fog; so that when airborne troops arrived in transport aircraft they met some opposition from anti-aircraft defences and suffered casualties.

In the capital, the German Ambassador had been up all night, impatiently awaiting the arrival of the naval squadron, before presenting an ultimatum to the King and Government. Out in the bay a naval attaché waited to board the German flagship to act as pilot. By 4.30 it was full daylight. News of fighting at Oscarsborg had come in, but there was no sign of the squadron.

By 4.45 the Ambassador could delay no longer. He waited on the King and presented his Memorandum but, without the backing of the naval guns and troops which had been expected, his demand for co-operation by the Government was sternly rejected. Instead, at long last, the Government gave the order for partial mobilisation. Even now, so unrealistic was the outlook of the Norwegian Ministers that the call-up was to be made *by post*! Reservists were required to report at their mobilisation centres by the 11th.

In a chance interview put out over the broadcasting system, the Foreign Minister, Dr Koht, spoke of general mobilisation, however, so that from all over the country, Servicemen began to converge on Trondheim, Bergen, Kristiansand and Oslo itself. On arrival many of them found that there were no arrangements for their reception and that their mobilisation centre was already in the hands of the enemy. The simultaneous descent by the Germans on all the key points had effectively paralysed the whole organisation for defence.

Only at Oslo, the gallant resistance at Oscarsborg gave a breathing space. As the first air transports arrived over the city and the anti-aircraft guns opened up, the Government was forced to realise that defence of the capital was hopeless. At 7.30 a special train rolled out of the station heading north for Hamar, carrying the Royal Family and most members of Parliament. The traitor Quisling was left to form a new government to collaborate with the enemy but with almost no support and robbed of any veneer of legality by the continuance in being of the proper government.

At noon the German airborne troops occupied the capital which had been declared an undefended, open city. Not until the late afternoon did news of the disaster to the *Blücher* filter through. The sorry remnants of her crew were brought to the German Embassy, their story casting a shadow over the triumph of Nazi ruthlessness.

Oslo was not the only invasion point where the German timetable went adrift, though it was by far the most important. At Kristiansand, Group IV, led by the cruiser *Karlsruhe*, met dense fog as they approached the coast. Groping their way shorewards, with sounding machines going, they reached the 100 fathom line off the entrance at 3.45 am. But not until 6, when the visibility improved, could they risk approaching the rocky mouth of the fiord.

As they loomed out of the mist passing between the lighthouses of Oksoe and Groenningen, the guns of the fortress island of Odderöy, commanding the approach to the town, opened such a heavy and accurate fire that Captain Rieve of the *Karlsruhe* hastily reversed the line and retreated seawards under cover of smoke. The Luftwaffe was then called on to bomb the batteries after which, at 7 o'clock, a second attempt was made to force an entrance. Again the Norwegian batteries spoke out and again the ships were forced to retire.

Captain Rieve now attempted to send troops ashore in torpedo boats covered by long-range fire from the cruisers. In the middle of this attempt, dense fog descended suddenly again. Blinded and out of touch with one another the ships turned back in a confusion of siren wails to await a clearance. For more than two hours they suffered this frustration. Then Captain Rieve lost patience and took his ship towards the shore, heading, as he thought, for the entrance of the fiord. A yell from a lookout in the bows and instant reversal of his engines saved him by the narrowest of margins from stranding on the rocky shore.

At last, at 11 o'clock, the sun began to suck up the fog. With torpedo boats leading, the German squadron again steered for the fiord. In the meantime a message had been received by the commander of the fort, 'British and French destroyers coming to your help. Do not fire.' The message being in Norwegian code, the commander had no reason to doubt its authenticity. When, instead of the *Karlsruhe*, torpedo boats were sighted approaching, fire was withheld while anxious eyes peered through the mist to distinguish what ensigns they were flying. Someone reported them to be French. Others were not sure, but there was sufficient doubt to keep the guns silent. In the confusion the *Karlsruhe* sped past into the harbour where she was safe from the batteries of Odderöy. When the soldiers tumbled ashore in the grim, steel-helmeted panoply of German shock troops, there was no resistance. By 5 o'clock in the afternoon the town and its defences had been occupied.

Along the coast at Stavanger, the Norwegian destroyer *Sleipner* had not long been in possession of the signal put out by the *Pol III* giving the alarm, when a merchant ship was sighted entering the harbour. Challenging her and getting no satisfactory reply or reason why a ship bound, as she claimed, for Murmansk should be putting in to Stavanger, the captain of the *Sleipner* took the heavy responsibility of sinking her on suspicion. The ship was the *Roda*, one of the seven Trojan Horses. In her holds were anti-aircraft and other artillery for the paratroops who were about to be landed on the Stavanger airfield.

In spite of this setback, however, the Germans were soon in possession of the finest airfield in Norway. It was shortly to be operating dive-bombers against the British fleet and driving it northwards where it could no longer be a threat to the scattered German forces which might otherwise have fallen victims to its superior strength.

The same fog which had so complicated the fight for Kristiansand had laid a welcome shroud over the movements of Group III for Bergen. Kept down to the speed of eighteen knots by the presence of the old cruiser *Bremse* and the transport *Karl Peters*, the squadron was forced to make its passage round the south-west corner of Norway in daylight. Had the weather been clear, air reconnaissance would have found them at 5 pm on the 8th a bare sixty miles from Edward-Collins' force of two cruisers and eleven destroyers just reaching the starting position for their northward sweep. Hampered by the presence of slow weak ships cluttered with troops and equipment, Rear-Admiral Schmundt commanding Group III would have been brought to action at a great disadvantage and been forced either to sacrifice his slower ships while the remainder made a dash for Bergen or to turn back and give up his mission altogether.

But it was not to be. Not until darkness fell to take its place did the fog clear. Undetected, the German force entered the Kors Fiord approach to Bergen at 2 o'clock in the morning.

There it was illuminated by searchlights and challenged by a patrol vessel; but a signal from the *Köln* identifying herself as HMS *Cairo* apparently satisfied the Norwegians and the ships swept on unhindered. Again at 4.30, when a Norwegian destroyer was encountered, a signal in English, 'I am proceeding to Bergen for a short visit' was sufficient to get them by without challenge.

By now daylight was growing fast. Such deception would not serve much longer. At the entrance to By Fiord, the last stretch before reaching Bergen, the squadron stopped while troops were landed to take from the rear the batteries at Kvarven on the south shore. This prudent precaution was thrown away, however. To wait for the fort to be overrun by the troops would put the operation behind schedule. Admiral Schmundt pressed on.

Though the batteries were taken sufficiently by surprise for the *Köln* and the torpedo boats of the squadron to get through unharmed, the Norwegians woke up in time to put three 8-inch shells into the *Königsberg*, inflicting damage which was to be of great importance in the ensuing operations, and one into the *Bremse*. In spite of this, however, the whole German squadron broke through into Bergen harbour and as troops were rushed ashore all resistance was quickly swamped. The people of the most important town and port in south-west Norway found themselves under German military rule as the sun rose on the morning of April 9th.

The port of Trondheim, like the others, was guarded by batteries of ancient but serviceable big guns sited at Narrows in the approach fiords. Had the garrisons been alert and well practised they could certainly have at least inflicted some damage on the *Hipper* and her four destroyers. But a past history of a century of unbroken peace and a universal determination to keep out of the war was not conducive to a well-conducted defence.

Spreading doubt and confusion by long flashlight messages, the *Hipper* led through the Narrows at twenty-five knots. Before the unskilled gunners could find the range of the ships starkly illuminated by their searchlights, the whole squadron had swept through and beyond the arc of fire of the guns. Too late, the Norwegian defenders awoke to the realities of the situation and when troops were sent against the forts they defended themselves with such spirit that it took two days' hard fighting and a bombardment by the *Hipper*'s 8-inch guns to force their surrender. But it was of little avail, as Trondheim itself had fallen without a shot.

So we turn to Narvik — Admiral Raeder's biggest gamble. The safe delivery of the assault troops was dependent not only upon surprising the Norwegian defenders but also upon a failure of British air reconnaissance to locate and shadow Group I on its long passage up the coast during daylight on April 8th. The stormy weather and low visibility which it encountered could not have been relied upon, nor could the good fortune which led to the only sighting of Group II on a westerly course, leading British naval dispositions astray. The unfortunate intervention of the Admiralty which withdrew the British destroyers from their patrol off the Vestfiord at the crucial moment was a further bonus of good luck for the Germans.

Thus it was that Commodore Bonte found himself unhindered to make his way through darkness and snowfall up the long fiords towards Narvik. On board his ships were troops of General Dietl's mountain division, specially trained to operate in conditions of snow. Many of the lights and beacons on shore were still burning in spite of an order from the government for them to be extinguished, so he had no difficulty in keeping to his schedule for the passage. The pilot station at Tranöy was passed at 3 in the morning. At 4.10 he passed Baröy and entered the long Ofotfiord. Two small patrol boats at the entrance signalled the alarm and for some reason — perhaps in the hope of delaying the Germans — informed them that there were eight warships in Ofotfiord.

At the Narrows of Ramnes, fortifications were reputed to exist but there was no sign of them as the flotilla sailed past. Bonte, however, detached three of his ships to land troops to locate and occupy them. They did not, in fact, exist, though both British and Germans believed them to do so. With the remainder of his ships Bonte led on. Coming abreast Herjangsfiord he detached others to proceed up it and send troops to the little township of Elvegaard where the regimental depot for the area, holding important stocks of equipment, was occupied without resistance. Then with his flotilla leader, *Wilhelm Heidkamp*, the *Arnim* and *Thiele*, he made for the harbour of Narvik itself.

Almost to the minute, at the allotted time of 5.15, a snowstorm parted its veil to reveal the harbour crowded with ships of all nationalities loaded with iron ore or awaiting cargoes. In the entrance lay a warship quickly identified as the 4000-ton coastal defence ship *Eidsvold* of the Royal Norwegian Navy, an ancient vessel dating from 1900 but mounting an armament of two 8.2-inch and six 5.9-inch guns. A signal lamp winked agitatedly, ordering the German ships to stop. A shot was fired across the *Heidkamp*'s bow.

Remembering Raeder's demand for ruthlessness, the Commodore stopped his ships and planned black treachery. A boat was sent to the *Eidsvold* with an officer to demand free passage. If negotiations failed, as they were almost certain to do, the officer was instructed to fire a red Very light as soon as he left the Norwegian ship.

While he waited for the signal, Bonte surreptitiously manoeuvred his ship to keep his torpedo tubes trained on the *Eidsvold*. As the red light soared into the sky, two torpedoes leapt away on their short run to the target. Before the Norwegians realised what was happening their ship had been blown up, broken in half and sunk with the loss of all but a handful of her company.

The roar of the explosion told the *Eidsvold*'s sister ship *Norge*, flagship of the Senior Naval Officer, Commodore Askim, at anchor inside the harbour, what she could expect. The *Arnim* was already going alongside the wharf, her decks plainly crowded with troops. On to her the *Norge* turned her guns, though ineffectively. The reply was instantaneous as a storm of shots from the quick-firing 5-inch guns of the destroyers fell on her, followed by two torpedoes. The *Norge* rolled over and sank leaving some fifty or sixty survivors only.

In sharp contrast to the devoted, if unskilled defence by the *Norge* and the uncompromising attitude of the captain of the *Eidsvold* in the face of hopeless odds, the commandant of the garrison, Colonel Sundlo proved to be a traitor. A follower of Quisling, he ordered the garrison not to resist. By the time orders came from Divisional headquarters removing him from his post, it was too late and General Dietl was in firm control.

So, during that fatal April 9th, every key position on the coast of Norway fell into German hands in accordance with the plans for Weserübung. Boldness, speed and ruthlessness had achieved their object as Raeder had forecast, in the face of Norwegian hesitancy and ill-conceived British naval strategy.

So far the loss of the *Blücher* had been the only serious casualty to the German fleet, and Grand Admiral Raeder had cause to be satisfied.

The most dangerous phase of Weserübung was still to open. The whereabouts of all German ships must be known to the British, whose powerful fleet was at sea to bar the way of return. Already *Gneisenau* and *Scharnhorst* were partly out of action, each with a turret inoperative and restricted to twenty-five knots. 'The third part of the operation is in progress and will probably entail further loss,' Raeder wrote, preparing his Fuehrer for the blows to come.

CHAPTER 5

While all the main centres of Norwegian population were falling at one blow into German hands, the British Home Fleet, its great opportunity missed, was concentrating out at sea in a latitude between Bergen and Stavanger. By now it was clear to the Commander-in-Chief that a full-scale invasion of Norway was in progress. He considered what steps could be taken.

At 6.30 am on April 9th, when Vice-Admiral Layton with the Eighteenth Cruiser Squadron — *Manchester, Southampton* and seven destroyers — joined him, Bergen was some ninety miles to leeward. Enemy warships were certainly there but in what strength he knew not. A signal asking for information was sent to the Admiralty with a suggestion that Layton's force might be sent in to the attack.

In London, the Chiefs of Staff had been roused from their beds at dawn as news began to come in from Norway. By 6 o'clock they were in session. The apparent situation which they had to consider was that Bergen and Trondheim were in German hands, but that Narvik was still unaffected. One battalion of the Guards Brigade, the 1st Scots Guards, was already embarked in a transport in the Clyde in accordance with the now disrupted Plan R4. It would 'leave at once for Narvik' — an optimistic and unrealistic pronouncement which was typical of many to come from the High Command in this first serious operation of the war.

The first object, however, was to prevent the Germans consolidating their positions at Bergen and Trondheim. The Commander-in-Chief's signal when it was read, fitted in with this decision which led to instructions being framed to *Prepare plans for attacking German warships and transports in Bergen and for controlling the approaches to the port on supposition that defences are still in hands of Norwegians. Similar plans as regards Trondheim should be prepared.*

At 10.15 the Admiralty approved the Commander-in-Chief's proposal for a force to go to Bergen and, at 11.30, Layton left the fleet with *Manchester, Southampton, Glasgow, Sheffield* and seven destroyers to carry out his mission. The fleet had continued to steer southwards during the morning so that Layton's squadron had now a long reach to make into the teeth of the northerly gale. His destroyers could make no more than sixteen knots into the heavy seas, and it would be dusk by the time the entrances to the fiords were reached.

Layton's orders were to send his seven destroyers up the fiords to Bergen, while his cruisers remained in support at both entrances — a half-hearted effort which lost much of its attraction when a reconnaissance aircraft reported that two enemy cruisers were in the harbour. Second thoughts in the Admiralty led to an annulment of the operation early in the afternoon and Layton turned to rejoin the fleet which at midday had swung north.

It was an uninspiring opening move in the campaign to aid the Norwegians and dislodge the Germans. Had Layton's cruisers penetrated to Bergen that first evening before the shore defences had been taken over by the Germans, they would have found only the *Königsberg* and *Bremse*, both damaged, to oppose them, and they might on their way in have met the *Köln* which sailed after dark.

In the meantime, however, the Home Fleet had been undergoing an experience which brought home for the first time the change in naval warfare wrought by the advent of air power. It is no part of this story to examine the reasons why the Royal Navy entered the war so gravely handicapped by a shortage of aircraft carriers, aircraft and pilots, a shortage which was to lead to fatal difficulties in every theatre and every phase of the war. It is sufficient to say that for naval air reconnaissance the inadequately equipped and trained Coastal Command of the Royal Air Force had to be relied upon. Fighter cover was limited, outside the short range of Hurricanes and Spitfires of Fighter Command, to such low-performance aircraft as Blenheims and Hudsons or to the handful of ill-designed aircraft which could be operated from the solitary carrier intermittently available to work with the fleet.

An unwarranted confidence in the efficacy of anti-aircraft gunfire had, paradoxically, led to warships being equipped with high-angle guns in inadequate numbers and with fire-control systems which could not cope with the high-performance aircraft brought against them. Cruisers and above had reasonable batteries of high-angle guns which could be brought into action against high-flying bombers, though they rarely had much success. Against the dive-bombing technique favoured by the Luftwaffe which could only be countered by massed machine-gun fire, they were singularly ill-equipped.

Destroyers in the fleet, even those completed in the years immediately before the war, had only the clumsy unreliable 2-pounder pom-pom guns and 0.5-inch machine guns to bring against air attack of any sort. Their main armament of 4.7-inch guns had a maximum elevation of only 40 degrees.

When, on the afternoon of April 9th, in clear, blue weather, the Luftwaffe, now able to operate from bases further north than ever before, sent their bombers against the Home Fleet, it was soon clear to the Commander-in-Chief that his ships could no longer operate so far south unless prepared to suffer considerable loss. The first British force to be found and attacked was Layton's squadron, steering to rejoin the fleet.

Fortunately, the main weight of attack was from high bombers; the Germans, like ourselves, had not yet appreciated the difficulty of hitting ships at sea, free to manoeuvre, with this form of attack. Two of Layton's cruisers, *Southampton* and *Glasgow*, were nevertheless near-missed and damaged. In the heavy sea running, anti-aircraft fire was wild and inaccurate. At the high speed at which the ships were steaming the destroyers, constantly swept by sheets of spray, could barely bring their guns into action at all, even in the limited role which poor elevation allowed.

The *Gurkha*, reducing speed to overcome this difficulty, dropped behind and out of the support of her consorts. Dive-bombers picked on her. Scoring direct hits they left her stopped, sinking and alone. In the rough sea, all hands would have been lost had not the cruiser *Aurora*, steaming to join the fleet, come across her by chance in time to save most of them.

Throughout the afternoon and evening the Fleet was under attack. *Rodney* was hit by an 1100-pound bomb which failed to penetrate her armoured deck and so did little damage. Though in the face of the gunfire of the fleet this was the only success scored by the German pilots, ammunition had been used up at an alarming rate, Layton's cruisers firing off nearly half their supply.

A proposal by the Commander-in-Chief that torpedo aircraft from the *Furious*, on her way to join him, should take on the task of attacking the ships in Bergen, had to be reconsidered. The only aircraft-carrier in home waters could not be exposed to so heavy an air threat. Trondheim, however, was not yet within the orbit of German air superiority. The torpedo attack would be transferred to the ships there, Bergen being left to bombers of the Royal Air Force and dive-bombers of the Fleet Air Arm from the Orkneys.

As for the important sea route to the southern ports of Norway through the Kattegat and Skagerrak to Oslo, Kristiansand, Stavanger and Bergen, along which were being transported the vital reinforcements and supplies without which the German hold on the country could not be consolidated, they would have to be left to submarines to disrupt. Thus early in the conflict the lack of naval air strength limited the Royal Navy's ability to wield sea power in its traditional fashion.

We shall see later how the Submarine Service strove to make up for the deficiency in conditions of great difficulty and hazard. For the moment interest centred on the air weapon which the British in their turn were to bring into play against enemy warships. The events of the night of April 9th and the morning of the 10th are of interest in contrasting the effectiveness of the various forms of air attack.

The Royal Air Force in its anti-shipping role pinned its faith on precision bombing from a height. There were several reasons for this, the most important being that only from a great height could armour-piercing bombs achieve sufficient velocity to penetrate to the vitals of a ship. This was perfectly true, though it applied only to attacks on heavily armoured ships of the battleship type. Unfortunately, hits were very rarely achieved even on stationary ships by this method, as was to be discovered by British, German, Italian and American Air Forces.

The Fleet Air Arm had for a long while pressed for a dive-bomber, following the example of the US Navy and the Luftwaffe. When at last such an aircraft reached them — the

Blackburn Skua — it was so designed as to double the role of fighter and dive-bomber. As a result it was satisfactory in neither. The pilots flying them were about to show, however, what might have been done had a dive-bomber been available to the Royal Air Force instead of the large twin-engined aircraft on which they relied.

We have already seen a force of thirty-five of this latter type of aircraft sent against the German Groups I and II on April 7th. Of these only twelve Blenheims had found the enemy, but with no success. Now on the evening of the 9th, twelve Wellingtons and twelve Hampdens were sent against the ships at Bergen. They found *Köln*, *Königsberg* and *Bremse* at anchor there and pressed home their attack with gallantry and zest, coming down to machine-gun the ships after dropping their bombs. The result, however, was negligible. One aircraft was shot down. Soon after the attack the *Köln* got under way; but learning from intercepted signals that British ships were patrolling off the entrances to the fiords, Rear-Admiral Schmundt contented himself with steaming south through the Inner Leads as far as Mauranger Fiord where he anchored to wait for the coast to be clear. Getting under way again on the afternoon of the 10th, he evaded detection and arrived home safely.

Meanwhile, at the Royal Naval Air Station of Hatston in the Orkneys there was considerable activity. Two squadrons of Skuas were stationed there in the absence of any carrier to embark them. They were commanded by Captain R. T. Partridge, Royal Marines, and Lieutenant W. P. Lucy, Royal Navy. The senior observer of Partridge's squadron, Lieutenant-Commander Hare, had been lent, with other naval observers, to a Coastal Command squadron engaged in reconnaissance of the Norwegian harbours and uncertain of their ability to identify enemy warships. Early on the 9th he had been over Bergen harbour and seen the three German cruisers at anchor there. Encountering the Home Fleet on his return passage he had been able to pass this news direct to the flagship.

As he climbed out of his aircraft at Lossiemouth, Hare was immediately bundled into a waiting transport plane and flown back to Hatston. His news had led the Commanding Officer of the station to seek and obtain permission for the two squadrons of Skuas to take off at first light for an attack on Bergen.

The double journey across the North Sea was just, but only just, inside the endurance of the Skuas. Its safe accomplishment was dependent upon an accurate landfall on the Norwegian coast, a swift attack and an immediate return. Any time wasted checking their position or searching for their targets would mean forced-landings in the sea for want of petrol. An observer who knew from personal experience not only the coastal features in the vicinity of Bergen, but also the berths in which the targets lay, was invaluable.

Before daylight on the 10th, fifteen Skuas roared off into the darkness and headed into the dawn. Under each was slung a 500-lb. bomb. Travelling above cloud for most of their two-hour journey and so dependent, in those early days, entirely upon dead reckoning and a forecast strength and direction of wind, they ran into clear weather off the Norwegian coast to make a perfect landfall. Flying up the fiord under Hare's directions to where he had seen the cruisers on the day before, there was a brief moment of dismay when the berths were seen to be empty. The *Köln*, as we know, had sailed after dark the previous evening; the *Königsberg* had shifted berth. Now, just when it began to seem that the journey had been in vain, she was sighted alongside a jetty in the harbour.

Without a moment's hesitation, Partridge led the formation in a long line of steeply diving aircraft. One after the other the fifteen aircraft pulled out at the bottom of their dive and released their bombs. Not until half of them had done so and were streaking away low over the water did the German gunners come into action to send streams of tracer shells climbing steeply into the air. Three bombs made direct hits on the cruiser; others hit the jetty or fell into the water close alongside. Before the last aircraft was out of sight the *Königsberg* was already rolling over on her side. In a few more minutes the first major warship ever to be sunk by air attack had gone to the bottom. Of the aircraft not one had been shot down, though one was lost by accident on the return journey.

It was an impressive demonstration of dive-bombing, but one which was to act as a warning of what our ships faced when operating within range of the German dive-bombers, the deadly Stukas, rather than pointing the way to the type of aircraft needed by the Fleet Air Arm. The Skua was soon to be withdrawn from service but never replaced by a true dive-bomber.

The third form of air attack against shipping, the airborne torpedo, was favoured by the Royal Navy as its principal 'strike' weapon and to a somewhat lesser extent by the Royal Air Force. It was *par excellence* the weapon for use against capital ships, which were largely immune to bombs owing to their armoured decks. In peacetime exercises, when delivered by a large number of aircraft coming in simultaneously from different directions, it had achieved a high degree of success. When war came, however, it was rarely possible to bring more than one carrier into action at a time so that attacks were attempted by mere handfuls of aircraft. Casualties were high, successes few. Furthermore, the wartime expansion of the

Fleet Air Arm led to the dispersal of the highly-trained teams of torpedo-bomber pilots to lead the newly-formed squadrons.

It was with a fairly powerful force of torpedo aircraft, however, that the attack on Trondheim was launched on the 11th from the *Furious*. Eighteen Swordfish aircraft roared and trundled down her flight deck and climbed heavily into the morning twilight at 4 am.

Reconnaissance the previous evening had revealed the *Hipper* at anchor off the town. But now, as the long fiord opened up under the eyes of the airmen, it appeared at first empty. Further search succeeded only in finding two of the German destroyers, anchored close in shore in shallow water. They were better than nothing and at the order of their leader the pilots took their aircraft slanting down through the 'flak' in their first encounter with the enemy. Unfortunately for them, the water was so shallow that many of the torpedoes in their first dive after being launched and before their depth-setting mechanism could bring them under control, hit the bottom and exploded. The first air torpedo attack of the war was a complete failure.

The fact was that Captain Heye of the *Hipper*, as soon as the troops had been safely landed, had been anxious to get his valuable ship back from its position so far north and exposed to the sort of counter-attack already being considered by the British. Fuel was running short in his ships owing to the nonarrival of the expected tanker. Two of bis destroyers had serious machinery defects and could not go to sea. Another was too short of oil to attempt the homeward passage. With the fourth, therefore, he got under way, as soon as it was dark on the 10th. In the black night he evaded British patrols off the entrances to the fiords and then, for some reason never explained, headed north-westward into the heavy seas still running.

Not only was this course impossible for his accompanying destroyer, so that she had to be sent back to Trondheim, but it led him within a narrow margin of encountering the Home Fleet as it steered through the night towards the launching position for the *Furious*' aircraft. Luck was with the *Hipper*, however. Turning south the next morning, running at high speed and aided by low visibility, she evaded all detection, and after joining the *Gneisenau* and *Scharnhorst* on the 12th, she reached Wilhelmshaven with barely 80 tons of fuel remaining.

The two German battle-cruisers, after lingering in the Arctic until midday on the 10th, then heard that, as will be recounted later, the destroyers in Narvik had been eliminated. They therefore similarly set off southwards through the northern mists, sleet and rain. Passing westward of the Home Fleet and close eastward of the Shetlands, they evaded all search and after making rendezvous with the *Hipper* at 8.30 am on the 12th reached Wilhelmshaven in company with her.

Thus three of Raeder's most valuable units returned from the venture to which he had, not without misgivings, committed them. It must have been a considerable relief to him, for other losses had been very heavy. The *Hipper*'s brand-new sister ship *Blücher* had been sunk in Oslo fiord, and the light cruiser *Königsberg* in Bergen harbour. There had been other calamitous news to give the Fuehrer since Hitler had congratulated him at his conference on April 10th on the great achievement of the navy. It was as well that the Grand Admiral had made it plain from the outset that losses were to be expected.

In the far north we left the situation around Narvik with the ten German destroyers and the troops of General Dietl in control of the town and harbour while, unknown to them, Captain Warburton-Lee with four ships of his flotilla was making up the Vestfiord with orders to sink or capture the solitary enemy ship believed to have reached Narvik. Meanwhile, to the British and Allied submarines, in the narrowly restricted and shallow waters of the Kattegat and Skagerrak, had been assigned the difficult and hazardous task of disrupting the German supply line to Oslo and of intercepting the enemy warships returning from their various missions.

The Home Fleet was steering north towards Narvik where it was hoped that the *Furious*' aircraft might be more successful against Commodore Bonte's destroyers than they had been at Trondheim. The cruisers of the fleet after an abortive search for non-existent German transports in the Inner Leads from Aalesund to the Vestfiord had been sent back to the Orkneys and Shetlands to refuel and prepare to escort a military expedition to Narvik.

CHAPTER 6

Men of the British Submarine Service have always prided themselves that they could take their boats and operate them where even the long arm of sea power in the shape of surface craft could not penetrate. During the Kaiser's War, they took their boats through the minefields and swirling currents of the Dardanelles into the Sea of Marmora where they played havoc among warships and transports in what had been previously a Turkish lake.

Another flotilla had sailed through the shallow, tortuous channels of the Sound into the Baltic, evaded the German patrols waiting for them and joined the Imperial Russian naval forces based on Helsingfors and Reval. There, under the leadership of Commander Max Horton, they had dominated the narrow waters of the Baltic, their exploits evoking jealous envy from irresolute, incompetent allies and grudging admiration from their enemies. The latter paid Horton the compliment of ruefully referring to the Baltic as 'Horton's Sea'.

In April, 1940, this same Max Horton was Vice-Admiral, commanding the British Submarine Service. He had no illusions therefore as to the hazards he was asking his crews to face when he stationed them in the restricted waters of the Kattegat and Skagerrak. But Operation 'Wilfred' was fully expected to bring an immediate reaction in the shape of a German descent on Norway by sea. The enemy forces would come from Kiel, passing up through the Great Belt into the Kattegat or from Wilhelmshaven along the west coast of Denmark and across the Skagerrak.

Horton had for some time been convinced — in advance of most of his colleagues — that a German invasion of Norway was imminent. He therefore fell in gladly with the Admiralty's wishes on April 4th for his submarines to be concentrated where they could intercept such movements. Three were sent to the Kattegat, three to the Skagerrak, one of which was the Polish *Orzel*, and three more off the west coast of Denmark. Furthermore, following his hunch, Horton gave them orders that, if warships and transports were encountered together, the latter were to be the primary targets.

The intelligence of German activity and movements, which was so unhappily disregarded by the Admiralty from April 5th onwards, was available also to Admiral Horton. He evaluated it more accurately and by midday on the 7th had no doubts that the invasion of Norway was to be expected very shortly. A further six submarines were ordered to sea. Unfortunately, Admiralty zeal to hit at the German heavy forces known to be on the move from the sighting report of the reconnaissance aircraft on the morning of the 7th, led to an adjustment of submarine patrol positions so as to cover the approaches to the ports in the Heligoland Bight at the expense of a close watch on the Norwegian ports.

Thus the approaches to Stavanger and Oslo were uncovered at the crucial moment. Nevertheless, as we have seen, the *Orzel* intercepted and sank the transport *Rio de Janeiro* at noon on the 8th, thus providing the first positive information that an invasion was in progress. At about the same time the *Trident*, on patrol in the northern Skagerrak, had intercepted the German tanker *Posidonia* laden with 8000 tons of fuel for supplying U-boats at Stavanger. In accordance with the instructions binding our submarines, the *Trident* surfaced, ordered the tanker to stop and gave her crew time to abandon ship, and incidentally make an SOS signal, before their ship was sent to the bottom with a torpedo.

This restriction on our submarines, in comparison with the German U-boats' adoption of unrestricted warfare from the outset, lost them many opportunities to attack the stream of supply ships and transports taking reinforcements to the first assault troops. With anti-submarine ships and aircraft flooding the area, they could rarely come to the surface during daylight and were forced to watch in impotence as fat targets steamed past their periscopes.

Not until 1.30 on the afternoon of April 9th was Admiral Horton able to get sanction to instruct his captains that any German merchant ship in the Skagerrak or Kattegat might be sunk without warning. The first to benefit from this order was Lieutenant-Commander Slaughter, commanding the *Sunfish* on patrol in the Kattegat, an area in which it was suicidal to surface by day. Through his periscope he was following the course of the German steamer *Amasis* passing by, laden, as he very well knew, with supplies for the German forces in Norway. Torpedoes were ready, the range was right, he was ideally placed for a shot — a shot which he was forbidden to take.

As the sights were coming on, a voice in his ear said, 'Signal, sir. Just come in. German merchant ships east of 8° East may be sunk without warning.' Without taking his eye from his eyepiece, Jacky Slaughter replied, 'Splendid, signalman,' and to the waiting tubes crews, 'Fire One.' A few minutes later the *Amasis* was no more. It was the first of four such sinkings by the *Sunfish*.

Even with this newly-won freedom to attack on sight and while remaining submerged, British submarines could net disrupt altogether the short sea routes from Germany to the

Norwegian coast. Every attack betrayed their position to antisubmarine craft which could be on the spot within a short time. Then only stillness and silence could save them from detection and crippling damage by depth charges. For hour after hour they had to lie quiet and endure, while the air got steadily fouler, bodies weaker and brains more torpid. Only with nightfall might there come an opportunity to float secretly and softly to the surface and suck in the clean air while they sneaked away in the darkness to recharge their exhausted storage batteries.

Once the Germans, by their bold tactics of surprise, had got their initial assault forces through, not all the efforts of British submarines could prevent enough of the follow-up reinforcements reaching them to consolidate their positions in the south. Admiral Raeder's plan had succeeded as he had foretold, though he had British and Norwegian inertia to thank more than the secrecy on which he had counted.

As he had foretold also, the most difficult part of the operation was the return of his warships to their bases. Aided by stormy weather and low visibility, *Scharnhorst*, *Gneisenau* and *Hipper* were, indeed, to evade all search and get safely home. The *Köln*, too, by a quick night dash, escaped interception. The ships in Oslo and Kristiansand were not to be so lucky.

Throughout April 9th, the submarine *Truant* had been on patrol off Kristiansand. Her captain, Lieutenant-Commander C. H. Hutchinson, had had a trying day. In his hydrophones the sound of fast-running propellers had never ceased. Whenever he risked a brief glance through his periscope, the sight of prowling anti-submarine craft met his gaze, and there was nothing he could do but stay quiet and avoid detection.

Towards evening there came a lull when the anti-submarine craft left to make a cast in a new direction. Taking the *Truant* up to periscope depth at 6.30, Hutchinson swept his eye round the horizon and was rewarded with the sight of the *Karlsruhe* heading his way, escorted by three torpedo boats. The well-practised attack routine went into action. The enemy's course and speed were estimated and fed into the calculating machine, from which the torpedo-firing course would be worked out.

The speed was something over twenty knots, but the enemy formation was zigzagging so that only at the last moment would the final calculation be made. For the next twenty minutes, as the periscope slid smoothly up and down at Hutchinson's command, the bearing and range of the enemy at each successive sighting was read and plotted, the submarine manoeuvring to put her into the perfect firing position off the cruiser's bow.

Torpedoes were ready, bow caps open, range just right and the moment to fire at hand when the *Karlsruhe* swung away on a new leg of her zigzag, leaving the *Truant* broad on her beam. The perfect firing position had been lost; but there was still a chance of a hit. At 6.56 Hutchinson gave the order to fire the first of a full salvo of torpedoes.

As he had feared, the torpedoes were sighted as they came racing up on the quarter of the *Karlsruhe*. She swerved to avoid them and nearly succeeded in doing so; but not quite, for one of them hit aft, wrecking her steering gear, putting both main engines out of action and splitting her hull open to let flood water in. With her pumps unusable, the *Karlrsuhe* lay motionless and slowly sinking. Unable to check the flooding, Captain Rieve gave orders to abandon ship and, when the crew had been transferred to two torpedo boats, her end was hastened by torpedoes from one of them.

Meanwhile, the torpedo boats, aided by the anti-submarine flotilla which had come hurrying back, were hunting the *Truant* remorselessly. For the next two hours depth charges erupted round her, shaking, tossing and hammering her, damaging her machinery and starting leaks. At a depth of 320 feet, near the limit which the submarine was designed to withstand, she crept slowly and silently, barely under control. Gradually the attacks became less frequent and further off as the hunting pack lost the scent. At 9.45 the crew had enjoyed a whole quarter of an hour without being rocked and shaken by explosions. It would be dark up top. Hutchinson gave the order to take the boat up near the surface. But as tanks were blown, the noise was heard on the enemy's hydrophones. Once again the crash of depth charges sent the *Truant* down to seek safety in the depths.

Though these fresh attacks were less accurate than the earlier ones, it was plain that the hunters were close enough to detect any slightest noise of machinery. There was nothing for it but to match patience with patience and endure to the limit. By 11.25 *Truant*'s battery was almost exhausted. It was nineteen hours since the coming of dawn had forced her to dive. Air was becoming foul. It was difficult to breathe. Nothing had been heard for a while. Once again the submarine was floated gently to the surface. As the blessed fresh air poured into the boat Hutchinson searched the dark horizon and found no enemy in sight. He headed through the night for home and urgent repairs and hoped to be clear out to sea before dawn.

The crew at once set to work to patch up the damage and were so successful on the homeward journey that by the evening of the 11th Hutchinson was able to signal *Defects rapidly being made good. Six torpedoes left. Morale high. Shall I return to patrol?* But Max Horton knew when it was time to give his terriers a breather. *All in good time*, he replied. *I want to see you first.*

As *Truant* was crawling home, another submarine was meeting the fate she had so narrowly missed. On patrol off the south-west corner of Norway as the first glimmer of light was growing on the morning of April 9th, the *Thistle* had sighted a German U-boat on the surface. Torpedoes were launched at once, but something warned the U-boat and, before they reached her, she had dived.

During the day *Thistle* was given orders to try to penetrate Stavanger harbour and attack German shipping believed to be there. When at dusk she was able to surface and acknowledge this order, she also reported her unsuccessful encounter and was thereupon told to return to the area in which it had occurred. Thus it came about that both *Thistle* and her same antagonist, *U4*, were prowling through the darkness on the night of the 9th seeking each other. This time the tables were turned. From the U-boat, the *Thistle* was sighted, silhouetted against the false dawn just after 1 o'clock in the morning. And this time there was no escape from the torpedo which exploded against her hull and blew her to pieces. It was the first British submarine loss of the campaign. There would be others.

Meanwhile, on April 10th, the submarines in the Kattegat found themselves in the midst of great activity. The delay in the reduction of the defences of Oslo fiord had held up throughout the 9th the stream of transports which it had been planned should follow the assault force with supplies and reinforcements. By the 10th the way was clear. A convoy of fifteen steamers with a strong sea and air escort started moving up the Kattegat.

Lying in wait for them were the same two submarines, *Triton* and *Sunfish*, which had reported the squadron comprising Group V as it swept by on its way to Oslo. Lieutenant-

Commander E. F. Pizey, captain of the *Triton*, had had two days to nurse his disappointment at seeing his torpedoes, aimed at that tantalising target, go astray. Now he was to have his revenge.

Breaking through the screen at 4.30 pm he loosed a salvo of six torpedoes, three of which found a mark. Two sank the steamers *Friedenau* and *Wigbert*, sending them to the bottom with 900 troops as well as their valuable supplies. A third torpedo blew an escorting patrol vessel to pieces. The enemy's reaction was immediate and prolonged. Seventy-eight depth charges had burst round the *Triton* before Pizey was able to give the slip to the infuriated escorts and get away to safety.

He owed his escape in some measure to the attention of the anti-submarine craft being transferred to the *Spearfish* in the adjacent patrol area off the Skaw. Some unwary movement had attracted them to this new target to which they fastened themselves with unhealthy firmness, dropping sixty-six depth charges round it between 5.30 and 6.40. Again at 8 o'clock the *Spearfish* was set upon. Her after-periscope damaged besides other injuries, the submarine was kept down hour after hour while the thrashing of propellers told of patrol vessels still on her trail.

Her situation was becoming desperate with foul air and dying batteries when at last, half an hour before midnight, the sounds of pursuit died away. Lieutenant-Commander J. H. Forbes brought her thankfully to the surface after more than twenty hours submerged, a very long time for those days before re-purification of the air in submarines was perfected.

Spearfish was not left for long to enjoy her new-found peace and quiet. An hour after surfacing the pale gleam of what was taken for the tumbling bow-wave of a destroyer was suddenly sighted on the starboard beam. Unwilling to dive with his batteries so low, Forbes put his wheel over to port to get away from this fresh menace. While *Spearfish* was swinging round, he kept his binoculars on the white streak and then realised that what he was looking at was not a bow wave but the stern wash of a ship travelling at high speed — and a big ship, too. It was a worthy target for his torpedoes. Remaining on the surface, he manoeuvred to bring his tubes to bear.

The pocket battleship *Lützow* — for such was the *Spearfish*'s target — had sailed from Oslo at 2.40 that afternoon, April 10th. She was urgently required at Kiel to be prepared for a foray into the Atlantic. Thus, although no suitable fast escorts were available for her, it was decided that high speed and darkness would be sufficient protection from prowling British submarines.

As she was leaving the Oslo fiord, news came in of *Triton*'s attack on the convoy in the Kattegat and of a further sinking by the *Sunfish*. Captain Thiele therefore took a wide sweep to the westward to avoid the danger area and so fell foul of the *Spearfish*. Unlike British ships at that time, the *Lützow* was equipped with an early version of radar, intended primarily for gunnery ranging. On this, when ten miles north of the Skaw, she detected some object fine on her starboard bow. As the range came down, Thiele ordered an alteration of course to port to avoid it. The swinging stern of the great ship at high speed raised a tall, tumbling white stern wave. It was this which had betrayed her to Forbes.

It was this alteration, too, which just gave time for the *Spearfish*'s crew to bring her torpedo tubes to the ready. When, three minutes later, the *Lützow* was brought back to her original course, Forbes was able to launch a salvo of six torpedoes, aiming them hastily by eye at the great ship racing by. One found its mark right aft in the pocket battleship, wrecking her propellers and rudder and causing heavy flooding. She lay, a helpless hulk drifting on the current towards the Skaw.

Still in no fit condition to dive and ignorant of the *Lützow*'s absence of escort, Forbes did not linger to admire his handiwork but hurried away westwards on the surface before the expected retribution descended on him. It was lucky for the *Lützow*. Her only protection was in fact her picket-boat which was hoisted out and set to patrol round her. It was not until 9 o'clock in the morning that a flotilla of destroyers and a Danish tug arrived to succour the crippled and well-nigh sinking ship.

Even now it was only by the narrowest margin that this valuable unit of Raeder's fleet was got back to her base. So parlous was her condition that Thiele nearly decided to beach her before she should sink. The knowledge that salvage tugs with powerful pumps were on their way held his hand. Carrying on, lying deep in the water, the *Lützow* did indeed ground involuntarily for a time but was hauled off. At a crawl the passage through the Belt to Kiel was made where she finally arrived on the evening of the 13th, so damaged that it was to be a full twelve months before she went again to sea.

Meanwhile, in conditions of ever-increasing difficulty and hazard, other submarines had kept up their efforts to disrupt the supply route. The narrow waters of the Kattegat were alive with anti-submarine craft. Overhead patrolling aircraft kept a continuous watch. In spite of this, the *Triad* had sunk the transport *Ionia* in the very mouth of the Oslo fiord in the early morning of the 11th. The same afternoon the *Sealion* had sunk the supply ship *August Leonhardt* in the Kattegat.

The following day, *Snapper*, failing to hit with two torpedoes the small tanker *Moonsund* with a cargo of urgently needed aviation petrol, boldly surfaced and sank her by gunfire, taking her crew prisoner. On the 14th, the *Sunfish* had her fourth success when Slaughter sent the transport *Florida* to the bottom with her ammunition and supplies. The Admiralty's warm signal to the Submarine Service, *You are all doing magnificent work*, was more than well deserved.

But as the German anti-submarine measures were stepped up, opportunities became harder to make, the dangers immensely greater. When the *Sterlet* attacked and sank the gunnery training ship *Brumme* on the 15th, she was overwhelmed by the weight of the counter-attack and destroyed with all hands. Surface patrols, aircraft and newly-laid minefields all combined to make conditions intolerable for the others. Days were long; darkness in which the submarines could surface and charge their batteries lasted only a few hours. With the enemy in occupation of all its shores, the Kattegat became a German lake, and though British submarines continued to haunt it at great hazard to themselves, they were unable to do much more to harry German communications with Norway.

When it is remembered that even in the broad waters of the Atlantic, German U-boats failed to disrupt Allied shipping sailing in convoy with comparatively weak escort, it is remarkable how much the British submarines did achieve in far more difficult conditions. The torpedoing of the *Lützow* and *Karlsruhe* was in any case a serious blow to Raeder's small surface fleet when added to the loss of the *Blücher* and *Königsberg*.

Far to the north, amidst the snows of Narvik, the German Navy had had to make further sacrifices on behalf of Hitler's grand strategy. There we must now turn to follow the events.

CHAPTER 7

During the night of April 9th the German assault forces everywhere were consolidating their hold on the Norwegian ports. The British Fleet, recoiling from the heavy air attacks of the afternoon, was steering away to the westward to rendezvous with the *Furious*. The *Karlsruhe* was being abandoned; the *Truant* was suffering her ordeal by depth charge, and the Fleet Air Arm at Hatston was preparing the Skuas for their epoch-making enterprise.

At Narvik the German destroyers were finding themselves in a position of increasing difficulty and danger.

The harbour to which they had penetrated lay far from the open sea, being reached by travelling first up the wide Vestfiord, formed by the sea area enclosed between the long line of the Lofoten Islands thrusting south-westward into the Arctic Ocean and the deeply indented mountainous mainland. Where the Vestfiord begins to narrow, the island of Tranoy juts out from the eastern shore and here pilots for the remainder of the journey were normally embarked.

A few miles further and the Vestfiord abruptly narrows at the island of Baröy and becomes the Ofotfiord. From here to Narvik the Ofotfiord runs eastward, a narrow waterway between precipitous mountain sides falling sheer into the sea and at that season mantled in deep snow to the water's edge.

The steep cliffs break back at intervals to form a number of side fiords. The first of these, on the southern shore, is Ballangen Fiord in which there is room to berth one or two small ships, though the little town of Ballangen has no harbour. Then on the same side comes a steep, narrow cleft.

The head of the Ofotfiord has now been reached and here three deep indentations push in between the hills. To the north, Herjangsfiord with the hamlet of Bjerkvik at its head and the Norwegian regimental depot of Elvegaard a mile or so from the sea. Eastward runs Rombaksfiord, deep and narrow; south-eastward, Beisfiord. On the hilly promontory between these last two is the town of Narvik, facing down the Ofotfiord, with the harbour formed by the bay just inside the narrow entrance of the Beisfiord. The long, restricted approach to the iron-ore port could easily be defended against an attacker; but exit from it could similarly be blocked.

Nine hundred miles from his base, and with the British fleet at sea in strength to intercept him, the German commander's only hope of breaking out was to sail at the earliest possible moment before the advantage of surprise had been lost. This he had been unable to do, for one of the two tankers which should have been at Narvik to refuel his ships had not arrived, and only the converted whaleship *Jan Wellen* from Murmansk was available. The destroyers each required between 500 and 600 tons of fuel. Not only was this far beyond the capacity of the tanker but her pumping arrangements were such that transfer of oil was very slow and only two destroyers at a time could be served.

Commodore Friedrich Bonte, however, was not unduly worried. He would sail on the night of the 10th when he was confident of evading enemy patrols by a high-speed dash through the night. The naval command would then arrange for tankers to meet his ships at sea. Meanwhile, U-boats were on patrol in the Vestfiord which would give him ample warning of any hostile forces and perhaps be able to damage them also. His powerfully armed ships could then be got ready to give a good account of themselves in the narrow waters of the Ofotfiord. It was unfortunate that the batteries commanding the Narrows did not exist; but to back up the U-boat pickets, one destroyer at a time would be stationed in the Ofotfiord, being relieved as necessary for the refuelling programme.

While waiting their turn to fuel, two destroyers would be berthed off Ballangen, ten miles to the westward of Narvik; others would be in the Herjangsfiord running north from the main fiord. The remainder, except the one on patrol, would be in the harbour of Narvik itself where the tanker lay.

To the Senior Officer of the Third Flotilla — one of the three flotillas of which the German force was composed — the duty was delegated of ensuring that these arrangements were carried out. Commodore Bonte was thus able to face the night — it was to be his last on earth — with a quiet mind, particularly as at 8.22 pm there came in a signal from *U51* reporting five British destroyers in Vestfiord steering south-west — away from Narvik. There was evidently no immediate attack to be expected, so the German flotilla settled down for the night. In the bitter cold and the falling snow, lookouts huddled in their thick clothing, cursing the fate which put them on watch on such a night when in any case they could see nothing but drifting snowflakes.

The ships which *U51* had glimpsed heading westwards between the snow squalls had been Captain Warburton-Lee's flotilla which we last saw heading up Vestfiord and intending to arrive off Narvik at 8 pm on the 9th. On his way, Warburton-Lee pondered the inadequacy of the information in his possession and its doubtful source. A Press report on the situation in a remote, minor port beyond the Arctic Circle, that 'one German ship had arrived and landed a small force', was neither dependable nor easily credible.

He bethought himself, therefore, of the pilot station at Tranoy in the Vestfiord. Arriving off it at four in the afternoon, he sent ashore to learn what the pilots could tell him. As he had suspected, the Germans were in greater strength than had been reported. Six warships, larger than those of the British flotilla, as well as a submarine had gone up the fiord, the pilots said, adding that the entrance to Ofotfiord was probably mined. The Germans also held the town of Narvik in considerable strength, and the English would need twice as many ships as they had, the Norwegians gloomily estimated.

The Germans were not the only ones, however, who knew the value of surprise. Signalling this fresh intelligence to the Admiralty, Warburton-Lee added *Intend attacking at dawn, high water*! High water would allow his ships to float over the moored mines, if they existed; dawn was the ideal moment for achieving surprise.

While off Tranöy, Warburton-Lee had a welcome reinforcement in the shape of the *Hostile*, commanded by Commander J. P. Wright. He had been on detached service with the cruiser *Birmingham*; but when that ship was sent home, he had hurried to join his flotilla leader. With his five ships, Warburton-Lee now turned seawards to await the hour at which he calculated he must turn back to arrive off Narvik at first light. Thus it was that *U51* had sighted him on a course away from Narvik which gave a false sense of security to Commodore Bonte.

At 9 pm, in reply to Warburton-Lee's signal, the Admiralty gave him orders which would have had most unfortunate results had they been obeyed. The flotilla was to patrol during the night in the entrance to Ofotfiord, lest the enemy should leave Narvik and by turning off through Tjelsundet, a channel leading north to Vaagsfiord, escape without encountering the British force. Fortunately, Warburton-Lee ignored this message. Otherwise he would certainly have run against the German destroyer on patrol, surprise would have been lost and calamity might have followed.

The message had ended, *Attack at dawn: all good luck*. This was sufficient for *Hardy*'s captain. Thereafter he had no doubts as to what he must do, even when the Admiralty in midnight session thought the operation was so hazardous that they began to have second thoughts and signalled, *Norwegian coast defence ships Eidsvold and Norge may be in German hands: you alone can judge whether in these circumstances attack should be made. We shall support whatever decision you take*. By the time this reached him, the flotilla was already past Tranöy and, in continuous snowstorms, was feeling its way into Ofotfiord.

Out at sea, Admiral Whitworth in the *Renown* had followed this interchange of signals and from the moment he had received Warburton-Lee's first signal at 6 pm had pondered whether he should send reinforcements to the Second Flotilla. He had the cruiser *Penelope* and destroyers under his command. By the time they could make their way up the Vestfiord through the blinding curtain of falling snow and join forces with the Second Flotilla delay would have been imposed on the operation.[3] He decided to leave well alone. In the light of later events it seems Unfortunate that the *Penelope* was not sent after the Second Flotilla even if she did not join it until the attack had been delivered.[4]

---

[3] The control of the operations of ships of his own force taken out of his hands by the Admiralty's direct orders to Warburton-Lee, Whitworth felt he might only confuse the issue by interfering.

[4] The Germans, working to a carefully prepared plan, were

At 1 o'clock in the morning they had groped their way past Tranöy. Following the *Hardy* was the *Hunter* commanded by Lieutenant-Commander L. de Villiers. In her wake came the *Havock*, Lieutenant-Commander Rafe Courage. The *Hotspur* was next, the ship of the second-in-command of the force. Commander H. F. N. Layman, and finally, the *Hostile*.

The shoreline was invisible behind the curtain of snow for long stretches of the tortuous passage. One nearly disastrous moment came when a white hillside loomed dimly out of the mists directly ahead of the *Hardy*, which swerved hastily away to avoid running aground. Astern of her, the others also only sensed their danger at the last moment and saved themselves by emergency manoeuvres which threw the line into temporary confusion.

Then the bright lights of a local passenger steamer suddenly appeared as it steamed right through the fine of darkened ships. Unaware of her narrow escape as wheels were put hastily over, engine-room telegraphs clanged and turbines screamed in reverse to claw the destroyers clear of collision, the steamer passed on and vanished into the snowfall.

The first grey light was growing as the flotilla passed through the Narrows into Ofotfiord — fifteen miles to go. It was here that Commodore Bonte must have believed that one of his ships was on guard in accordance with his instructions. The Commanding Officer of the German Third Flotilla must have thought so also; he was later to state that the *Roeder* had been

---

implementing it with speed and vigour, at Narvik as elsewhere. The British, 'caught on the wrong foot', groped blindly and irresolutely. Boldness might have brought them glittering success at Bergen and Trondheim. At Narvik it was left to Warburton-Lee and his little force to gather the laurels but their triumph would have been more complete and less costly if they had been in greater strength.

told to remain on patrol until relieved by the *Lüdemann*. But in the *Roeder*'s diary there was the entry 'Am relieving *Schmitt* from 0400 as anti-submarine patrol until dawn.' (German times were an hour ahead of the British which are used throughout this book.)

So at 4 o'clock British time, as dawn was breaking, the *Roeder* turned towards harbour, leaving the patrol position empty. A bare mile or so behind her, hidden in the snow and mist, the British destroyers were following. As the *Roeder* came to anchor at 4.20 the snowfall was beginning to clear and visibility was increasing as daylight grew.

Nothing had been seen of the British ships when at 4.30 the harbour suddenly erupted in shattering explosions and shell splashes. The sleeping crews came clattering on deck to action stations, shocked and dazed, unable to distinguish any enemy and believing at first that they were under air attack.

Commodore Bonte's flagship, *Heidkamp*, at anchor in the harbour, was the first to suffer as a torpedo exploded in her after magazine, blowing it up, causing fearful casualties, including the death of the Commodore himself. Then the *Schmitt* seemed to leap bodily in the water as a torpedo burst in her engine room and another in her boiler room, breaking her in two pieces which sank at once. Other torpedoes were bursting against merchant ships in the harbour and against the shore, while salvoes of shells rained on the *Roeder*, starting fires and wreaking heavy damage.

There came a brief lull. Not a shot had been fired as yet from the German ships, taken completely by surprise. Then gun flashes were seen in the harbour entrance and at last the German gun crews came into action; but with no clear targets in sight their shooting was wild and inaccurate, whereas they themselves were repeatedly hit. The two ships which had been alongside the Jan *Wellen* taking in fuel had slipped their wires at once, but one of them, the *Lüdemann*, had a gun knocked out and a fire started which necessitated flooding the after-magazine. The other, the *Künne*, escaped being hit but the concussion of the torpedoes which sank the *Schmitt* had put her engines temporarily out of action.

It was the *Roeder*, however, which bore the brunt of the attack. One of the first hits had wrecked her cable gear so that her anchors could be neither weighed nor slipped. With fires raging and heavy damage she was moved astern, dragging her anchors behind her, to the pier, where her condition seemed so perilous that her captain gave the order to abandon ship.

Most of this damage had been caused by three of Warburton-Lee's destroyers. Going in alone in the *Hardy* at the outset, he had been able calmly to manoeuvre among the tightly packed merchant ships in the harbour and bring his torpedo tubes to bear before his first gun salvoes woke the sleeping enemy to action. Of the seven torpedoes fired, two had hit and sunk the *Schmitt*, another had blown off the stern of the *Heidkamp*, and others had hit merchant ships. He had then withdrawn to let *Hunter* and *Havock* take his place. Both fired torpedoes, though it does not seem that any of the German destroyers were hit by them, and both continued the gun action in which the *Roeder* was so severely damaged.

In reply the *Roeder* also fired torpedoes in the direction of the harbour entrance, but those which found their target were seen to run under the British destroyers without exploding. They were either set too deep, or like the torpedoes supplied to German U-boats at the beginning of the war, they were fitted with magnetic pistols which failed to function in high latitudes.

The two remaining ships of Warburton-Lee's flotilla, *Hotspur* and *Hostile*, had been left on guard outside the harbour to neutralise batteries believed to be mounted on the north shore of the Narvik peninsula. Finding that these were not in fact in existence, the *Hostile* had joined in the gun action and had seen her 4.7-inch shells plunge home in the boiler room of the *Roeder* to start a devastating fire. As the others withdrew, *Hotspur* and *Hostile* covered them with a smokescreen from the German fire which was at last becoming more effective. At the same time the *Hotspur* took the opportunity to send four torpedoes into the mass of shipping in the harbour.

In the low visibility, it had not been possible for any examination to be made of the side fiords. But this did not seem of any great importance as five out of the total of six German destroyers reported by the pilots of Tranöy had been located and engaged. Warburton-Lee therefore now led all five of his ships to the harbour entrance for a further bombardment as they steamed past. They were greeted by a fairly intense fire but it was still ineffective and they had suffered little damage when they withdrew two or three miles down the fiord.

There Warburton-Lee surveyed the situation and called for reports of the number of torpedoes each ship still had aboard. Though *Hardy* had only one and the *Hunter* none, *Hotspur* had four, *Havock* three and the *Hostile* had her full outfit of eight. Most of the enemy destroyers had apparently been located in the harbour and were sunk or damaged. The British flotilla having spent more than an hour in the vicinity without meeting any serious opposition, there seemed nothing to prevent a final attack before withdrawing. Once more, therefore, he signalled for single line ahead and, at fifteen knots, led the way back to the harbour entrance. Mist had thickened over Narvik but occasional targets showed up and were engaged as the destroyers turned to port in each other's wakes. The *Hostile* sent four of her torpedoes shorewards and saw another enemy torpedo pass harmlessly under her.

Well satisfied with the success achieved by daring and surprise, the British commander prepared to withdraw. But the luck which had attended him so far had run out. As he turned away from Narvik to head seawards, three fresh enemy ships suddenly appeared out of the mist to the northwards.

The three German ships, *Zenker*, *Giese* and *Köllner*, which had been berthed for the night in Herjangsfiord had heard and seen nothing of the action until 5.15 when the alarm was finally got through to them. Fifteen minutes later they had got under way and now arrived in time to engage the British flotilla as it turned to retire. Considerably larger than the British ships and each armed with five 5-inch guns as compared to the four 4.7-inch guns of the *Hardy* class, they were at first identified as a cruiser and three destroyers. As such, Warburton-Lee reported them to his commander-in-chief, adding *Am withdrawing to westward*. Signalling for thirty knots, he led the flotilla seaward.

A running fight developed, but in the low visibility neither side achieved any success. The German destroyers were among those which had not refuelled. Their tanks were all but empty so that they could not stay long in chase. The British flotilla was about to escape almost unscathed, when suddenly out of the mist ahead there loomed a further two German destroyers across their path. The British were trapped.

The two ships in Ballangen Fiord, *Thiele* and *Von Arnim*, had not sighted the British destroyers on their way in, but they had received the alarm signal. Thick fog had delayed their getting under way until 5.40, so that only by the narrowest margin did they finally appear on the scene to turn the tables.

At first sight of them, Warburton-Lee hoped they might be reinforcements coming to him — as well they might have been had Admiral Whitworth's decision gone the other way. A signalled challenge from the *Hardy*, however, was answered by an accurately placed salvo of 5-inch shells. With only their forward guns available to engage the enemy, the leading British ships were at first seriously outgunned. The signal, *Keep on engaging the enemy*, had just broken out at the *Hardy*'s yardarm when a shell hit squarely on her bridge with devastating effect.

Warburton-Lee was mortally wounded and every man on the bridge with him was either killed or wounded. From the *Havock*, third ship of the line, Lieutenant-Commander Courage, who was manoeuvring his ship to avoid a shoal of German torpedoes, which were fortunately seen in good time running on the surface, thought that one of them had hit the leader as a great explosion and a huge column of smoke broke out amidships in her. It was in fact a salvo of shells which had hit and started a raging boiler-room fire.

On the *Hardy*'s bridge with his captain was the Secretary, Paymaster-Lieutenant G. H. Stanning. At the explosion of the first shell he was lifted clean off his feet to fall asprawl the gyro compass binnacle. Gathering himself together he found his left foot hanging lifeless; but he had otherwise escaped serious injury — a miracle it seemed as he surveyed the shambles around him, his captain terribly wounded and the navigator lying kicking on the deck, apparently dying.

From the wheelhouse below the bridge there came no sound and no reply to orders. The ship was careering along at high speed with no one in control, the rock-bound shore close on the port side. Paymasters were neither trained nor expected to take part in fighting or control of the ship. Their duties in action were to cipher and decipher messages and perhaps keep a record of events. They were non-executive officers. The

Secretary was usually given the expressive sobriquet of 'Scratch'.

In the absence of any executive officer, Stanning, with great initiative, at once took action. Dragging his wounded leg behind him, he struggled down from the bridge, took the wheel from the lifeless hands of the Coxswain and steered down the fiord until a seaman arrived to relieve him, when he again made his painful way to the bridge to resume control.

The second salvo of shells had cut the steam pipes to the engines and now the *Hardy* was rapidly losing way. It seemed that she must soon come to a standstill, a blazing hulk to be hammered to a wreck by the concentrated fire of the enemy. The torpedo officer, Lieutenant G. R. Heppel, assuming that the bridge steering position had been put out of action, had made his way aft to connect up the auxiliary steering position, but finding the ship answering to the wheel, returned to the bridge in time to approve an order which Stanning had just given, to run the dying ship ashore before she sank.

Meanwhile, as the crippled *Hardy* sheered away, the *Hunter*, now leading the line, drew the enemy's fire and was almost at once set on fire and disabled. Astern of her, Commander Layman in the *Hotspur*, his telegraphs set to Full Speed Ahead, saw the *Hunter* swerve across his path as her speed fell away. He called an order to the Coxswain at the wheel which would take his racing ship clear.

At that moment a shell burst below his bridge, cutting not only the controls between the wheel and the steering gear, but twisting and jamming the engine-room telegraph connections. Unable either to steer or to give orders to stop engines, Layman saw his bow cleave deep into the *Hunter*'s hull.

The two ships were locked together, the *Hotspur*'s forward way spinning them slowly round. To get control of his ship again, Layman left the bridge to run aft to where he could give verbal orders to the engines and the auxiliary steering position right aft. Hardly had he left when a shell hit on the bridge, bursting against the pedestal of the gun director, killed every soul left on the bridge and in the director tower.

The German destroyers were now pouring a devastating fire into the two crippled ships. Reaching the after superstructure where 'X' gun was mounted and whence the two after guns were being kept in action and controlled by the wounded Sub-Lieutenant L. J. Tillie, Layman was able to control his engines by verbal orders passed down the engine-room hatch. He managed to disengage his ship from the now sinking *Hunter*, then, by the cumbrous method of passing messages down to the tiller flat in the extreme stern, he was able to shape a wavering course down the fiord away from the hail of shells which was rapidly reducing the *Hotspur* to a wreck.

Of the British flotilla, two ships only, *Havock* and *Hostile*, had avoided serious damage. Swerving past the interlocked *Hunter* and *Hotspur*, they had found themselves running clear of the action to the westward after engaging the *Thiele* and *Arnim* at point blank range as the Germans ran past on an opposite course to join the three ships from Herjangsfiord. *Havock*, now at the head of the line, turned back to bring support to the two injured ships, but finding both his forward guns out of action, Courage turned westward again, screening the *Hotspur* with smoke and continuing to engage the enemy with his after guns.

Then, his forward guns repaired, he followed the *Hostile* round as the two ships boldly steered towards the greatly superior enemy force so as to cover the escape of the *Hotspur*. The enemy showed no enthusiasm to continue the fight. The three ships from Herjangsfiord were so short of fuel that they could not chase the *Hotspur*, while the *Thiele* and *Arnim* had both suffered so heavily in the gun action that they left the fight and made hastily for harbour. The *Thiele* had been repeatedly hit, had two guns out of action, was on fire and had a magazine flooded. The *Arnim* had been five times hit and had a boiler room out of action.

The fight had ended with three out of the five British ships escaping seawards. The *Hardy* was aground and on fire, and last seen with one gun still in action while her crew scrambled ashore. The majority escaped and were rescued a few days later as will be related elsewhere. The *Hunter* had sunk in mid fiord, the bitter cold of the ice-flecked water claiming all but fifty of her crew who were picked up by the Germans, ten of them dying later.

Warburton-Lee's gallant leadership earned his memory a posthumous Victoria Cross, the first to be awarded in the War.

As for the ten ships of the German flotilla, two had been sunk — *Heidkamp* and *Schmitt* — three had been so damaged as to make them unseaworthy or nearly so — *Roeder*, *Thiele* and *Arnim* — and another, the *Lüdemann*, had a flooded magazine and other damage. The *Künne* had her engines temporarily disabled and had suffered damage from shell splinters. Only the *Zenker*, *Köllner* and *Giese* were undamaged and they had shot away more than half their ammunition.

A further German calamity was to make this latter handicap all the more serious. As the three surviving British ships were passing through the Narrows on their way to sea, a large merchant ship was sighted making up the fiord. Commander Layman, his ship much damaged, being controlled from aft and with no means of signalling, had delegated command of the flotilla to Commander Wright of the *Hostile* who now brought the merchant ship to with a shot across her bows. When another shot from the *Havock* hit her in the bow and set her on fire, the crew were seen to abandon ship. They were picked up by the *Havock* whence an armed boats' crew was sent to examine the ship, now identified as the German supply ship *Rauenfels*. She was burning so furiously, however, that the boat was recalled. Getting under way again, Lieutenant-Commander Courage ordered two rounds of high explosive shell to be fired into her.

The result was spectacular and left no doubt of the German ship's cargo as she blew up with a shattering explosion, sending a column of flame and debris up to a height of 3000 feet. The *Havock* was indeed fortunate to escape with slight damage to her hull and no casualties.

Thus ended the first Battle of Narvik. That it was a material victory for the British flotilla must be conceded. Out of the ten destroyers of Commodore Bonte's squadron, only four remained fully battleworthy and the damage to the four others surviving could not be made good, cut off as they were from repair facilities.

Warburton-Lee's initiative and dash were to have wider repercussions. The Norwegians, hitherto dazed by the sudden, unprovoked German attack on their country, took heart to resist. The detailed German plans for Narvik were completely disrupted. The morale of their destroyer crews was so shaken by the suddenness and surprise of the assault that they were bereft of the skill and resolution which might have enabled them to extricate and save the seaworthy survivors of the battle. While they fumbled and hesitated, nemesis approached.

CHAPTER 8

News of the Second Flotilla's gallant exploit, arriving at about the same time that the success of the Fleet Air Arm aircraft from Hatston became known, seemed a bright gleam in an otherwise black horizon. But in spite of its superior strength, the Home Fleet had failed to prevent the German naval forces from reaching any of the key ports on the Norwegian west coast although information which should have enabled them to do so had been available in time.

A fleet cannot be kept continuously at immediate notice for sea. The steady flow of doubtful rumours of enemy movements since the beginning of the war, much chaff containing a few grains of truth, requiring the check and double-check of every piece of intelligence before action was taken, had delayed-appreciation of the true meaning of the German fleet's sortie. By the morning of April 9th, however, news of the invasion of Norway had come in to confirm the Commander-in-Chief's opinion reached on the previous afternoon. Admiral Forbes had at once appreciated that the enemy forces at Bergen, less than a hundred miles to leeward of him, might be trapped if a British force were sent in after them.

Unfortunately, he hesitated. The Nelson dictum — 'Lose not an hour' — was forgotten. Not one but many hours were lost while the Admiralty was asked for details of the enemy's strength. It was nearly noon before Admiral Layton's cruisers were detached; it would have been dusk before they reached the entrance to the fiords. In face of the air attacks which were about to be delivered on the British fleet, however, this might well have been a positive advantage.

But now the Admiralty made one of the repeated interventions which were to hamper the initiative of their sea commanders. The attack was annulled. Unreasonable fear that the shore defences would have been already taken over and made effective by the Germans, was the principal reason. The daring and vigour which had given the Germans their success was sadly lacking in the British High Command at this time.

It may be argued that the British force would have been subjected to an intolerable weight of air attack on the following day, but it would have been no more severe than what they were to suffer in the later stages of the campaign without unacceptable losses. It is certainly true that the Commander-in-Chief's orders to Admiral Layton to send only his destroyers up to Bergen, keeping his cruisers at sea, was open to criticism, but it would have been within the Admiralty's sphere to have ordered the strength of the attack to be increased. To cancel the operation altogether seemed weak-kneed in the extreme. Letting 'I dare not' wait upon 'I would', the Home Fleet was left to patrol uselessly at sea and to be driven from the area by air attack.

Trondheim was the next target considered. It was politically and strategically even more important than Bergen and not yet so strongly dominated by German air power. Had the port been invested by the main body of the Home Fleet and a force sent up the fiords on the following day, April 10th, the valuable cruiser *Hipper* would have been trapped. Instead, it was decided to employ the torpedo bombers from the *Furious* and a whole day was wasted waiting for her to join the fleet. The negligible results and the escape of the *Hipper* have been already recounted.

What a different approach had been that of Warburton-Lee — *Intend attacking at dawn*! His initiative and daring had turned Narvik into a mortal trap for nearly half the total German destroyer strength. Yet even now the harvest which Warburton-Lee's sowing had prepared was nearly lost to the British through indecision and hesitation. *Hardy*'s last signal, reporting a cruiser and destroyers, reached Admiral Whitworth at 6 am. He at once ordered Captain Yates of the cruiser *Penelope*, with his screen of four large Tribal class destroyers, to 'support the retirement of the Second Destroyer Flotilla, counterattacking the enemy as necessary'. He was then to establish a patrol off the minefield (at the entrance to Vestfiord) 'with the object of preventing further enemy forces reaching Narvik'.

When Yates met the three survivors of the Second Flotilla, there was, of course, no enemy immediately in view to counterattack. Having agreed with Commander Layman's proposal to take the battered *Hotspur* to the shelter of Skjelfiord in the Lofoten Islands for temporary repairs, with the *Hostile* to escort her, he therefore proceeded to dispose his available destroyers — the four of his screen, Captain Bickford's four mine-laying destroyers and the *Havock*, in accordance with Whitworth's instructions. These were amplified by a signal at midday. *Present situation. Enemy forces in Narvik, one cruiser, five destroyers, one submarine. Troop transports may be expected. Your object is to prevent reinforcements reaching Narvik. Establish destroyer patrol across Vestfiord, and a warning antisubmarine patrol thirty miles north-east of it.*

This unambitious objective was slightly modified when an Admiralty message originated early in the morning reached Whitworth at a few minutes before 1 pm. This ordered him to concentrate on 'allowing no force from Narvik to escape', which did not, however, entail any great alteration in Yates' dispositions.

Meanwhile in Narvik where, on the death of Commodore Bonte, the naval command had descended on Captain Bey, commanding the Fourth Flotilla, desperate efforts were being made to get the eight surviving destroyers battleworthy. The three undamaged ships were taking in fuel. Two of them, the *Giese* and *Zenker*, had completed early in the afternoon of the 10th. The third, the *Köllner*, would not be ready until midnight. Of the remainder the *Roeder* was too badly damaged to be made seaworthy and she was relegated to the role of harbour defence from a berth alongside the jetty; the other four would require two days' work with the resources available to make them seaworthy, let alone fit for battle. An immediate attack by *Penelope* and her destroyers would have found the enemy disorganised, some immobilised through machinery damage, others with only a portion of their armament ready and all critically short of ammunition.

The daylight hours of the 10th were allowed to pass with the British light forces passively awaiting a further move by the enemy. Although at 7 pm the Admiralty signalled to the Commander-in-Chief that recapture of Narvik took priority over that of Bergen and Trondheim, and that an expedition was being prepared, they expressed concurrence with the arrangements made by adding that it was of primary importance in the meantime to prevent Narvik being reinforced by sea.

An hour later more forceful counsels began to prevail in Whitehall, no doubt coinciding with the arrival of Mr Churchill in the War Room for his night's labours after his customary afternoon sleep. A signal was soon on its way to *Penelope*: *If in light of experience this morning you consider it a justifiable operation, take available destroyers in the Narvik area and attack enemy tonight or tomorrow morning.*

Yates was not long in replying. At 11.10 pm he signalled. *Consider attack justifiable though surprise has been lost. Navigation dangerous from wrecks of ships sunk today, eliminating chance of successful night attack.* So far, so good; but the signal continued, *Propose attacking at dawn Friday (12th) since operation orders cannot be got out and issued for tomorrow in view of present disposition of destroyers on patrol.*

Another day was thus to be granted to the Germans in which to repair their battle damage and consolidate their position ashore for the sake of written operation orders when a few signals passed down the line on the way up the fiord would have been enough. *Lose not an hour.*

Meanwhile, a further element of doubt was befogging strategical thought. Admiral Whitworth, exasperated at the way control of the ships under his command was again being bypassed by these direct communications between the Admiralty and one of his cruiser captains, felt bound to point out that his force as a whole had now been given three different tasks not wholly compatible with each other — to prevent the Germans from escaping from Narvik, to prevent fresh forces reaching them there and now to attack them. 'In my view,' he later said, 'the situation required clarifying.'

He therefore signalled to the Admiralty that the orders to *Penelope* conflicted with the official policy previously decided that the primary object was to prevent Narvik being reinforced by sea, a policy with which he agreed. Further casualties to ships of his force, which would probably result from an attack on Narvik, would jeopardise the achievement of that primary object.

Nevertheless, the Admiralty stood by their plan and approved Yates' proposal to attack at dawn on the 12th.

While these signals were being exchanged, the enemy in Narvik were stirring. During the afternoon Captain Bey had received orders to put to sea that night with any of his ships that were seaworthy. Only the *Giese* and the *Zenker* could be got ready in time, and with these he set out soon after dark. Down the Ofotfiord and through the Narrows he passed, finding no sign of an enemy. At Tranöy the Vestfiord opens out into a wide estuary. The snowstorms had cleared and, though it was dark, to the north there was the glow of the Arctic night. Against it Bey sighted the *Penelope* and two destroyers on patrol. By keeping close inshore where the outline of his ships would have merged with the dark background of the land, Bey could almost certainly have slipped away unsighted. With no radar the British would have been most unlikely to have detected the two destroyers which in any case had full speed available and so risked only a running fight through the darkness.

But Bey's heart failed him, his nerve shaken by the disastrous events of the morning. He turned back to Narvik. At noon on the 11th, though more of his ships were by then fit for sea, he signalled to his Commander-in-Chief that a breakout that evening was impossible. It betrayed a lack of enterprise surprising in a destroyer man whose career had been spent almost exclusively in those racing, lively craft which relied on speed and daring for success. It was to cost Raeder's Navy dear.

For, meanwhile, a further delay in British plans had intervened. During the night of the 10th the British destroyer patrol off Baröy, outside the narrows of Ofotfiord, of which the senior officer was Commander McCoy of the *Bedouin*, had

had an experience which was falsely interpreted. Unknown to them, they had been sharing their patrol area with a German submarine — *U25*. Soon after dark the U-boat had fired torpedoes at its unsuspecting target. Explosions which followed had led the U-boat commander to believe that two of the destroyers had been sunk.

Fortunately for the British, however, German torpedoes at this time were suffering from two serious defects. The magnetic pistols in the warheads were failing to function correctly owing to the difference in the earth's magnetic field in those northern latitudes from that in German waters. Furthermore, the depth-keeping mechanism of the torpedoes themselves was unreliable. We have seen, during the Battle of Narvik on the morning of the 10th, some German torpedoes passing harmlessly under the British destroyers and others scuttering along the surface so that they were easily avoided.

So recurrent were these defects that the U-boats were virtually unarmed. Reading his commanders' reports, Admiral Doenitz, their chief, had exploded, 'I do not believe that ever in the history of war have men been sent against the enemy with such a useless weapon.'

However, *U25*'s torpedoes were not without their effect. Exploding harmlessly near the *Bedouin*, they had led Commander McCoy to believe that his ships were in the middle of a minefield electrically controlled from the island of Baröy where he saw unusual activity taking place.

Not only did McCoy deem it wise to withdraw his force from the area, thereafter keeping further out in Vestfiord and so clearing the way for Bey's two ships to clear the Narrows undetected had they tried, but he signalled his conclusions to Captain Yates. The shore defences were fully prepared, it seemed to him, and an operation on the lines of the Second Flotilla's attack 'could no longer be carried out effectively'.

Accepting McCoy's unfortunate interpretation of his experiences, Yates signalled them to the Admiralty, agreeing with his conclusions. Though the Admiralty felt they could not go against the opinion of the men on the spot, they evidently doubted its validity as they told Yates to have all preliminary arrangements made in case an attack should be ordered. But in fact Yates' opportunity to lead a force into victorious action had gone, never to recur.

While he procrastinated, news had reached Admiral Whitworth through Commander Wright of the *Hostile* in Skjelfiord which he considered merited immediate action by *Penelope* elsewhere. The Norwegian police had told Wright that a warship had been seen on the 10th in Tennholm Fiord, fifty miles down the coast, that a large tanker was lying there, hoping for a pilot to take her to Narvik, and that several large transports had arrived at Bodo at the entrance to Vestfiord. Early on the 11th Yates was accordingly told to get a pilot at Tranöy, take two destroyers and attack the transports reported at Bodo, after which he should try to capture the tanker in Tennholm Fiord. Lest there should be doubt as to his first object, Admiral Whitworth concluded his message with the instructions that 'attack on enemy transports must take precedence over attack on Narvik'.

It was to prove a calamitous wild-goose chase. Failing to find a pilot at Tranöy, the *Penelope*, with *Eskimo* and *Kimberley*, sailed south to try to get one at Fleinvaer, a few miles from Bodo, or, if necessary, to go up the fiord without one. At 3 o'clock in the afternoon the cruiser struck a rock and was so badly damaged that it was only with great difficulty that she was able to struggle back to Skjelfiord in tow of the *Eskimo*.

Meanwhile, the *Kimberley* made her way up to Bodo where it was learnt that only one merchant ship had called there since the invasion began. This was the supply ship *Alster* which early that morning had been intercepted and captured by the destroyer *Icarus* in Vestfiord.

Procrastination and misfortune were by no means confined to the British. In Narvik the vacillating German commander had again refused to risk a breakout during the night of the 11th though by this time seven out of eight of his ships were reasonably seaworthy and the way had been cleared for them by the elimination of the *Penelope*. This latter fact was not known to Bey who shrank from a possible encounter. Though his Commander-in-Chief was pressing him to get all seaworthy destroyers away, seizing any opportunity of bad visibility to break out, Bey seemed to have lost all fire and resolution. He gloomily surmised that with the short nights at that season, he would have to wait for some time for suitable conditions.

Then during the night of the 11th fate delivered a blow which one might think comprised the just deserts of his lack of enterprise. While manoeuvring in the harbour two of his undamaged destroyers ran aground. The *Zenker* damaged her propellers and would be restricted to twenty knots; but the *Köllner* had so damaged herself that she was irreparably unseaworthy. There was no question of her getting back to Germany. She was therefore to be moored at Taarstad, down the fiord, as a floating defence battery as soon as she could be sufficiently patched up to move.

Thus delays on the British side were more than cancelled out by the inertia of the German commander. By now the Admiralty had bestirred themselves to give instructions to the Commander-in-Chief, Home Fleet, to prepare a fresh attempt against Narvik from the sea, using a battleship heavily escorted by destroyers with a synchronised dive-bombing attack by the aircraft of the *Furious*.

Admiral Forbes, since the unsuccessful air attack on Trondheim, had been coming north with the *Furious* whose aircraft were to attempt a similar operation against the considerable German force, believed to include two cruisers, in Narvik. Early on the 12th he was joined by Admiral Whitworth's two battle-cruisers. That evening the air attack was launched. It suffered from the same makeshift arrangements which were to bedevil the whole of the British operations in Norway. No previous reconnaissance of the area was made; there were no maps so that the airmen had to rely upon photostat copies of charts on which no contours were shown.

With low cloud blanketing the steep mountainsides and snow squalls sweeping across below the overcast, the first squadron of Swordfish aircraft set off at 4 pm on the 150-mile flight to Narvik. Flying blind at times between the precipitous cliffs of the narrow fiord, they broke into clear weather in the nick of time to see the harbour stretched out below them. Climbing steeply up into the blue, pursued by anti-aircraft fire, the slow, ponderous biplanes, never designed for dive-bombing, banked over and shuddered their way earthwards to release their bombs at heights of between 1200 and 400 feet. It is not surprising that the inexperienced airmen, who had gone into action for the first time in their lives at Trondheim on the previous day, scored no hits.

The second squadron from the *Furious*, leaving half an hour later than the first, found weather conditions worse and could not win their way through to Narvik at all. In darkness the two squadrons landed on their carrier again far out at sea, the first night deck-landing any of them had made.

While this abortive but gallant effort was taking place, the Commander-in-Chief had been issuing orders for an assault by surface ships on the morrow, April 13th. Admiral Whitworth was to transfer to the battleship *Warspite* and would have under his orders four Tribal Class destroyers, *Bedouin*, *Cossack*, *Eskimo*, *Punjabi*, and five smaller destroyers, *Hero*, *Icarus*, *Kimberley*, *Forester* and *Foxhound*. The squadron would make rendezvous inside Vestfiord, some 100 miles from Narvik at 7.30 in the morning, and would head up the fiord, the destroyers going ahead, some screening the battleship, others with sweeps out against the suspected minefield.

In the meantime, during the 12th, news had reached Admiral Forbes that at last a military expedition was on its way to Narvik. An advance party of half a battalion of the Scots Guards with the Military Commander, General Mackesy, had sailed from Scapa Flow in the cruiser *Southampton* and would reach the Narvik area on the 14th. At about the same time the cruiser *Aurora* had sailed from the Clyde, flying at her masthead the Union Flag of an Admiral of the Fleet, the Earl of Cork and Orrery, who had been designated Naval Commander of the expedition, and by reason of his rank and the absence of any appointment of a Supreme Commander, was also overall commander of the operation. On the day after, a convoy of five troopships carrying the remainder of the Guards Brigade and another Brigade, the 146th, would also arrive.

To cover the passage of the convoy, designated NP1, the Commander-in-Chief had detached the *Valiant*, *Repulse* and three destroyers.

High hopes that the military force might be rushed quickly to Narvik to take advantage of the dismay and demoralisation spread among the enemy by naval victory had led Winston

Churchill to give the expedition the code name 'Rupert' after the dashing Cavalier leader. Alas, an overseas military expedition can never be quickly mounted; still less so, when its dispatch follows upon a preceding disbandment and dispersal, as in this case.

Even so, great expectations were harboured in naval circles that, following destruction of the German naval force in Ofotfiord, Narvik would fall 'like a ripe plum' to British troops thrown ashore. Such expectations were not shared by the War Office or its chosen commander, Major-General P. J. Mackesy. Though to his official instructions was added a manuscript note from the Chief of the Imperial General Staff, General Ironside, in which occurred the sentences

> You may have a chance of taking advantage of naval action and you should do so if you can. Boldness is required [the key phrase in his orders ran]. It is not intended that you should land in the face of opposition.

Thus, while Whitworth's force prepared for action which was expected to destroy the remnants of German naval strength in the north, the two commanders of the expedition to capture Narvik were speeding through the night to the scene of action with very different ideas as to the task ahead of them. The seeds of controversy had been truly sown.

CHAPTER 9

The Germans' ability to decipher many of the British naval messages at this time brought ample warning to Captain Bey that a formidable attack using a battleship, destroyers and aircraft was planned for the afternoon of April 13th. He at once gave orders for the best possible disposition of his force which would at least make the enemy pay heavily for any success. The battleworthy ships would disperse into the side fiords — Ballangen and Herjangs — where they might hope to encircle the British force, as by good fortune they had managed to do at the last on the 10th. The *Köllner* was to be moved at once to Taarstadt where she could lie in ambush.

Such were Bey's orders, but his own fatalistic, even despairing attitude would seem to have spread to the force under his command. When, at 1 pm, the *Köllner*, escorted by the *Künne*, on her way to Taarstadt, sighted the British force approaching through the Narrows, the remainder of the German destroyers had not yet raised steam for their move from Narvik harbour where all six of them lay concentrated. On receipt of the alarm from the *Künne*, all but the immobilised *Roeder* were ordered out by Bey; one by one, as sufficient steam became available, they got under way — first the *Lüdemann*, followed by *Zenker* and *Arnim*. The *Thiele* and *Giese* were still more unprepared and did not follow them for some time.

Meanwhile, the *Künne* had retired in face of so greatly superior a force, exchanging ineffective fire at the limit of visibility, some six miles. The *Köllner*, patently unable to offer battle in her damaged state, had headed for Djupvik Bay on the south side of the fiord where she could lie unsighted until the

British ships passed at close range when her captain hoped to be able to use his torpedoes to good effect before himself being overwhelmed. His hopes were doomed to be shattered. From the *Warspite* had been launched the Swordfish floatplane she carried, and now it was scouting ahead. Its observer, Lieutenant-Commander W. L. M. Brown, was to send back invaluable information.

Having reported the two enemy ships, the Swordfish had flown on up the fiord, reported the enemy dispositions and turned for a reconnaissance of Herjangsfiord. There the delighted airmen saw a submarine, *U64*, lying fully surfaced. Putting his clumsy machine into the nearest approach to a dive of which it was capable, the pilot, Petty Officer F. R. Price, released his two 350 lb. anti-submarine bombs. A direct hit sent the U-boat to the bottom within half a minute.

Returning down the fiord, the crew of the aircraft were just in time to see the *Köllner*'s retirement into ambush and signal a warning to the *Warspite*. Thus, when the leading British destroyers, *Bedouin* and *Eskimo*, rounded the point of Djupvik Bay it was with torpedo tubes and guns trained to starboard and ready to open fire. Torpedoes splashed into the water from both British and German ships and at the same moment guns on either side flamed into action. It was a hopeless fight for the *Köllner*. She had got only one salvo away when the combined fire of the *Bedouin* and *Eskimo* smashed her into silence. Then the first torpedo arrived, blowing off the *Köllner*'s bow. As the *Warspite* nosed round the corner the monstrous blast of her 15-inch guns split the air and went bellowing away, the thunder tossed back and forth from mountainside to mountainside. In a few minutes, the *Köllner* rolled over and sank. Her own torpedoes had missed.

The British squadron swept on, all eyes peering into the mist for a first sight of the enemy. The *Künne*, retiring, met the *Lüdemann* and *Zenker*. She turned into line with them and the three ships together awaited the coming fight. As the first British ships came dimly into sight, the Germans, now joined also by the *Arnim*, turned to bring all their guns to bear and to fire torpedoes; but with ships of both sides firing independently, the German destroyers weaving back and forth in a confusing pattern, and the British swerving to avoid the flights of torpedoes whose tracks could be seen streaking past or under them, spotting the fall of shot was impossible. As the Germans retired before the advancing British, keeping at the limit of visibility, the shooting on both sides became wild and quite ineffective. Frost and snow blurred gun and director telescopes. The gunfire echoed and rolled round the steep sides of the fiord, an occasional shattering blast as the 15-inch guns of the *Warspite* found a target adding to the sound and fury. The concussions dislodged clouds of snow from the hillsides which blew blindingly across the scene.

As Narvik was approached and the German destroyers stood for a time to fight, the range came down and ships came into clearer view of each other. The Germans began to take heavy punishment while they themselves were coming to the end of the meagre supply of ammunition left to them after the battle of three days before. At the same time, to add to the confusion of the scene of smoke and gun flashes from the weaving destroyers, the force of ten Swordfish led by Captain Burch, Royal Marines, arrived from the *Furious* to deliver their attack.

They had had the same frightening flight through the fiords as on the day before, under low clouds streaming down the mountainsides and through snowstorms. At the scene of action the cloud base had lifted sufficiently for them to climb to 2000 feet before diving down on their targets. But it was a wasted effort. As the Luftwaffe, equipped with properly designed dive-bombers as they were, had already discovered, ships free to manoeuvre were difficult targets. For the slow-moving and highly vulnerable Swordfish, whose proper weapon was the torpedo, this form of attack was even more ineffective. Though bombs fell close to the *Künne* and *Arnim* they did little damage and there were no direct hits, while two aircraft were shot down.

By now the German ships were suffering heavily from the gunfire of the British ships. *Zenker*, *Arnim* and *Künne* had expended all their ammunition when Bey gave the order to retire up Rombaks Fiord, the narrow inlet stretching eastward past the town of Narvik. The *Künne* had already retired up Herjangsfiord, pursued by the *Eskimo*, and her captain now beached his ship and ordered his crew to escape ashore. A torpedo from the *Eskimo* completed her destruction.

The British destroyers had not escaped unscathed. On the *Punjabi* had fallen a fierce and accurate rain of 5-inch shells. The first, plunging into her hull below the bridge, had burst between decks, splinters killing one man and wounding three others in the transmitting station whence the guns were controlled. While two of these were having their wounds dressed on the mess deck nearby they were more seriously injured by a second shell which had burst on the upper deck at the foot of a steel locker containing ready-use cordite charges for the guns. Tearing a hole in the deck, it had showered splinters between decks killing two of the ammunition supply party and wounding others. Cordite charges from the locker blazed up, starting a fierce fire.

Almost simultaneously, the ship shook to another hit right forward which shattered a watertight bulkhead and caused flooding. A fire then broke out between the funnels from a bursting shell. Right aft another shell had plunged into a storeroom starting a blaze which threatened a magazine which had to be flooded. Fire and repair parties were thus all fully occupied when a fifth hit, bursting on the starboard motor boat and setting it alight, sent a jagged fragment through the upper deck, smashing a steam pipe and engulfing the engine room in a roaring cloud of steam. Other splinters had swept across the decks, killing two of the pom-pom crew and wounding two others as well as three of the torpedo-tubes' crew.

A message from the engine room had just reached Commander H. T. Lean, *Punjabi*'s captain, that the engines would shortly have to be stopped owing to the burst pipe, when torpedoes were seen approaching, running on the surface. With imperturbable skill, Lean swerved his ship out of their path, but the time had come to consider what best to do for his ship in its precarious situation. The engineer had been sent for to report on the situation below. With fires blazing forward, amidships and aft, all fire hoses slashed and useless, extinguishers exhausted, the guns' crews were urgently needed to help the parties fighting the flames by means of buckets of water. The guns were, in any case, in local control and largely ineffective owing to the damage to the transmitting station.

As the engineer officer arrived, oil-streaked, grimy and wild-eyed, a sixth shell burst on the upper deck below, savagely wounding him in the back and arms. He was just able to confirm his diagnosis of the damage to the steam system before collapsing. The chief stoker in charge of the party fighting the fire amidships was instantly killed and several more men wounded.

There was urgent need for a respite in which to get the situation under control. Lean put his wheel over and retired, signalling his predicament to the Admiral. Heroic efforts were then able to master the fires. The steam system was repaired and the magazine pumped out. Within an hour *Punjabi* was steaming into action again, though her speed was restricted to fifteen knots by the jagged hole in her bows.

While the four other German ships were retreating up Rombaks Fiord, the *Giese*, with steam on her engines at last, came alone out of the harbour to be received by the smothering fire of six British destroyers. Her guns quickly silenced, her hull riven and on fire, she was soon abandoned and left drifting.

But now, as the British ships closed the harbour entrance, the *Roeder* began to give a good account of herself from her berth alongside the pier. Her gunfire being taken for that of a shore battery, the *Warspite*'s great guns were turned on her; but when the *Cossack* nosed her way between merchant ships and wrecks in the harbour, the *Roeder* was still in action. Before she could silence the enemy, the *Cossack* had herself suffered eight hits from 5-inch shells — two seriously damaging. The first had exploded against the fore-end of the forward superstructure making a shambles of the ammunition supply party inside. The other had burst in the forward boiler room, killing the stokers. At the same time it had cut all leads from the bridge to the steering engine and engine-room telegraphs and had fractured the main steam pipe.

Unable to steer or to give orders to stop the engines until emergency repairs could be made, the ship swung uncontrollably away to run hard aground on the south shore of the fiord opposite the harbour. There she was to remain for the next twelve hours, sniped at by troops ashore and exchanging shots from time to time with field guns, while efforts were made to repair her damage and get her afloat again. It was fortunate for her that the German troops had no heavy artillery and most of the mountain guns for General Dietl's troops had been swept away by the heavy seas encountered by the German destroyers on their journey north.

Commander R. St V. Sherbrooke of the *Cossack*, seeing that the *Roeder*, silent and burning, had been abandoned by her crew, now ordered the *Foxhound* into the harbour to board her. Lieutenant-Commander Peters accordingly nosed her in between the wrecks littering the harbour, only their masts above water to show their positions, and shaped up to put *Foxhound* alongside the enemy destroyer. As he did so, he saw several Germans emerge from below, hurry ashore, jump into a car and drive off. With some inkling of what this might portend, Peters brought his ship up some fifty yards clear of the *Roeder*.

Suddenly came the bark and crackle of heavy machine guns and rifle fire from the neighbouring quay and from houses along the waterfront. While the remainder of the *Foxhound*'s hands dived for cover, her guns' crews went into action. Returning the fire in good measure they were able to silence the guns ashore, but one of *Foxhound*'s crew was killed in the first burst of fire.

While this exchange of fire was going on, the *Roeder* suddenly erupted in two shattering explosions. A great cloud of smoke billowed out and when it drifted away on the wind, where the German destroyer had lain, only twisted wreckage was to be seen. Peters congratulated himself that he had not, as he had first intended, gone alongside her. There was nothing further for him to do in the harbour. An offer to try to tow *Cossack* clear was refused as Sherbrooke feared she might sink by the bow if floated off before repairs had been made. After sending her doctor to the *Cossack* to attend to the wounded, *Foxhound* was taken out into the fiord where she was ordered to pick up survivors from the abandoned *Giese*. Two officers and nine ratings were made prisoner but two of these died later from wounds and exposure.

Of the remainder of the British destroyers, Commander Micklethwait of the *Eskimo*, while finishing off the *Künne*, had seen the enemy retiring up Rombaks Fiord and was the first to go in after them through the smokescreen left by the German ships. He was followed by the *Forester* and *Hero* and then by *Bedouin* and *Icarus*.

Some five miles from the entrance Rombaks Fiord narrows to a neck barely 500 yards wide. While passing through it, a ship would have little freedom of manoeuvre and would be at the mercy of an enemy waiting beyond. Furthermore, only one ship at a time could negotiate the narrow channel and she could bring only her forward guns to bear. Though *Warspite*'s aircraft overhead, keeping him posted as to the enemy's movements beyond the smoke, gave Micklethwait the welcome news that two out of the four German ships had gone right to the head of the fiord, he also knew that the remaining two had turned at bay some three miles beyond the narrows. These were the *Lüdemann* and *Thiele*. As the *Eskimo* was seen rounding the bend at the narrows, both opened fire with their last remaining rounds of ammunition but with no better success than they had achieved earlier in the action; whereas the *Eskimo*, soon backed by *Forester* and *Hero* as they followed her into the inner fiord, at once began to batter the enemy. The *Lüdemann* received a number of hits before she fired her remaining torpedoes and retreated up the fiord to join the

Zenker and *Arnim* who were scuttling themselves and sending their companies ashore.

The *Thiele*, more severely damaged and on fire fore and aft, had also got torpedoes away before her captain, himself wounded and all his bridge staff killed, rang down to the engine room for full speed ahead and ran his ship on to the rocks where she capsized and sank.

None of the British ships had been hit by the German gunfire; but as the *Eskimo* was being brought round to fire her last torpedo, thus turning beam on to the enemy and leaving little room to manoeuvre, the three torpedoes fired by the *Lüdemann* were seen approaching. With a burst of full speed ahead, followed by a reversal of his engines just in time to prevent his ship running on the rocks, Micklethwait avoided these. Astern of him, *Forester* and *Hero* were full in the path of the oncoming torpedoes, and with no space in which to turn. Their captains rang down for full speed astern and speeding backwards down the fiord managed to outrun them. The second flight of four torpedoes from the *Thiele* could not be so successfully evaded. Though Micklethwait had taken his ship astern as close in as he could to the south shore of the fiord, one of these torpedoes found its mark under the *Eskimo*'s forecastle. In the fierce blast which followed, the whole fore part of the ship was blown off and hung down in a tangle of wreckage. Between decks where the ammunition supply and damage control parties were stationed there was fearful loss of life. The forward pair of guns were put out of action. At the next gun mounting, 'B' gun on the fore superstructure, there was not a moment's hesitation or dismay. As Lieutenant-Commander E. B. Tancock of the *Forester*, who was watching, said in his report later, 'B gun's crew magnificently continued firing as if nothing had happened.'

On the bridge, Micklethwait, with the greatest *sangfroid*, continued to manoeuvre until his torpedo sights came 'on' and his last torpedo was launched before steering his mangled ship stern first back down the fiord. He safely negotiated the awkward bend at the neck of Rombaks Fiord, but then the mass of wreckage hanging down from where his forecastle had been, with his anchors and cables swinging below it, took the ground in ninety fathoms and brought the ship to a standstill. There she perforce had to remain for the time being with *Forester* and *Punjabi* standing by on guard while *Hero*, *Icarus* and *Kimberley* went on to the head of the fiord.

A mile or two beyond Soldvika, where the *Thiele* had met her end, they could see two of the enemy aground, silent and deserted. Up the valley road beyond they could see their crews wending their way inland. The nearer ship was the *Lüdemann* which was lying on an even keel, smoke billowing from a fire aft. Armed boats' crews were sent away to examine her. As they approached, the other ship in sight, the *Zenker*, rolled slowly on to her beam ends, slid off the rocks and sank, to reveal the third ship, also scuttled and aground behind her. The whole enemy force had been destroyed.

The boats' crews boarded the *Lüdemann*, hoisted the White Ensign over the Nazi flag and searched her for documents — but the Germans had been thorough. Before abandoning her, they had burnt all documents, as a heap of charred paper on the bridge revealed. Though still upright, the *Lüdemann* was hard aground with her engine room flooded. Salvage was beyond the capacity of the British force. With the fire threatening to explode her depth charges, she was regretfully left after the ensign had been removed, and a torpedo put into her to ensure her total destruction.

So the last of Bey's ships met her end. Taking their shortage of ammunition into account, the squadron's fate had been inevitable once Bey had shrunk from attempting a dash through the night past the British patrols. Had the Germans shaken off their lethargy and made ready to receive the expected attack, they might well have made Whitworth pay more heavily for his success.

Surprisingly, Bey seems to have emerged with an untarnished reputation. Promoted in 1943 to Rear-Admiral he was to meet his end, on December 26th of that year, in the battle-cruiser *Scharnhorst* as the result of equally inept tactics in pursuit of a convoy to Russia.

As the last echoes of the explosion rumbled away among the snow-curtained mountainsides the wonted silence settled again on the desolate scene, broken only occasionally by the crack and whine of a light field gun taking pot shots at the grounded *Cossack* and the echoing crash of a 4.7-inch gun in reply. The *Warspite* floated on the outer water of the Rombaks Fiord like some monstrous black swan and called her cygnets round her while Admiral Whitworth considered his next move.

The town of Narvik, the treasured prize for which the campaign in Norway had been primarily launched, lay quiescent under his guns. Surely, with the backing of eight 15-inch guns, a dozen 6-inch and nearly half a hundred 4.7-inch, a landing party from the squadron could take and hold it until the military expedition arrived? It was a tempting idea. The small party which could be spared, however, would be greatly outnumbered by the 2000 troops under General Dietl, augmented by the crews of the sunken destroyers to more than 4000. A landing party could only remain concentrated, holding a strip of waterfront against the inevitable powerful counter-attack. Naval support would wreak havoc in the town and perhaps cost many innocent Norwegian lives.

There can be little doubt that Narvik could have been taken but for the vacillations of the British High Command which had first discarded Plan R4 and then taken three days to reembark the troops in conditions of great confusion. Had the First Cruiser Squadron with its troops embarked been kept at Rosyth until the situation had clarified itself, they could have been off Narvik on the 13th to take advantage of Admiral Whitworth's success.

The Mayor of Narvik, Theodor Broch, has described in his fascinating book, *The Mountains Wait*, the state of demoralisation of General Dietl's troops at the end of the day.

'Bands of beaten Germans continued to drift through the town and up Fagernes Mountain. Laboriously they trampled a path for themselves, zigzagging their way up the steep slope. Their dark rows stood out against the snow like curving snakes.

'An old woman came down the hill with her mattress on a sled. She owned a little cabin up on the ridge, but now it was packed with Germans. She told us they had asked about the way to Sweden and that she had pointed skywards.'

Such was the situation which a landing force would have found. Even the ill-organised brigade which was on its way in troopships might have been able to complete the demoralisation of Dietl's men, sending them to seek sanctuary across the border in Sweden. But it was not to arrive for another two days, by which time the shock of defeat and destruction of the naval support on which Dietl had been counting had worn off.

To help Admiral Whitworth decide against any fruitless lingering in the fiord, there came a signal from the *Foxhound*. A

German officer prisoner from the *Giese* had spoken of submarines in the fiord. In fact the *U51* had been in Narvik harbour when the British attack began. Thinking at first it was an air raid, the captain had taken his boat to the bottom and some time later had slid quietly out into the fiord, undetected. The *Warspite* and her brood of destroyers would make easy targets for a bold U-boat commander as they lay off Narvik waiting to support a landing.

Before the squadron could leave, there were wounded men from *Eskimo* and *Cossack* to be brought aboard the battleship. The *Cossack* was still aground opposite the harbour of Narvik, her crew striving manfully to get sufficient repairs done, bulkheads shored up and the ship lightened so that she could safely be refloated. Steam had been raised again in one boiler, allowing dynamos to be restarted. Meanwhile, the grim evidence of battle casualties was cleared away. Twelve men had lost their lives. Those of the wounded who could be moved had been sent off by boat to the *Punjabi*.

Soon after 8 pm there had been an unsuccessful attempt by the *Kimberley* to tow *Cossack* off. During the night further efforts to lighten the ship had gone on without pause. At 3.15 the following morning, towards high water, Sherbrooke decided to try to steam the ship off. He rang for the engines to be put astern. The water frothed under her stern. The ship shook and trembled for a brief moment and then slid off into deep water to a heartfelt cheer by her company.

Manoeuvring always astern, Sherbrooke took her out into the fiord and alongside the *Warspite* where the remainder of the wounded were disembarked. Then, in company with the *Forester*, the *Cossack* set off on her long journey stern first, to Skjelfiord for repairs.

The *Eskimo* had got away earlier. Shortly after her pendant wreckage had grounded she was got away into deep water with the aid of *Forester* and *Punjabi*. But it then appeared that she was slowly sinking by the head. By ruthlessly jettisoning all possible heavy gear on the upper deck the process was halted, but the chances of remaining afloat seemed so slim that Micklethwait ordered the destruction of all secret and confidential books. Repairs were pressed on, however, and by the evening the ship was made reasonably watertight — sufficiently so, at any rate, to steam stern first. After transferring all wounded and all hands not required to steam the ship, the *Eskimo*, a weird sight with no forecastle, backed away down the fiord and eventually reached Skjelfiord on the following day.

While all this was going on, there had come happy and unexpected news of yet other passengers for the flagship. From the destroyer *Ivanhoe* came a signal saying that survivors of the crew of the *Hardy* were in the township of Ballangen. This was great news for it had been presumed that they must have been taken prisoner by the enemy.

The story of these men since we left them scrambling ashore from their grounded and burning ship had been one of endurance and resource. When the order to abandon ship had been given it had meant swimming 400 yards to the snowbound shore through icy water for those who could do so, wounded being towed ashore by the uninjured. Of boats there were none.

The captain and the navigating officer, Lieutenant Gordon-Smith who had an ugly head wound, had been brought down from the bridge. The former, strapped in a stretcher, was taken ashore by the gunner, Mr McCracken, but was dead when he reached the land. Gordon-Smith also seemed so severely injured that Heppel, the last to go ashore, decided to leave him on the deck for the time being rather than subject him to the shock of the icy water which was likely to be fatal.

Meanwhile, the German destroyers had continued to shell the burning *Hardy*. The chief stoker, Styles, and the doctor, Surgeon-Lieutenant Waind, had both been wounded. They were got ashore together and the injured doctor, one arm shattered, stayed to tend the chief stoker on the beach while shelter was sought.

The remainder of the survivors, wounded and unwounded, had made their way to a group of wooden houses a little way inland. There they were taken in, given blankets, curtains, any material that could be found to replace their soaked clothes, and soup and warmth to bring back life into their frozen bodies. A Norwegian girl set off on skis to fetch a doctor. A party was sent to fetch in the chief stoker and the Surgeon-Lieutenant. Styles was found to be dreadfully injured, and there was little to be done for him but to ease his passing, which came during that afternoon.

When the Norwegian doctor arrived he brought the glad news that at the township of Ballangen, where there were no Germans, there was a hospital. He telephoned for help, receiving promises of ambulances and doctors. While awaiting them, Heppel collected volunteers to go back aboard the *Hardy* to rescue the navigating officer who, to their astonishment, could now be seen stumbling about the quarterdeck. Finding a dinghy abandoned on the beach they got Gordon-Smith safely ashore, and it was later discovered that his injuries were confined to a cracked skull from which he eventually made a complete recovery.

The Norwegians were as good as their word and by midday all the wounded except for three men and the Surgeon-Lieutenant had gone off in the care of doctors and nurses and the return of the ambulance for the remainder had been promised. As the afternoon wore on, however, and the ambulance did not return, Lieutenant-Commander Mansell, the first lieutenant, began to fear that German troops from Narvik would be arriving to take the ship's company prisoners. He decided that he must get the unwounded men away. Calling them together, he shared out among them the cash which had been brought ashore from the ship's safe and they were marched off on the fifteen mile road to Ballangen under Lieutenant Heppel. Though many of them were ill-shod for such a march and were mostly exhausted after their ordeal, they reached Ballangen safely that evening, cheered on their way by hot soup and food offered by the inhabitants of cottages they passed.

Meanwhile, Mansell waited with the remainder of the officers and the three wounded men. When a party of men was seen advancing up the road from Narvik it seemed certain it must be a German patrol coming to take them prisoners. Then there was a hail in English. Mansell went out to meet the newcomers and found to his relief that they were, in fact, the officers and crew of the British merchant ship *North Cornwall* who had escaped from their captors during the confusion of the battle.

They had had a remarkable escape. When the Germans first arrived, the crews of all the British merchant ships had been sent to the *North Cornwall* where they were held prisoner under guard. Of the eight torpedoes which the *Hardy* had fired with such good effect into the harbour, one had been aimed at their ship but had fortunately gone astray, passing only a few feet ahead of her as she lay at anchor. Now the *North Cornwall*'s crew were joining the men who had all unwittingly attempted their destruction a few hours earlier.

As the action progressed, the Germans had ordered all the merchant crews ashore. Their guard was a young, inexperienced soldier. When he trustingly gave his rifle to one of the British sailors to hold while he clambered over the side into the boat, the *North Cornwall*'s men realised it would not be difficult to give him the slip and at a suitable moment they had done so. Now, after a rest after their long march, they were directed on to join the others at Ballangen.

It may be noted here that survivors from the *Hunter* had a similar experience during the second battle. When they were put ashore from the destroyer which picked them up, a kindly-disposed German officer had said to them with a grin as they left, 'That road leads to Sweden,' pointing up the south shore of Rombaks Fiord. In the panic and confusion which swept over the Germans on the 13th as the terrifying thunder of the *Warspite*'s guns rolled and echoed back and forth across the fiord, they had remembered the hint and set off. They got clear away into Sweden and eventually back to England.

By 3 o'clock in the afternoon it seemed clear to Mansell that the promised ambulances were not coming. The wounded were in great pain and getting worse. He decided that somehow the officers must get them to Ballangen. Enquiries produced a sledge and a horse. The kindly villagers provided mattresses and coverings, the wounded were made as comfortable as possible on the sledge and the little party set off. The rough and rutty road inflicted tortures on the wounded for the next four and a half hours, but by 9 pm they had all found sanctuary in the blessed comfort of the cottage hospital at Ballangen.

For the next three days the crews of the two ships were housed and sheltered by the kindly inhabitants. Food was plentiful and its cooking and serving looked after with great efficiency by the chief steward of the *North Cornwall*. But always there was the anxiety that the Germans would arrive to take them prisoner. It was therefore in a crescendo of excitement that news began to come in of British ships approaching. Then came the thunder of guns down the fiord. German destroyers were seen steaming out and then retreating under heavy fire and finally the majestic shape of the *Warspite* came into view.

Norwegians reported that a German destroyer had been sunk. Whereupon two boats put out from Ballangen, one manned by Norwegians and another by British naval and merchant seamen. The latter returned in triumph with an undamaged power boat from the *Köllner*, ashore down the fiord. In it they found a box signal lamp with which the *Hardy*'s yeoman of signals repaired to the attic of the schoolhouse to set up a signal station.

Meanwhile Heppel with the captain and first officer of the *North Cornwall* set out in the German motor boat to obtain help. Thus it was that at dusk the yeoman of signals was able to take in a signal from the *Ivanhoe* that an armed guard was being sent in. Boats were soon plying to and fro and by 1 am all except the severely wounded who were left in the hospital, had been embarked.

As soon as all had been gathered in, *Warspite* and her screen of destroyers went back to the open waters of Vestfiord to await the arrival of Admiral Lord Cork in the *Aurora* and to hold themselves ready to operate against Narvik when required.

Meanwhile, the usual evening messages from the Admiralty had opened up with one to the Commander-in-Chief, urging on him the desirability of occupying Narvik at once to ensure an unopposed landing later by the main expedition. It was alas but a pipe dream. Had the military expedition been able to leave for Narvik 'at once' on the 9th, as the Chiefs of Staff had envisaged, it would have been a different story. As Whitworth signalled on the evening of the 13th, knowing that troopships were on the way, *My impression is that enemy forces in Narvik were thoroughly frightened as result of today's action and that presence of Warspite was the chief cause of this. I recommend that town be occupied without delay by main landing force.*

Unhappily, the main landing force could not arrive before the 15th. Being equipped and loaded for an unopposed landing in friendly territory it was heading for Vaagsfiord and the town of Harstad to the north of Narvik, where the troops could be landed, and their equipment sorted out before they were ready for action. Not appreciating this, Whitworth again signalled on the morning of the 14th, *Information from Norwegian sources estimates 1500 to 2000 troops. I am convinced Narvik can be taken by direct assault without fear of meeting serious opposition on landing.*

Heading for the area to assume command of operations was another Admiral with similar ideas. 'Ginger' Boyle, as he was known to the Service, with a reputation for drive and vigour, and now recalled to service as Admiral of the Fleet, the Earl of Cork and Orrery, had hoisted his Union Flag in the *Aurora* and sailed from the Clyde on the 12th.

From Scapa on the same day had sailed the military commander, Major-General P. J. Mackesy, in the *Southampton* with an entirely different view of the task facing him. His instructions were that no landing in the face of opposition was contemplated. All the ingredients were thus present for an ugly brew of misunderstanding and cross-purposes, a state of affairs stemming from the clumsy arrangement for the higher direction of the war described by Sir Winston Churchill at the beginning of Chapter 23 of his first volume on the *Second World*

War. As First Lord of the Admiralty, his dynamic personality had made itself felt in every action taken by the Navy — too much so, and not always with happy results it can fairly be said. Although until April 15th he presided over the military co-ordination committee, he had no power to take or enforce decisions on military or air matters. It may be that, had he at this time been Prime Minister, his great fund of energy would have been more evenly divided over the whole field of operations to their great benefit, while he would have had less time to intervene in the detailed movements of his sea commanders, in which sphere his touch was less sure.

Be that as it may, the fact remains that the campaign in Norway about to unfold was to show that Britain had much to learn in the art of making war. The lesson was to be painful but invaluable, for this first campaign of the war was clearly to show the shape of things to come in that all three Services were involved in a common enterprise. Operating each under their own separate command systems, they had no joint supreme commander and no combined headquarters.

Indeed, had such a system been set up, it can be surmised that once the opportunity for an immediate counter stroke had been missed, the campaign, except perhaps for the capture of Narvik, would never have been undertaken. It would have been made clear to the Navy and Army that the Air Force could do little or nothing to dispute German control of the air once they had gained possession of the airfields in southern and central Norway. The Navy, which already on April 9th had experienced the weight of air attack the enemy could deploy, might have warned the soldiers what they might expect to suffer with no anti-aircraft defences. Finally, the complete absence of training or equipment of the troops for operating in the Arctic conditions still prevailing in Norway and the absence of any plan might have given a supreme commander pause.

CHAPTER 10

The purely naval phase of the campaign of Norway was over when the last of the German flotilla at Narvik was destroyed. Hitler's fleet had been made to pay heavily by the Norwegian defenders and the submarines and light forces of the Royal Navy. But the speed and ruthlessness demanded by Grand Admiral Raeder of his captains had achieved a strategical success of lasting value to the Germans for the remainder of the war. Though the secrecy he had also relied upon had been lost at a dangerously early stage, the creaking, reluctant pace at which the rusty war machine of the democracies was turning had saved him from the consequences.

The Allies now sought desperately for some means of retrieving the situation. Narvik, which had been the original bone of contention, was lightly held by German troops whose artillery had been lost and whose supply ships had failed to reach them. They must rely for supply and reinforcement on hundreds of miles of snowbound mountainous roads, while to the British, Narvik was accessible over a sea route which the Royal Navy still controlled. The senior officer on the spot, albeit not a soldier, had signalled his belief that it could be taken by direct assault. A military expedition was on its way to the area carrying two brigades of infantry.

Such was the situation when the news of the second Battle of Narvik reached the Chiefs of Staff and the Cabinet in London. Complicating it, however, was an urgent desire from all quarters to attempt the recapture of Trondheim. This, the third largest town in Norway, was of prime importance from the political and strategical standpoint. The ancient capital of the country and the crowning-place of its kings, it was strategically placed where the two main routes from Oslo, a main route from Norway to Sweden and the only road and rail route to the North all met. It provided a large, safe harbour with extensive docks and quays. Its recapture from the Germans would obviously nullify the greater part of the advantage they had secured.

Already on April 10th the Admiralty had signalled to the Commander-in-Chief, Home Fleet, ... *it will be necessary to take Bergen and Trondheim. Narvik will also be taken.* Bergen had been crossed off when it became clear that the fleet could not operate so far south in the face of German air superiority. Trondheim remained. The Service staffs had been instructed on the 11th to examine — though not to prepare for — the possibilities of landing a force in its vicinity, the operation to be called 'Maurice'.

Thus, when a message reached the Government on the afternoon of the 12th from their Minister in Norway that the Norwegian Government urgently desired the recapture of Trondheim to maintain their authority in the country, it was in accord with their own views. It was further backed by the opinion of the Norwegian Commander-in-Chief, General Ruge, who asked for a British division to be sent to attack Trondheim from the north while he himself would hold himself ready to attack from the south.

The following day, therefore, Vice-Admiral Edward-Collins was ordered to Rosyth from Scapa with the *Galatea* and *Arethusa*. There his two cruisers and the troopship *Orion* were to embark the 148th Infantry Brigade under Brigadier Morgan — previously embarked for Stavanger in the First Cruiser Squadron but sent ashore at the first alarm on the 8th. The destination of this force was to be Namsos, a little town some sixty miles north of Trondheim, at the head of the Namsen Fiord. There, for the time being, we must leave Brigadier Morgan and his force, carrying out the third set of orders they had received — and soon to be given yet another.

The news of Admiral Whitworth's victory at Narvik had caused a wave of optimism to sweep through the minds of the Ministers and Chiefs of Staff directing operations. Half of the force of two brigades in Convoy NP1 would be sufficient to take Narvik from the demoralised German occupying force, it was considered. The other half could be diverted to Namsos in place of Brigadier Morgan's force, which, in turn, would now form the southern arm of a pincer movement against Trondheim, landing at Aandalsnes at the head of the Romsdal Fiord and joining General Ruge.

Accordingly, on the evening of the 14th, Vice-Admiral Layton, escorting Convoy NP1, was instructed to divert the two transports, *Chrobry* and *Empress of Australia* carrying the 146th Brigade, to this new objective. With these two ships, his flagship *Manchester*, the cruiser *Birmingham*, the anti-aircraft cruiser *Cairo* and three destroyers he bore away south, leaving the remainder of the force to go on to Vaagsfiord. We will return later to follow events there and at Narvik; but for the present the centre of interest lies round Trondheim.

There, since the evening of the 12th, a force of two cruisers, *Glasgow* and *Sheffield*, and six destroyers, under the command of Captain Pegram of the *Glasgow*, had been engaged in searching The Leads for enemy shipping from Stadtlandet northwards. Reports from Royal Air Force aircraft on reconnaissance had reported a pocket battleship, a cruiser and many merchant ships in his area. The 13th was spent searching for the warships which were in fact imaginary, while his destroyers were sent to Aalesund at the entrance to the Romsdal Fiord after the merchantmen which proved to be Norwegian.

While thus engaged, Pegram received orders to land a force of sailors and marines from his two cruisers at Namsos to secure the quays there and at the neighbouring town of Bangsund and to hold the bridge across the River Namsen and the road leading south until the main landing force arrived. As soon as the fiord was secured his cruisers were to withdraw to seaward while a daily contact by destroyer was to be maintained with his men.

It was not until the following day, the 14th, that Pegram was able to comply, when his destroyers returned to him. With the last of the light the landing party under Captain Edds, Royal Marines, of the *Sheffield*, was ferried ashore. With them went two army staff officers who were to report on prospects for the main force. They were Colonel Peter Fleming, the writer and explorer, and Captain Martin Lindsay, the traveller. They found no Germans in the place to oppose them but after consultation with some Norwegian officers they signalled home a gloomy report. There was no concealment for any large force from the daily air reconnaissance sent over by the Germans. The deep snow blanketing the countryside restricted all movement to the road and railway (except on skis or snowshoes). Any forward move by more than a battalion at a time would be slow and conspicuous from the air.

The operation had been decided upon, however, and the officer to command it, Major-General Carton de Wiart, VC, was already on his way by flying boat. As soon as the naval party had been landed, all Pegram's destroyers except *Somali*, Captain Nicholson's ship, returned seawards to join him and to steer to join the escort of Layton's convoy which was coming south. Nicholson remained to meet the General and to make arrangements for the landing of 'Mauriceforce' as the main expedition was called.

He was thus to be the first to enjoy the daunting experience which was soon to be a commonplace, of being penned in his ship in the narrow fiord, the target for day-long attacks by dive and high bombing against which his meagre anti-aircraft weapons and unsuitable main armament could do little but attract bombs which might otherwise have been directed upon the defenceless troops ashore.

Like all the ports on Norway's rugged coast, Namsos lay at the landward end of a long, narrow fiord. Its principal function was to load the timber which was the main export of the area and which covered the snowclad hillsides down to the waterline. For this purpose there was a single stone quay at which ocean-going ships could berth, a smaller, wooden quay at Namsos and another at the neighbouring hamlet of Bangsund on the other side of the Namsen River. These landing places were, of course, conspicuous from the air and would make perfect aiming points during any disembarkation of troops and stores by daylight.

With ammunition soon running low, Nicholson signalled his opinion that facilities for landing from troopships were inadequate at Namsos, and unless command of the air were secured, there would be grave risk to the town and transports. He recommended that the troopships should be sent elsewhere, the troops embarked in destroyers and thence put directly ashore at Namsos and Bangsund at dusk, whence they could be moved forward before daylight.

General de Wiart who arrived in the middle of an air raid during which his flying boat was machine-gunned on the water, his staff officer wounded and he himself penned in the aircraft until the enemy had exhausted his ammunition, readily agreed with Nicholson's views. In fact, the Admiralty had already sent orders to Layton to take the troopships to the remote anchorage of Lillesjona, some 100 miles north of Namsos, and act as suggested by Nicholson.

The destroyers with Pegram accordingly went in with the convoy to Lillesjona on the evening of the 15th. The *Somali*, now quite out of high-explosive shells and reduced during her last hours at Namsos to firing practice shells 'for moral effect', arrived with General de Wiart. He transferred to the *Afridi* where Captain Philip Vian assumed command of the destroyers while *Somali* returned home to replenish her magazines. She was replaced by the *Nubian* which had escorted the oiler *War Pindari* to Lillesjona. *Afridi*, *Sikh*, *Matabele*, *Mashona* and *Nubian* refuelled from the tanker, and then went alongside the troopships to embark the Lincolnshire and the York and Lancaster Regiments. Enemy aircraft found them even so far north. The destroyers left in a flurry of frothing stern wash, curving bow waves and the tall thudding splashes of bomb bursts for their high-speed run down the coast to Namsos where they arrived during the night of the 16th. By daylight their troops had all been landed, the men dispersed from the quay sides and all traces of their arrival obliterated. The German reconnaissance which flew over the next morning suspected nothing.

Back at Lillesjona the air raids, though never very heavy, had been almost continuous. They failed, surprisingly, to hit the large targets offered by the two liners; but near misses constantly shaking them shook also the morale of the young inexperienced soldiers, receiving their baptism of fire cooped up helplessly aboard. To wait for the return of the destroyers would have subjected them to this ordeal throughout the 17th. Layton therefore decided that the King's Own Yorkshire Light

Infantry from the *Empress of Australia*, a large, unhandy ship, should be transferred to the *Chrobry* which was carrying the bulk of the stores. The *Chrobry* would then go up the fiord at dusk, land the troops during the night and be clear away to sea by daylight.

Before daybreak therefore the force put out from Lillesjona and stood out to sea for the day. *Afridi*, with the General aboard, and her consorts joined during the day. When the convoy put about so as to reach Namsen Fiord at sunset, the *Empress of Australia* was sent home though still carrying 170 tons of stores for 'Mauriceforce'. While Admiral Layton's cruisers remained at sea, *Afridi* led the way in to Namsos. The *Chrobry* anchored off the town and through the night the destroyers ferried the troops and stores ashore. The troops were all landed but there were still some 130 tons of stores in the *Chrobry* when the military working parties were withdrawn so that they could be under cover before daylight and the inevitable return of the Luftwaffe. All ships thereupon turned seawards and by noon on the 18th had rejoined the Admiral.

The next troops to join 'Mauriceforce' were three battalions of French Chasseurs-Alpins under General Audet. They were on their way in four troopships, the *El d'Jezair, El Mansour, El Kantara* and the *Ville d'Oran*, and should have arrived on the 18th. They were a day late, however, so Layton took the opportunity to send the *Chrobry* in again that night to complete unloading her stores.

So far no troopships had been exposed to prying eyes in German reconnaissance aircraft and no sign of the nightly activities was left at daylight. The bombers had thus concentrated on any warship seen in the fiord, but there was no hiding this sizable convoy when it arrived off the coast well before nightfall. Bombs were soon pitching round the troopships as they filed up the fiord led by the anti-aircraft cruiser *Cairo*.

The enemy failed to damage the troopships, but the escorting cruiser *Emile Bertin* was hit by a bomb. Though not seriously damaged, she retired from the scene leaving the *Cairo* and four French destroyers to complete the operation. The troops landed safely during the night but their arrival could no longer be hidden from the enemy. A few hours after the ships had sailed again, the Luftwaffe descended on the town of Namsos. Completely unopposed, the German aircraft reduced the place to a rubble and set it ablaze. The base for 'Mauriceforce' was largely obliterated, making reinforcement and supply almost impossible.

The further experiences of this expedition up to the time of its evacuation a fortnight later are no part of this story which is confined to the naval aspects of the campaign. It is sufficient to say that the British troops, totally inexperienced in any form of warfare, let alone the specialised Arctic version facing them, without anti-aircraft guns or artillery, advanced to the Trondheimsfiord, endured with passive courage bombardment by German naval guns and aircraft and attack by highly trained and mobile German ski-troops, held their positions for a time and finally retreated in good order to be re-embarked. The Chasseurs-Alpins were well trained for operation in snow, but had been landed without some essential strap for their skis. Relying normally upon mules for transport, they were immobilised by the lack of them. As Carton de Wiart has ruefully recorded, 'They would have been invaluable to us if only I could have used them.'

The General, indeed, had quickly summed up the possibilities of Operation 'Maurice'. Informed on the 17th that he was to be an Acting Lieutenant-General he did not bother to put up the badges of his rank as he 'felt in his bones that the campaign was unlikely to be either long or successful'.

In the long run it was the total German superiority in the air which doomed the operation to failure. Their aircraft roamed and bombed at will. When the destroyer *Nubian* came back to Namsos on the night of April 20th to give what anti-aircraft support her unsuitable armament could provide, her captain, Commander Ravenhill, recorded, 'The whole place was a mass of flames from end to end and the glare on the snows of the surrounding mountains produced an unforgettable spectacle.'

The General came aboard to say that 'the storehouses and jetties had been destroyed and that, owing to the evacuation of the Norwegians, all his transport had disappeared; in consequence any stores landed would be exposed to almost certain destruction before there was any hope of removing them.... Unless the Germans could be drastically restricted in their air activities within a very short time, the expedition was doomed.' Signalling in this vein to the War Office, de Wiart concluded, *I see little chance of carrying out decisive or, indeed, any operations unless enemy air activity is considerably reduced.*

From a soldier of de Wiart's reputation and courage, who inspired his men with awe by his cool contempt for danger during air attacks, these were grim words. From a naval point of view the position was equally untenable. Though warships could, in varying degrees, according to their armament, fight back at the enemy bombers, they were invariably selected as a primary target and were under attack throughout the hours of daylight. Had the Luftwaffe dive-bomber pilots attained the skill they were to display later in the war, not a ship up the fiords could have survived.

Ravenhill's report described 'the very great strain imposed on personnel of these anti-aircraft ships. Owing to the high mountains no warning can be obtained of the approach of aircraft.... Ships must be kept under way day and night and when attacks come there is little room for manoeuvre. There is continued tension and the knowledge that... nothing can come to your assistance is trying to the nerves.'

During the 21st the sloop *Auckland* arrived to relieve the *Nubian*. Attacked continuously with bombs and machine guns throughout her passage up the fiord, she arrived miraculously undamaged. Perhaps the most certain result of the stationing of ships off the harbour was that attacks which would otherwise have been directed on the troops were expended — fortunately for the most part fruitlessly — on them.

The complete domination of the area by the Luftwaffe and the impossibility of maintaining ships for long under attacks opposed only by their guns had been an unpleasant surprise to the Navy. Though the gun was entrusted with the task of holding off air attack, most British warships were most inadequately supplied with suitable weapons. In the latest destroyers the main armament had a maximum elevation of 40 degrees. The only anti-aircraft mountings were a few unwieldy 2-pounder pom-poms and 0.5-inch machine guns. Even in larger ships where batteries of six or eight 4-inch high-angle guns were mounted, it was soon discovered that this was not sufficient defence against resolute attack. Only fighter cover could bring immunity. For distant operations such as those in Norway, this meant aircraft carriers with the fleet; but these were few and for the most part antiquated. The handful of obsolete fighters they were able to deploy at this time could do little to affect the situation. Unfortunately the Royal Air Force, which might have been able to help, was woefully short of long-range fighters. Those they had — Blenheims and Hudsons — had a performance little superior to the bombers they had to meet, while their crews were untrained in naval co-operation and unhappy operating over the sea.

The story of the cruiser *Suffolk*, sent to bombard the airfield at Stavanger, illustrates the relative capabilities of ships and aircraft at this time. The *Suffolk*, a cruiser with a main armament of eight 8-inch guns and an anti-aircraft battery of eight 4-inch high-angle guns, commanded by Captain J. W. Durnford, sailed from Scapa Flow on the afternoon of April 16th escorted by four destroyers. She carried two Walrus amphibian aircraft which would spot for the bombardment. A RAF Hudson aircraft was to drop a flare over the airfield to assist its identification at zero hour.

The cruiser arrived on time in the area and contact was duly made with the submarine *Seal*, acting as a mark-boat. The first Walrus was catapulted as dawn was approaching. The sea was calm, the sky was clear. Then things began to go wrong. Warning rockets and anti-aircraft gunfire from the defences of Stavanger prevented the identification of the Hudson's flare. Wireless communication with the Walrus could not be established. The second Walrus was catapulted but again there was a wireless failure.

In spite of this, the bombardment started at 5.13 with the first of the light. Visual communication with the aircraft took the place of radio and with its aid considerable damage was done to the airfield, casualties were inflicted on the German air contingent and two petrol dumps were set ablaze. A few minutes after 6, the force began its withdrawal at thirty knots.

Orders had been received to conduct a sweep northwards up the coast on completion of the bombardment. After running seawards for an hour, Durnford turned northwards to comply and signalled his position, course and speed at 7.20. Fighter escort by RAF aircraft had been arranged, but no fighters materialised. They had been sent out indeed, but not finding the *Suffolk* close inshore where they had expected, they had flown on up the coast and took no further part in the proceedings.

At 8.25 the first enemy air attack arrived. For the next six hours and three quarters, the *Suffolk* was under almost continuous attack. After the first hour and a quarter Durnford had stood out to sea. Of the thirty-three separate attacks, twenty-one were fortunately of the high level type. Not only was the cruiser's powerful anti-aircraft battery well suitable for deterring this form of attack — though as far as is known none of the enemy were shot down — but, as was to be demonstrated again and again during the war, high level bombing very rarely achieved hits against ships free to manoeuvre. Though near misses were numerous, it was not until 10.37 that a dive-bomber put a heavy bomb into the *Suffolk*.

It was a catastrophic blow. Plunging down through the upper deck at the base of 'X' turret, it drove on through the wardroom and warrant officers' flat to burst in a storeroom close to the bulkhead of the after engine room. The explosion penetrated forward into the engine room where it inflicted heavy damage, casualties and flooding, and downwards to hole all oil fuel tanks in the vicinity. The blast aft was the most devastating. Breaking through into the shell room of the turret it vented through into the cordite handling room, where a cordite charge exploded, sending a searing flame up through the hoist into the turret itself. Another charge there exploded. The roof of the turret was lifted up the blast. A column of flame shot up as high as the gaff on the mainmast where the ensign was burnt up and destroyed. Casualties throughout the turret spaces were grievous. Altogether thirty-three officers and men were killed and thirty-eight wounded by this one bomb.

As fires raged, the magazine of 'X' turret had to be flooded. Water poured in through holes in the hull, 1500 tons in twenty minutes.

The *Suffolk*'s speed was reduced to eighteen knots. As she struggled on westwards still under attack, repeated appeals for fighter protection brought no response. At 1 pm flooding put her steering gear out of action. For the next twenty minutes while emergency repairs were made, Durnford could only steer by varying the speed of his engines and could no longer manoeuvre to upset the enemy's aim. It was nearly fatal. A bomb missed by only five yards, wreaking further heavy damage. Other near misses blew in lower deck scuttles. The whole after end of the ship became flooded with 2500 tons of water.

At last, at 2.15 in the afternoon, the first fighters appeared on the scene. Even then they could not bring immunity and one of the most accurate and dangerous attacks took place when nine of them were in company. The worst was then over. The following day the *Suffolk* limped into Scapa Flow, her quarterdeck awash, the first visible evidence to the fleet that a new era had dawned in naval operations. The gun was no longer the master at sea — as naval airmen had been trying to persuade the Admirals for many years.

To return to Namsos, a further body of French troops had sailed from Scapa in the liner *Ville d'Alger*, and arrived off the fiord on the 21st. But de Wiart, already considering the desirability of a withdrawal, would not at first accept them. The ship was taken out to sea again and when finally brought in on the following day only the soldiers were disembarked and she sailed again without landing her heavy stores, among them some anti-tank guns and an anti-aircraft battery.

These were the last troops to be landed at Namsos. Almost daily de Wiart reported his opinion that there was 'no alternative to evacuation unless he could have superiority in the air'.

The Romsdal Fiord area, 200 miles further south, which had been selected as the landing point for the other arm of the pincer movement against Trondheim, was strategically of great importance, Aandalsnes being connected by rail with the main line from the south to Trondheim at the junction of Dombaas, 60 miles away. German progress up the main line to bring badly needed reinforcements to their small force at Trondheim was being opposed by a section of the hastily mobilised Norwegian Army under its Commander-in-Chief, General Ruge. It was envisaged that an allied force would advance up the branch line from Aandalsnes to Dombaas and then turn north to attack Trondheim.

Romsdal Fiord seemed at first an excellent landing point and base. Two small timber ports with suitable quays were available — Molde at the entrance on the north side of the fiord and Aandalsnes at the head. The little town of Aalesund, near the entrance on the side opposite to Molde, seemed suitably placed to house the crews of a naval battery of 4-inch guns which could be set up to dominate the approaches.

Like the Namsen Fiord, however, the deep cleft between mountains which it comprised formed a trap for any ship afloat on its waters exposed to the attack of dive-bombers. There was little sea room in which to dodge and manoeuvre. The steep shore, climbing up in places to 2000 feet and more, enabled aircraft to approach unseen and to swoop swiftly and suddenly before guns could be brought to bear.

Furthermore the Romsdal Fiord was within easy reach of Stavanger airfield, whence the dive-bombers could keep up a sustained effort throughout the hours of daylight.

It will be remembered that the 148th Infantry Brigade under Brigadier H. de R. Morgan had been embarked in the cruisers *Galatea* and *Arethusa*, of the Second Cruiser Squadron, and the transport *Orion* at Rosyth on April 14th with orders to land at Namsos. They did not sail, however, until the 17th, by which time their objective had been changed — for the third time — to Aandalsnes, and it had been decided not to send the *Orion* but to substitute the two AA cruisers, *Curacoa* and *Carlisle*. Their operation was designated 'Sickle'.

As at Namsos, however, the force was not intended, equipped or loaded to make a landing against opposition. The Navy was therefore to put a small force of sailors and marines ashore first to ensure a friendly reception. The operation was given the happy vernal name of 'Primrose' which must have seemed a grim piece of humour among the snowstorms and bitter weather of Norway. On the 16th a force of cruisers and destroyers had been sent to the area with orders to prevent any enemy force forestalling the British expedition. On the morning of the 17th the destroyer *Ashanti* had been sent up the Romsdal Fiord to land a few sailors to hold Aandalsnes and prepare for the arrival of 'Primrose'.

Meanwhile, Captain A. L. Poland, commanding a flotilla of sloops comprising the *Black Swan*, *Auckland*, *Flamingo* and *Bittern*, at Rosyth, had at 10 o'clock on the morning of April 14th received verbal orders for transporting 'Primrose' force, 700 seamen and Royal Marines from battleships refitting under Lieutenant-Colonel A. W. Simpson, RM. Their first destination was to be Aalesund where they would land the 4-inch defensive battery before going on to Aandalsnes. An hour later the first stores and equipment began to arrive, soon followed by the naval detachments by train and an anti-aircraft detachment by lorry from Newcastle, all accompanied, of course, by baggage and equipment — 4-inch guns, 37-inch howitzers, 2-pounder pom-poms and their respective mountings.

Six and a half hours after the first inkling of the intended operation had reached Captain Poland, the first of his ships to be loaded, *Auckland*, intended to arrive in the area twenty-four hours before the remainder, had sailed with a contingent from the battleship *Barham*. By 3.20 the following morning the remainder had sailed. With their draught a foot deeper than the normal maximum, heavy gear cluttering the upper decks and affecting their stability, and their mess decks jammed with 170 passengers each, they headed out into a rising gale and steered north.

As the little ships plunged and rolled their way northward in heavy and increasing seas, it quickly became evident to Poland that unless he took shelter until the weather moderated, equipment would be lost and, as for the landing force cooped up on the waterlogged mess decks, many of them helplessly sick, the 'Primrose would be a very wilted flower on arrival'. Overhauling the *Auckland*, where Commander Hewitt, her captain, realising that in the wild weather he could not reach his destination at dawn on the 16th as scheduled, had hove-to to await the remainder of the flotilla, he took the whole force into Invergordon for the night of the 15th. There he was joined by Captain M. M. Denny for passage to Molde at the entrance to Romsdal Fiord where he was to set up a naval base. There, too, he first heard that the landing was to be at Aandalsnes, not Aalesund, and Colonel Simpson had his first opportunity to meet his officers and to explain his plans to them.

There can seldom have been a landing ordered with less foreknowledge. Simpson and his officers knew little of the country for which he was bound. He had no maps. For knowledge of the terrain he had to rely upon the Sailing Directions for the Norwegian coast. Fortunately, the Royal Marines can take such difficulties in their stride.

The weather had not greatly moderated when Poland set forth again the following morning, but he was able to make fifteen knots and towards evening on April 17th the steep, snowbound coast was in sight. By 10 pm *Black Swan* and *Bittern* were alongside the quay, giving place to the other ships as each completed disembarking troops and stores. By dawn they were clear and Simpson's party were already mounting their pompoms and moving off by platoons to occupy strategic points including the power station at Verma, eighteen miles up the railway towards the important junction of Dombaas.

Meanwhile, the 4-inch guns and the crews to man them were taken to Aalesund in the sloops, only to find that the local inhabitants strongly objected to the mounting of the battery there, claiming, not without reason, that they would only bring the German bombers down on them. In the event, though the guns and crews were landed, they were found to lack vital parts of their mountings; nor, in fact, did any enemy ships present themselves as targets during the brief history of the expedition.

Thus all was ready for 'Sickleforce' when *Galatea*, *Carlisle* and the destroyers *Arrow* and *Acheron* arrived at 8 pm on the 18th. At the same time *Arethusa* and *Curacoa* berthed at Molde whence their troops were sent to Aandalsnes in local craft. Before daylight the ships were again at sea. The speed of the operation and the absence of any troopships successfully hid from the Germans the fact that a landing had been made. For the time being the town was not seriously attacked from the air and the troops were able to push forward unmolested to Dombaas where they were in a position to swing north towards Trondheim as originally planned. (They got no further owing to the necessity of turning south to the support of the Norwegians trying to hold up the main German advance from the south — but that is outside the scope of this story.)

Meanwhile, the Luftwaffe turned their attention to any warships remaining in the Romsdal Fiord. This meant at first the *Black Swan*, which for two days fought a solitary and successful battle with the enemy bombers, shooting down several and escaping damage herself, until with ammunition running low she was relieved by the anti-aircraft cruiser *Carlisle*. From then onwards either one of these cruisers, mounting eight 4-inch high-angle guns, or a sloop of the *Black Swan* class with six 4-inch, stood guard in the harbour. Their anti-aircraft armament sounds formidable, but when it is remembered that they lay between the steep cliffs of the fiord sides, rising to 2000 feet or more, behind which the dive-bombers could take cover until they made their sudden swoops, the difficulty of bringing the guns into action in time can be appreciated. Under such conditions the ships' companies stood at action stations for the eighteen hours from dawn till dusk never knowing when next the rising scream of a Stuka's engine would herald yet another attack. Ammunition was used up at a startling rate. Gun barrels were soon worn almost smooth, making accurate shooting impossible.

It was now that the Commander-in-Chief received an ominous message from the Admiralty. Ammunition stocks for the high-angle guns were running low. There were only 7000 rounds remaining in the armament depots. Such news given out to the fleet would have had a lamentable effect on the morale of ships' companies already being tested to the limit by their long ordeals. Sir Charles Forbes kept it to himself and hoped that relief might come in good time.

It was against the background formed by this ominous news and reports of day-long fights between his scattered ships and the Luftwaffe that Forbes had been urged to consider a more hazardous operation than any so far attempted — a direct assault up the fiords against Trondheim.

CHAPTER 11

The two hastily organised, ill-equipped expeditions we have seen thrown ashore at Namsos and Aandalsnes were the sort of improvisations forced upon a belligerent who has been 'completely outwitted' by the enemy, as Churchill had been forced to admit was the case. Caught off balance, the Allied plans emerged slowly and uncertainly, coloured by an agonised indecision as to which area was to be the main objective. They thus fell between two stools, sending an inadequate force to Narvik for the sake of a half-hearted thrust at Trondheim.

The Germans, on the other hand, saw clearly that Trondheim was the key to Central Norway and concentrated all their efforts on consolidating their position there. As early as April 12th they had learnt from intercepted Allied signals that a landing at Namsos was planned. Soon afterwards they knew that another expedition was to go to the Narvik area.

The failure of their supply arrangements through the loss of so many of their transports had left the German detachments at Trondheim and Narvik critically short of ammunition, artillery and transport. Of the four ships destined for Narvik, the *Rauenfels* with ammunition had been blown up by the British Second Destroyer Flotilla on the 10th. The *Alster* with General Dietl's transport had been captured, and the *Barenfels* had got no further than Bergen where she was sunk by air attack on the 14th — while discharging her cargo. The tanker *Kattegat* had been intercepted by the Norwegians and scuttled to avoid capture.

The ships for Trondheim had been almost equally unsuccessful. The *Sao Paulo* had struck a mine and sunk off

Bergen. The *Main* had been sunk by a Norwegian destroyer. The tanker *Skagerrak* had been intercepted by a British cruiser and had been scuttled. Only the supply ship *Levante* reached Trondheim on the 12th, three days behind schedule. German anxiety for the safety of their two most northerly detachments was intense.

Directions were therefore issued on the 14th to the Army to strain every nerve to advance from Oslo taking possession of the railway through Dombaas; to the Navy to concentrate U-boats round Trondheim and Aalesund and to use others to transport the most urgently needed supplies; the Luftwaffe was to destroy any troops already landed, to prevent further landings in the Aandalsnes area, to occupy Dombaas with paratroops and to send reinforcements by air to Trondheim. So serious did the situation seem to them that on April 22nd they were discussing emergency methods of reinforcing their troops at Trondheim even to the extent of trying to rush troops there in the huge liners *Bremen* and *Europa* escorted by every available ship of the fleet.

It was not long, however, before the British Government also came to appreciate the crucial importance of Trondheim. Though twenty minutes before midnight on April 13th a signal to the Commander-in-Chief, Home Fleet, was initiated in which the landing at Namsos was envisaged as the main expedition against Trondheim with the 'Sickle' force as a diversion, April 14th was not two hours old when a further message said, 'Intention up to present has been to land at Namsos for the Trondheim area. For many reasons it would be advantageous to land the force inside Trondheim Fiord. Do you consider that the shore batteries could be either destroyed or dominated to such an extent as to permit transports to enter? And if so, how many ships and of what type would you propose to use?'

Thus the Commander-in-Chief, at sea off the Lofoten Islands in his flagship, was suddenly posed with the age-old problem of whether ships should be sent against shore fortifications. In war after war throughout history the question has been raised and from time to time warships have engaged forts. Except for a brief period when ships were first sheathed in armour while explosive shell had not been perfected — in the Crimean War — the answer had been the same. Ships could not effectively engage forts.

The most recent example had been at the Dardanelles during Churchill's ill-starred Gallipoli adventure in the First World War. Battleships had on that occasion failed to force the Straits in face of shore fortifications and minefields. The Navy had been almost unanimous in condemning the attempt. An exception had been Roger Keyes who had been Chief of Staff to the Commanding Admiral and who passionately believed that the attempt had been abandoned just when victory was in sight. Subsequently Keyes had gained great renown for his leadership of the raid on Zeebrugge.

Now he was Admiral of the Fleet Sir Roger Keyes, and was at the First Lord's elbow urging an operation which had much in common with that in the Dardanelles. Admirals of the Fleet are always on the Active List and the gallant Keyes was burning to lead a squadron against Trondheim. Another Admiral of the Fleet, Lord Cork, had already been given command of the expedition to Narvik so that it would create no new precedent if Keyes, greatly senior to Sir Charles Forbes, were also to fly his flag in a ship of the Home Fleet.

But even Churchill's unorthodox approach to naval matters could hardly permit him to launch such a project without the concurrence of the Commander-in-Chief.

Forbes' reaction was discouraging. Just as it is arguable that the Dardanelles could have been forced if further attempts had been made, so Forbes was prepared to agree that battleships could destroy or dominate the shore batteries defending Trondheim, though an essential preliminary would be the provision of special high explosive bombardment shell which none of his ships at that time carried. But just as at the Dardanelles, the forcing of the Narrows was not an object in itself but a means to permit further operations — operations of doubtful value and great hazard — so at Trondheim the real difficulty would come after the fleet had passed the defences. Then, as Forbes pointed out, untrained troops would be committed to the perils of an opposed landing, bad enough in itself, but made infinitely worse by continuous air attack by dive-bomber pilots trained for just such a role.

Even though an aircraft carrier would be available in support, the few obsolescent fighters' carried would be quite insufficient to give cover to the landing force and the carrier herself. Forbes concluded his reply, 'I do not consider operation feasible unless you are prepared to face very heavy losses in troops and transports.'

Churchill, with Keyes' urgings in his willing ear, was not convinced. At 1.21 am on the 15th a signal which bears the unmistakable stamp of his hand replied, 'We still think that the operation described should be further studied. It could not take place for seven days devoted to careful preparations. Danger from air would not be appreciably less wherever these large troopships are brought into the danger zone; in fact it might be greater while the aerodrome at Trondheim is in action. Our idea would be that, in addition to RAF bombing of Stavanger aerodrome, *Suffolk* would bombard with high explosive at dawn, hoping thereby to put Stavanger aerodrome out of business. The aerodrome at Trondheim, which is close to the harbour, could be dealt with by Fleet Air Arm bombers and subsequently by bombardment.

'High explosive shell for 15-inch guns has been ordered to Rosyth. *Furious* and First Cruiser Squadron will be required for this operation.'

'Pray, therefore, consider this important project further.'

This message was full of misconceptions of the facts of modern war at that date. The submission of large troopships immobilised in a narrow fiord to attacks by dive-bombers — and the enemy could be expected to throw in everything they had to defend so vital a spot — was little short of suicidal. Furthermore, airfields were not nearly so vulnerable to bombing attack or bombardment as was implied, though it is fair to say that this was not appreciated until the Germans failed to put British airfields out of action for any length of time during the Battle of Britain.

Admiral Forbes' reply made the former point clear. After asking for further details of the project and suggesting the substitution of the *Glorious* for the *Furious* as the latter had no fighter squadron embarked and her bomber squadron was in need of re-equipment, he went on to say:

'I think you have misunderstood my 1157/14. I do not anticipate any great difficult from the naval side, except that I cannot provide air defence for transports while approaching and carrying out an opposed landing — the chief air menace being JU88s from Germany. And I know, from personal experience, what an opposed landing is like, even without air opposition.

'The naval force required would be *Valiant* and *Renown* to give air defence to *Glorious*; *Warspite* to carry out bombardments as she is the only 15-inch ship in the fleet with 6-inch guns; at least four anti-aircraft cruisers; about twenty destroyers and numerous landing craft.'

Meanwhile, the greater part of the fleet was ordered home to prepare for the operation. The Commander-in-Chief himself arrived at Scapa on the 17th, having asked for a member of the Admiralty staff to bring to him details of the plan. Accordingly, Rear-Admiral Holland arrived aboard the flagship the next day with the latest Admiralty intentions and a personal letter from the First Lord strongly advocating the proposed operation.

Forbes found that his principal objection had been met in that the assault troops would be carried in a force of four cruisers, seventeen destroyers and five sloops. Only the follow-up troops would be brought in troopships. But on the other hand the 'seven days for careful preparation' for this highly intricate combined operation, in which the smooth co-operation of all three services was essential for success, had vanished. Embarkation of the troops was to begin on the 21st at Rosyth and the bombardment of Stavanger airfield had already been carried out by the *Suffolk* at dawn on the 17th.

But, whatever its merits, Operation 'Hammer', as the Trondheim project had been called, had not been conceived under a lucky star. The first military commander appointed, Major-General Hotblack, fell ill in London on April 18th. His successor was flown north on the following day, but was seriously injured when his aircraft crashed on landing at the airfield at Hatston in the Orkneys. Before this, something of what was being risked was brought home by the arrival of the *Suffolk* in Scapa Flow from the Stavanger operation, being barely kept afloat, her quarterdeck awash and with seventy casualties.

In London the stakes were being more carefully considered against the odds offered. A large portion of the fleet was already committed to operations of considerable hazard in support of the landings at Namsos and Aandalsnes. Now almost the whole of the remainder was to be sent in to the restricted waters of Trondheim Fiord. Losses from air bombing were highly likely. Stocks of anti-aircraft ammunition were critically low. The War Office, too, began to get cold feet at the thought of an opposed landing under air attack. The experiences of their troops at Namsos after landing were filtering back to them. The question to be answered was whether the objective was worth the price which might have to be paid for it.

At this point a basic misconception of what had been achieved at Namsos and Aandalsnes was to cloud the issue. At both places the troops had been put ashore without loss and had been able to press forward towards their initial objectives. Why therefore attempt to open a fresh gateway into central Norway at great peril when two had already been established?

That both Namsos and Aandalsnes were quite inadequate as bases and that both were shortly to be obliterated by the Luftwaffe was not yet realised. Nor was it yet appreciated that Arctic conditions and the lack of transport were combining to put British troops at a hopeless disadvantage in the open country against the well-equipped and ski-trained German troops even apart from the German advantage in possessing complete air supremacy. It still seemed, therefore, that the risks involved in Operation 'Hammer' were not worth while when the objective could still be obtained through 'Maurice' and 'Sickle'.

Whether 'Hammer' would have been persisted with had this fallacy not been held, it is impossible to say. Up to April 17th, in spite of Admiral Forbes' doubts, the Chiefs of Staff and, beyond them, the First Lord of the Admiralty who was the vitalising influence in the War Cabinet, were unanimously in favour of the attempt. Winston Churchill in *The Gathering Storm* has been at pains to make the point that the project was never his own brain-child. The War Cabinet and the Staffs produced it unprompted by his restless, thrusting personality. 'Although Narvik was my pet,' he has written, 'I threw myself with increasing confidence into this daring adventure and was willing that the Fleet should risk the petty batteries at the entrance to the fiord, the possible minefields, and most serious, the air.' Again he writes, 'Left to myself I would have stuck to my first love, Narvik; but serving as I did a loyal chief and friendly Cabinet, I now looked forward to this exciting enterprise to which so many staid and cautious Ministers had given their strong adherence.'

It is difficult to picture him being led in such a matter by 'staid and cautious Ministers'. Certainly by the 18th when, as he has described, 'a vehement and decisive change in the opinion of the Chiefs of Staff and of the Admiralty occurred' leading to an abandonment of 'Hammer' the next day, he was 'indignant' and 'bitterly disappointed'. 'Having gone so far,' he believed, 'we ought to have persisted in carrying out Operation Hammer.'

Against this must be put the considered opinion of the naval Commander-in-Chief, as set down later in the Home Fleet Narrative, '…. that it was a gamble that might have succeeded, but probably would not. It appeared to him that it was only in the fleet which had practical experience in the matter, that the scale of air attack that the enemy could develop on the Norwegian coast was properly appreciated.

'An opposed landing with very slightly superior forces had to be undertaken which, from previous experience and in view of what happened at Narvik, was bound to be a hazardous operation and withal the combined operation had to be hastily planned and then performed without any practice at all.'

The pros and cons of Operation Hammer can be lengthily argued. What is certain is that its abandonment spelt the doom of Maurice and Sickle. The former had been launched on the assumption that, on reaching the Trondheim Fiord, it would find the Royal Navy afloat on its waters. Instead, it was met by German destroyers, who could bring speedy reinforcement to the troops ashore and could bombard the British positions with 5-inch guns at their leisure. Mauriceforce could advance no further.

Sickle had been originally envisaged as a diversionary operation only. It soon found itself engaged in a holding operation to check the German advance from the south while Trondheim was reduced by Maurice and Hammer. With the abandonment of Hammer the usefulness of both Maurice and Sickle dissolved. Evacuation of both should have at once been decided upon; but as we have noted above, their limited capabilities had not yet been brought home to the War Office in spite of Carton de Wiart's forthright opinions.

Instead, therefore, it was decided to send the troops released from Hammer, some 4000 men of the 15th Brigade, to reinforce Sickle. They were to be transported in two waves by cruisers of the Second and Eighteenth Cruiser Squadrons and destroyers. With them were to go a new force commander, Major-General B. C. T. Paget, and a Divisional Headquarters.

The fortunes of Sickle had already become clouded. Though the first infantry reinforcements had arrived on April 21st in two small transports and, aided by snowstorms and low cloud which had kept the Luftwaffe grounded, had been safely landed, the freighter *Cedarbank* which had accompanied them had been sunk by a U-boat during the voyage. With her had gone nearly all Brigadier Morgan's motor transport, antiaircraft guns and equipment. On the following day the antiaircraft sloop *Pelican*, on her way to the Romsdal Fiord carrying the personnel of the Naval Base party for Molde, was crippled by a dive-bomber and suffered heavy casualties.

Though something was known of the ordeal being suffered by Brigadier Morgan's force from the attentions of JU87s, the Stuka dive-bombers, which the enemy had so efficiently trained to operate in support of their ground troops, it was not yet appreciated to what extent unopposed air attack completely immobilised infantry confined to roads and railway. It was still thought that the fresh 15th Brigade, composed of three regular infantry battalions withdrawn from France, would be able to stabilise the situation south of Trondheim and with the aid of the Norwegian Army hold off the enemy advancing from the south long enough for Carton de Wiart to break through to Trondheim.

Furthermore, the Royal Air Force was now to make an effort to join in the campaign. Up to now the possession by the Germans of all airfields in southern and central Norway had made the operation of Allied fighter aircraft in the Trondheim area impossible.

The Fleet Air Arm, had it been developed before the war to the extent that the Navy's aviators had urged in vain, would have been able to transform the situation by operating fighters from carriers. As it was, only one carrier, the *Furious*, had been available at the opening of the campaign and she had no fighter squadrons embarked. The *Ark Royal* and *Glorious* joined the Home Fleet from the Mediterranean and arrived off the Norwegian coast for the first time on April 24th. Their fighters, however, were too few in number and of too low a performance greatly to affect the situation, though the pilots fought with sustained gallantry, shooting down a great many enemy aircraft and suffering heavy casualties themselves.

But fighters working from carriers which were necessarily kept some 150 miles out at sea could not hope to bring such continuous aid as could aircraft from airfields close to the scene of action. In default of such airfields it was decided to make use of the frozen Lake Lesjaskog hard by the road and railway connecting Dombaas and Aandalsnes. A single squadron of eighteen obsolete biplane Gladiator fighters was all that the Air Ministry could make available at short notice. It was a quite inadequate number for the purpose but in view of the organisational shortcomings and the operational difficulties which attended the project, leading to its total failure and loss, it was as well that no more were sent.

The first item in the task given to the cruisers, of reinforcing Sickleforce, was the transport of the ground staff, stores and equipment for this squadron. It was entrusted to the *Arethusa*, which embarked the RAF personnel at Rosyth on April 20th. With them came fifty tons of aviation petrol in boxed, two-gallon cans many of which were leaky and some forty so bad that they were rejected. This load of inflammable material piled high on her quarterdeck was viewed with undisguised disgust by the crew of the *Arethusa* particularly when from ships returning from the Norwegian coast came ribald comments as to the joy with which the Luftwaffe would greet such a succulent target. However, the passage was in fact made in safety, the petrol being thankfully discharged at Aandalsnes on the night of the 22nd, together with a large quantity of stores for Sickleforce.

But the administrative chaos which was to dog the Gladiator expedition throughout its brief life was already in evidence. Nine tons of stores arrived too late to be embarked in the *Arethusa* and had to wait to go a day later in the *Galatea* which was sailing with *Sheffield* and *Glasgow* to take the first wave of the 15th Brigade.

On the 21st these three ships took on board some 2000 men and 200 tons of stores and equipment and sailed early on the 22nd. Haste and confusion coloured the operation as it had everything to do with the military side of the campaign so far. Eighteen lorries rolled up for embarkation for which there was no space on the cruisers' crowded decks. By disembarking her aircraft, the *Sheffield* managed to house two of them. Another was found room in the *Glasgow*, but the remainder had to be left behind.

Twenty-five tons of lubricating oil for the Gladiators failed to arrive in time. *Glasgow* and *Sheffield* were ordered to land the few gallons they carried for their own aircraft on arrival — a very inadequate substitute. During the night of the 23rd, the cruisers discharged their loads at Aandalsnes and Molde and sailed again before dawn.

The arrival of these reinforcements for Sickle was the signal for the Luftwaffe to redouble their attacks on any shipping remaining in the fiord at daylight. Throughout the 24th, attack followed attack unceasingly. Three anti-submarine trawlers were sunk and the Norwegian torpedo boat *Trygg*. Any small craft that moved out from the shelter of cliffs or narrow inlets was at once pounced upon. All day long the blistered guns of the anti-aircraft cruiser *Curacoa* blazed skywards as squadrons of Stukas swooped on her, determined to eliminate her; but not until late in the day after they had been made to pay dearly for their efforts did they succeed. A bomb hit below the bridge superstructure and burst between decks killing thirty of her crew and wounding as many more. The cruiser limped home for repairs, being replaced by the sloop *Flamingo*.

As yet, however, owing largely to the fact that no large troopships had been sighted making for Romsdal Fiord by the German scouting aircraft, the importance of Aandalsnes and Molde as allied bases had not been appreciated by them. The two towns themselves had escaped relatively lightly, and even the vulnerable wooden piers had been kept undamaged by the efforts of Colonel Simpson's Royal Marine anti-aircraft gunners.

Thus, when the cruiser *Manchester* berthed at Molde on the night of the 25th to land General Paget and his headquarters, while the *Birmingham* and *York* went on to Aandalsnes with the third battalion belonging to the 15th Brigade, Captain M. M. Denny, the naval officer in charge, was able to tell the General that although naval losses were mounting steeply, his proposed base was still largely intact. It was in a fairly sanguine mood, therefore, that General Paget took passage from Molde to Aandalsnes in the Norwegian destroyer, *Sleipner*, and moved on up to the front, leaving the developments of his headquarters under the command of Brigadier Hogg.

He was thus not in Aandalsnes when, on the 26th, the Germans, at last appreciating from the growing dumps of stores and the large bodies of troops moving forward that a major landing had been taking place, concentrated their bombers on Aandalsnes and Molde in a determined and largely successful attempt to wipe them both out. By the end of the day both places were ablaze, devastated by bomb bursts and the explosions of ammunition dumps. By midnight naval and military officers at the base were in agreement that all hope had gone of supporting the expedition through the two ports for any length of time. The following morning Brigadier Hogg on his own initiative made the first signal to the War Office warning them that evacuation was the only course open.

Paget, though he had himself warned London that 'arrangements to evacuate should be prepared if aerial supremacy is not ensured forthwith', had not yet realised how unsuccessful the attempt was to be. He promptly signalled to the War Office in the opposite sense to Brigadier Hogg, but urging the need for effective action to deal with enemy aircraft. In fact, the air effort represented by the eighteen Gladiators of No 263 Squadron on Lake Lesjaskog had already petered out.

The squadron had flown off from the deck of the *Glorious* on the 24th during a snowstorm. Guided by two Skuas of the Fleet Air Arm, they reached their makeshift airfield at 6 pm and landed safely between the banks of heaped up thawing snow marking the runways which had been cleared by the ground crews. Though the enemy reconnaissance planes had been over and seen the preparations, they left them in peace that day. They could afford to, for with darkness the bitter cold there, nearly 2000 feet above sea level, combined with the administrative shortcomings in the arrangements for dispatch of the squadron would largely do their work for them. In 30 degrees of frost the aircraft parked out in the open were quickly frozen solid. Controls became immovable and carburettors blocks of ice. The starter trolleys sent with the ground equipment had batteries uncharged and no acid with which to fill them. A single trained armourer was available to service the seventy-two Browning guns.

Thus when daylight reached the valley at the bottom of which lay the lake airfield, two hours of strenuous endeavour only succeeded in getting one or two aircraft into the air to oppose the first bombing attack. A bomber was shot down, but others dropped their loads on the ice to start the process which was soon to make the airfield unusable. At 8.30 came the enemy's main effort as Heinkel twin-engined bombers attacked at their leisure while the majority of the Gladiators lay exposed and immovable. A few got into the air, but others, unable to start, were destroyed or put out of action where they lay.

It was, alas, an inglorious episode; for the ground crews, many of them strangers to the unit and unfamiliar with their aircraft, were demoralised. Taking shelter among the trees on the shores of the lake they remained there while the officers and sergeants were left to the work of refuelling, rearming and starting up the aircraft. On the other hand the naval crews of the two Oerlikon guns supplied for anti-aircraft defence and the Royal Marine platoon for guarding the petrol supply, with Lewis guns, stuck valiantly to their posts and gave a warm reception to any bomber which ventured low to machine-gun the airfield.

In spite of all discouragement, the pilots of those aircraft which did get into the air performed brilliantly while their ammunition lasted, shooting down a number of enemy bombers and bringing relief to the harassed, Stuka-dominated troops. By the afternoon of the first day, not only was the airfield barely usable, but the belted ammunition for the Gladiators' machine guns was already exhausted. The pilots nevertheless took off and did what they could to distract the bomb-aimers by making feint attacks.

Meanwhile, an alternative landing ground on the parade ground of a Norwegian army camp at Setnesmoen, just outside Aandalsnes, had been prepared. Towards evening the five remaining serviceable aircraft were flown there and the ground staff followed after destroying thirteen damaged Gladiators on the lake. But it was of little avail. By the next evening but one aircraft remained serviceable.

At nightfall on the 26th, the ill-starred effort to base fighter aircraft in Central Norway was at an end. A project to replace the Gladiator squadron by one of Hurricanes based on a makeshift landing ground near Aandalsnes was not proceeded with on the grounds that evacuation had been decided upon and Hurricanes were too valuable to be risked. If the organising ability behind it was no better than that which supported 263 Squadron, it was a wise decision. Royal Air Force support for Sickelforce was confined, for the remainder of its brief history, to occasional one-hour patrols of Blenheim fighters, working from Hatston airfield in the Orkneys. The cliche, 'conspicuous by its absence', was never more aptly applied to air support than by the unfortunate troops cowering in roadside ditches from the unceasing snarl of Stuka engines and the deadly chatter of their machine guns as they pounced on every moving thing. What it was like has been vividly described by Brigadier Dudley Clarke in his book *Seven Assignments*.

'The German pilots flew now just as they liked, up and down that one narrow road along which everything had to move. In relays of two and three they would come out to bomb the bridges and the crossroads and then, with the bombs spent, they would drop down on their remaining petrol for the sport of shooting up anything left in sight. The hum of engines soon became so regular that there was no more chance to stop the car and streak for shelter before each made his initial run in.

'That first attack either got you or it missed you; and only then, after it was over, would there follow the exhausting process of tumbling out and ploughing through snow to the nearest tree or wall, or even the roadside drain, in the few minutes that were left before the next one…

'Looking back upon it I believe the "Evil Eye" feeling was the worst part, the sensation of being watched at every turn by birds of prey who could swoop with deadly suddenness whenever they chose the moment. It was largely that which drove us to the flimsy cover of trees and sheds, and it was that which reduced Sickleforce to something near complete immobility during each eighteen hours of daylight.'

It is not surprising, therefore, that with the final elimination of the Gladiator squadron it became clear to the authorities in London that evacuation was inevitable. The German Army was being steadily reinforced across the short safe sea route to Oslo and was being brought up the road and railway towards Trondheim in ever increasing numbers, with tanks and artillery. Winston Churchill, explaining the decision to Sir Charles Forbes, said: 'It is impossible for 3000 or 4000 men without artillery or air superiority to withstand the advance of 70,000 or 80,000 thoroughly equipped Germans.'

At Namsos, Carton de Wiart's force, similarly dominated by enemy air power, had been thrown back from its position on the Trondheim Fiord. Without artillery or anti-aircraft guns, it could do no more than stand grimly on the defensive. Behind them their base lay in ruins. For a few days more, however, they were to have to endure.

CHAPTER 12

While the troops of Maurice and Sickle forces and the sailors and marines of the base Staffs were thus undergoing the grim ordeal which seems always to be the lot of the armed forces of democracies in the early phases of any war, the ships supporting the expeditions were bearing their share. The careless years of peace had to be paid for in material and lives.

Afloat, the brunt had to be taken by the little ships, the antiaircraft light-cruisers, the destroyers, sloops and trawlers. At the opening of the Namsos expedition it was destroyers from the Home Fleet which had first felt the weight of the Luftwaffe. Meagrely and unsuitably armed for defence against them, they had yet more than held their own against the bomber pilots who were themselves facing naval gunfire for the first time. The ships had escaped direct hits; and not all the German aircraft had returned to base.

As the airmen's skill increased, however, and above all with the arrival on the scene of the JU87 Stuka dive-bomber, which could attack with great accuracy at an angle so steep that the destroyers' guns could not retaliate, it was as well that ships armed with batteries of high-angle guns could be brought in to take the place of the destroyers.

The old 'C' class light-cruisers which had come to sea towards the end of the Kaiser's War had had their battery of five 6-inch guns removed and replaced by eight 4-inch high-angle guns. It had seemed a formidable armament to the gunnery experts who believed the principal air threat to come from formations of bombers flying at a steady course, speed and height to deliver their salvoes of bombs. Although before the war radio-controlled aircraft targets had flown back and forth unscathed while such guns blazed ineffectually at them, and it had been cause for jubilation when on rare occasions one had been shot down, the air threat was thought to have been mastered.

First, the Stuka dive-bomber and then the torpedo aircraft when properly used in massed attack were to prove this belief mistaken. Slow-firing large-calibre guns alone could not defeat either of them. A large number of heavy automatic weapons was the only antidote in the absence of fighter cover, and this British warships did not have. They had unreliable, unwieldy 2-pounder pom-poms and perhaps a four-barrelled 0·5-inch machine gun. That ubiquitous and splendid weapon which was later to drive the Stuka from the skies, the 20-millimetre Oerlikon, had been rejected by the Royal Navy on technical grounds. Only slowly, also, did the 40-millimetre Bofors gun become standard equipment.

The sloops of the *Black Swan* class which had also been equipped as anti-aircraft ships with six 4-inch high-angle guns were similarly meagrely supplied with automatic weapons.

It was to the anti-aircraft cruisers of the Twentieth Cruiser Squadron under Rear-Admiral Vivian and the flotilla of sloops under Captain A. L. Poland which had transported the Primrose force, that the task was given of defending the anchorages at Namsos and Aandalsnes. As long as their ammunition lasted a ship from one or other of these remained, keeping under way off the town for the eighteen daylight hours of each day, twisting and turning to avoid the hundreds of bombs aimed at them while their guns spat skywards till their barrels were red-hot and worn smooth. They were almost the only air defence for the two bases. Consequently the enemy strained every nerve to eliminate them. By night there was little rest for their crews, particularly in the sloops, which were required to ferry troops and stores ashore from transports, which could only venture into the fiords after dark.

Though it could only be a matter of time before a lucky hit by a Stuka's bomb got home to sink or cripple these ships, they stuck to their posts without flinching, following the age-old tradition of refusing to desert the troops they had put ashore. Only immediately prior to the evacuation, when it was of paramount importance to keep themselves intact for it, did they allow themselves to be driven out to sea during daylight.

The price they paid was not light, though only one ship, the *Bittern* at Namsos, became a total loss. Here, throughout April 30th, the Stukas in formations varying from three to nine aircraft had kept up an almost ceaseless attack. There had been rarely a moment when their ugly, broken-wing shape had not been in sight as they circled and waited for a suitable opportunity to bank over and scream down in their steep, plummeting dive.

By the late afternoon they had still failed to hit the indomitable little ship and at least two of them had been shot down. Still further waves of them kept appearing over the mountain tops, while the haggard, red-eyed gun crews groaned with weariness. At about 5 o'clock a formation of three Stukas split up and, while two came hurtling down on the *Bittern*'s port bow, the third crossed over, wheeled steeply round and dived from right astern of her.

Bittern's four forward guns opened up at the two ahead putting up a barrage which was enough to put the pilots off their aim. The solitary Stuka astern was engaged by the after pair of guns and the 0.5-inch machine gun. The attack was but one of a dozen similar ones which had been successfully beaten off during the day, but at last the *Bittern*'s luck had run out. There was no avoiding the bomb released by the Stuka coming in from astern. It struck the quarterdeck at the base of a steel locker holding high explosive demolition charges. There were two tremendous concussions as first the bomb and then the TNT charges exploded and a great flash streaked forward the full length of the ship, the blast reaching to the bridge where it threw the captain to the deck.

When he picked himself up he could see that the stern had been blown off his ship and smoke was pouring from her, aft. Depth charges on what was left of the quarterdeck were burning fiercely. Fire then spread between decks to the small arms magazine where ammunition began to explode. The ship's motor boat was blazing on the upper deck. All fire pumps had been put out of action and the fires were quickly out of control. The executive officer, Lieutenant T. Johnston, with Stoker Petty Officer Hopgood plunged through the exploding inferno to release three men trapped in the after 4-inch magazine before flooding it.

The ship was soon untenable and Lieutenant-Commander R. H. Mills gave orders for all hands except the forward guns' crews to abandon ship. Fortunately, the destroyer *Janus* had come in during the day and her captain now brought his bow alongside that of the *Bittern*, allowing the survivors to transship. The *Bittern* was now finally abandoned, her fires burning uncontrollably. Soon afterwards, the *Janus* was ordered to sink her with a torpedo.

The *Bittern* was the only major warship to be put out of action off Namsos, though not for a single day had the anchorage been left without its guardship. Admiral Vivian's flagship, *Carlisle*, which had shared the burden with *Bittern* during the 28th, but had had to withdraw to refuel the following day, had already returned to take the sloop's place by the time she had been hit. We shall be meeting the *Carlisle* again, when the time comes for evacuation of Namsos, as Admiral Vivian was then put in charge of the operation.

At Aandalsnes Captain Poland's *Black Swan* had been the first to stand guard. At first there had been only high bombers to contend with, which concentrated their aim on his ship, leaving the town alone. In consequence he had complaints that his gunfire was breaking windows in the houses. Little did the unfortunate inhabitants realise what was in store for them.

As the Luftwaffe organised itself, the dive-bombers began to appear. Three days of incessant attack had nearly exhausted the *Black Swan*'s ammunition when the *Curacoa* arrived to relieve her on April 21st. The cruiser's luck was quick to run out. The following day she received the hit on account of which we have seen her limping home with her damage, her dead and her wounded. The *Flamingo* took her place. By the time *Black Swan* was back again on the evening of the 26th to take another turn, *Flamingo* had been reduced to firing smoke shells and practice ammunition at her attackers.

As darkness fell, Poland could see from the glare of fires at Molde and Aandalsnes that the enemy effort had been stepped up even from the high level he had experienced before. With daylight the Stukas were back, their first object being to drive the ship seawards or eliminate her altogether so that they could come down low to finish the destruction of the town and base which they had started on the previous day.

At each attack the six 4-inch guns flamed into action, joined by every light machine gun in the armoury, the captain himself occasionally relieving his feelings by manning a pair of Lewis guns mounted on the bridge. Brigadier Clarke, in the book which has already been quoted, describes one of these attacks which he watched from the shore.

'On one occasion we were treated to a grandstand view in brilliant sunshine of a Stuka attack on an anti-aircraft sloop in the fiord which was almost reminiscent of a "set-piece" in an RAF display at Hendon. I think it was the *Black Swan* and she seemed to be the focus of every aircraft which visited Aandalsnes. This time they made a determined effort to get her. One pilot came out of the sun almost vertically and held to his course right down to mast-top height in spite of a mass of flak coming up from the ship. He went so low that for a moment it looked as though he were hit, but he dropped his bombs and zoomed up again, while spurts of water hid the sloop completely.'

Throughout the 27th, this scene was repeated again and again. By dusk five enemy aircraft had been seen to crash and several had been sent away smoking, clawing their way upwards to get over the mountain tops, but the ship had escaped with a shaking and numerous holes from jagged bomb splinters. Amazingly, there had been but one minor casualty, a member of the pom-pom's crew with a splinter wound in his arm.

More than 1000 rounds of 4-inch ammunition had been fired away during the day. Fortunately, some 400 rounds had been left ashore for ships needing replenishment. Before the weary crew could rest that night it had to be embarked. All but twenty rounds were used the following day.

Before the sun had topped the snowclad mountains to thaw the bitter cold of night, the Germans were back. Once again there began the endlessly repeated rising snarl of the Stuka engines, the staccato bark of the 4-inch guns, the chatter of machine guns and the deep concussion of the bombs as their delay-action fuses burst them below the surface of the sea, all echoing back from the steep sides of the fiord to make a wild bedlam of sound.

In the *Black Swan* neither the guns' crew nor the guns were as fresh as they had been on the previous day, but while the former could pull out reserves of strength and endurance, the guns, smoking hot and blistered, their recoil mechanisms beginning to falter, needed rest and repair. By noon Poland had been forced some distance seawards where he hoped for a respite. The Commander-in-Chief, realising that the limit of endurance was being reached, had signalled *Black Swan* to 'withdraw', but as Poland has said, 'As we were thirty miles inland from the coast, this was not easy. Each time we made for the sea a fresh lot of Huns would arrive and we had to start circling and twisting again.'

Ammunition was already running short again. The *Black Swan*'s Gunner had just reported 'Only eighty rounds of H.A. left' when a formation of twin-engined JU88s was seen approaching. 'Sorry as we were for the town of Molde and for the SNO and his staff there,' said Poland afterwards, 'we were very relieved to see the formation pass over just ahead of us to drop their load on that unfortunate town and not on us.'

He now considered the possibility of sheltering up a deep narrow inlet while he made the necessary repairs to his guns, repaired his wireless aerials which had been all shot away, and generally got into shape to make the most of his rapidly diminishing supply of ammunition. During a lull in aerial activity, he had turned the ship and was about to back her up the selected inlet when a reconnaissance plane passed right overhead, making his plan abortive. Instead, he again set off seawards. The twisting and dodging from successive attacks began once more.

At about 4 o'clock a covey of Stukas gathered overhead and circled like evil vultures while the *Black Swan*'s crew stood to their tired guns and wondered if they were to be the selected prey. Suddenly, the leading aircraft banked steeply over, hung for a moment and then plummeted seawards, followed by the remainder coming in from every angle. The guns barked defiance as best they could but their fire was slow on account of defects too great to remedy. Nor could they engage every one of the aircraft.

As one on the starboard bow pulled out of its screaming dive and the black, blunt bomb came away from its belly, Poland, pumping Lewis gun bullets at him, and Tennyson, the navigating officer, conning the ship in tight circles, together yelled, 'That one's got us.'

The bomb slanted down towards the stern and vanished. Nothing happened for a brief moment; no flash, no smoke. Then the ship seemed to pick itself up, leap bodily upwards and shake itself like a dog coming out of water — and then resumed its progress at full speed as though nothing had happened. Poland and Tennyson grinned at one another and decided that they had survived yet another of the long succession of near misses which was all the Stukas had so far been able to achieve.

Then, as the last Stuka roared away down the fiord, Mr Duggan, the Gunner, arrived breathless on the bridge. 'Sir, do you know No 3 magazine is full of water?'

'No. How is that, Gunner?' replied his captain. His apparent unconcern surprised Duggan for a moment.

'Didn't you know we had been hit?' he blurted, looking from one face to another on the bridge.

Hurrying aft, Poland found it was only too true. The bomb, hitting at an angle on the starboard side of the quarterdeck, had plunged on downwards through the wardroom where it had left a large hole in the middle of the mess table, through a fresh water tank, through the after 4-inch magazine — luckily nearly empty — and out through the ship's bottom, after passing between the two propeller shafts. Leaving a jagged hole some four feet square, its delay-action fuse had finally exploded it well below the surface.

It was a miraculous escape — not by any means the last in the wartime career of Poland, who probably had more bombs aimed at his various ships than any other naval officer. Though the ship's bottom was bent and corrugated, the propellers, shafts, rudder and steering gear were all intact, a great credit to the ship's builders. Perhaps even more amazing was the casualty list from this direct hit — one broken ankle. It was the last attack of the day and, unmolested further, the *Black Swan* reached the open sea to await darkness before returning.

Through the bomb hole in the ship's bottom, water flooded in, but so long as the ship kept steaming at full speed, the suction of her progress kept it down to below the level of the wardroom deck. Looking down to where dim green daylight could be seen through the hole, Poland pondered what would happen when the ship stopped. Bulkheads around the damage were shored up as strongly as possible. Speed was reduced to Slow. Sure enough, the water level rose at once; but at the level of the wardroom deck it stopped. Stop Engines was rung down while anxious eyes watched. The water sluiced up until the deck was covered to a depth of a few inches. Relief was heartfelt when once again it ceased to rise further.

With ammunition almost exhausted, the *Black Swan* was relieved that night by the sloop *Fleetwood* and steamed home for repairs.

Such was a not untypical day in the life of an AA guardship off Aandalsnes or Namsos, though direct hits were in fact achieved at astonishingly rare intervals by Luftwaffe pilots. Undoubtedly they preferred the sport of shooting up infantry formations or military cars and lorries which could neither move so fast nor hit back so hard as the bigger game. One target there was afloat on the fiords, however, against which they could make comparatively safe practice, though even this was not so defenceless as the troops ashore.

A lack of appreciation of what was possible in waters dominated by enemy aircraft had led to the dispatch to Namsos and Aandalsnes of a number of anti-submarine trawlers to patrol the entrances to the fiords against U-boats. The fact that in the narrow, confined waters of the fiords their asdics were for technical reasons almost totally ineffective was a minor miscalculation compared to that of exposing them to unopposed air attack. A few Lewis guns and in some cases a single Oerlikon 20-millimetre were the only defence against aircraft which these little craft possessed.

From the moment dive-bombers arrived in the area these slow, vulnerable vessels were first chased all day up and down the fiords and then, when several had been sunk or crippled and it became clear that during daylight hours at least they could perform no useful function, they were forced to take shelter under overhanging cliffs, camouflaged with fir trees, to evade the bombers' attentions and to rest their weary crews. In spite of this, out of the twenty-nine trawlers sent to the two places, eleven were sunk or driven ashore and few escaped without damage and casualties.

Manned by fishermen of the RN Patrol Service for the most part and officered by RNR officers from the Merchant Service and trawler skippers, with a retired RN commander in charge of each group of four, they suffered a grim ordeal, their days haunted by prowling Stukas, their nights as often as not spent at the beck and call of senior officers requiring them to give a hand in transporting troops and stores from ship to shore.

Their experiences were all so very similar that it will suffice to tell those of one of them, Lieutenant-Commander R. B. Stannard, commanding officer of the trawler *Arab*, who was to be awarded the Victoria Cross for his gallantry and leadership at Namsos. The Fifteenth Anti-Submarine Striking Force, the grandiloquent title of the group of four trawlers, *Aston Villa*, *Gaul*, *Angle* and *Arab*, under Commander Sir Geoffrey Congreve, arrived off Namsos at about 2 am on April 28th in company with a similar formation, the Sixteenth A/S Striking Force under Commander Martin Sherwood. The *Arab* was at once ordered alongside the *Carlisle*, flagship of Admiral Vivian, to ferry to the shore stores, ammunition and other equipment brought by the cruiser for the French troops.

Daybreak at 4 am brought the first air attack and *Arab* was hastily cast off to give *Carlisle* freedom to manoeuvre as she went into action. When it was over the trawler went back to complete embarkation of the stores and, at 6 am, was alongside the wharf astern of the French transport *Saumur* which had brought ammunition and supplies on the previous day.

As no one appeared to disembark his load, Stannard went ashore, routed out some French and British soldiers and set them to work. His ship was still at the wooden pier when a bomb landed squarely among the ammunition stacked there and set it blazing. Fortunately, there was not much of the trawler projecting above the pier level. The blast and storm of splinters flew harmlessly overhead therefore.

At the air-raid alarm, the master of the *Saumur* had slipped his wires to get away out into the fiord. In his haste he had wrapped a wire round his propeller. There he lay immobilised while the fire threatened to engulf him until the *Arab* and *Angle* went to his rescue. Finding that the *Angle* was able to tow the *Saumur* clear by herself, Stannard now placed the bow of his own ship against the pier, his engine running slowly ahead to keep it there, while his crew fought the fire. For two hours while bombers circled overhead and tried to complete the work of destruction, they played their hoses on it with apparently little result, though Admiral Vivian in his report credits their efforts with saving that small part of the pier which was to prove of inestimable value during the final evacuation.

Other work called. The *Angle*'s tow-rope had parted. *Arab* was required to take her place holding the *Saumur* in the middle of the fiord while efforts were made to cut the wire clear from her propeller. It was well into the afternoon when this was completed, and *Arab* could cast off as more bombs splashed and burst around the two ships.

By this time Admiral Vivian had received the news that evacuation of Namsos was to take place on the nights of May 1st and 2nd. A French battalion of 850 men were in the town. They were unlikely to get into action. With two French transports in the harbour it seemed sensible to get them away in them, to which both Carton de Wiart and General Audet agreed. *Arab* and *Angle* therefore spent the night transporting men and equipment from shore to ship.

It was their second night without sleep. A long day of bombing was ahead of them, and their turn would follow to relieve *Aston Villa* and *Gaul* on patrol. Stannard decided to seek shelter under a cliff but had failed to find a suitable spot before the first bombers arrived. In the first hour after daybreak sixteen near misses had shaken the *Arab*, cracking castings in the engine room and damaging rudder and propeller. She could still keep going, however, and Stannard took her to seek his senior officer in the *Aston Villa* in an inlet near the mouth of the fiord. There Congreve detailed him to relieve *Gaul* on anti-submarine patrol the following morning — a patrol that was destined never to be performed.

Chivvied to and fro by dive-bombers all morning, he escaped damage. The *Aston Villa* was not so lucky, as he discovered when he found her later alongside a wharf near Namsos, where Congreve was busy camouflaging her with fir trees. Near misses had fractured most of her engine room castings and she could move only with difficulty and at low speed.

The *Arab*'s crew were by now dropping with weariness and haggard with the unremitting threat from the Stukas which pounced whenever the ship moved. The departure of the *Carlisle* early that morning to refuel had left the trawlers the only target afloat for the Luftwaffe. Stannard was glad to get orders to seek shelter where he could until dark. This he found alongside a cliff; but of rest there was little, for the enemy were over every hour in flights of six and nine. The *Gaul* was hit and with a fifteen-foot hole in her bow, had retired to the shelter of a small inlet with only her forward bulkhead keeping her from foundering.

In the late afternoon the arrival of the *Bittern* brought promise of an easement of the trawlers' condition. As soon as it was dusk, Stannard took the *Arab* alongside her. To be able to hit back at his tormentors was his one idea by now. In concert with Lieutenant-Commander Mills, captain of the *Bittern*, he arranged that when daylight came he would place his ship some 400 yards to the westward of the sloop where he would be nicely placed to bring his Oerlikon and Lewis guns to bear on the Stukas as they flattened out of their dives from the direction of the sun.

At 7 o'clock the next morning he had his reward when sixteen dive-bombers concentrated on the *Bittern*. As they flattened out over the sloop after dropping their bombs, they were each momentarily an easy target. With grim satisfaction Stannard saw the glitter of his 20-millimetre Oerlikon shells as they burst against their fuselages. More than one Stuka certainly never reached its base from that attack.

This satisfactory state of affairs did not last long, however, for his group commander needed his services. From the *Aston Villa* Congreve embarked in the *Arab* to be taken to inspect the damage to the *Gaul*. While thus engaged, they came upon the trawler *St Goran* of the other trawler group sheltering under a tree-clad cliff and evidently badly damaged. Closing her they found her boat containing some badly wounded men and Carley rafts with the remainder of her crew. A direct bomb hit on her bridge had killed her skipper, the coxswain and two other ratings.

While rescue work was going on, further bombs were falling all round and Stannard hastened as soon as he could to take cover under a cliff. The destroyer *Janus* passing by on her arrival, she was appealed to for medical aid and sent her medical officer and a sick-berth attendant before going on up to Namsos. When the *Carlisle* arrived two hours later the doctor was able to take the wounded to her.

Informing the Admiral of the parlous state of the trawlers, Stannard received a somewhat astonishing reply, *Enemy ships and submarines expected. Keep a good lookout and prepare to engage the enemy*. The time had passed when any such action was imaginable, but the Admiral had clearly not yet appreciated to what a state the dive-bombers had reduced the trawler force. Bare survival had become the only possible aim.

With the arrival of more important targets with whom to share the ration of bombs — it was at this time that the *Bittern* was sunk — Stannard had some leisure to consider how he could best employ the resources remaining to him. He decided that machine gun posts at the summit of the cliff would best defend his ship and the damaged *Gaul* hard by from the dive-bombers and give the crews some protection. As he was landing the guns he came upon a large cave in the cliffside in which to install the crew by night and those off duty by day.

Stannard now bethought himself of some boxes of French equipment still aboard the *Arab*. Breaking them open he was delighted to find some automatic rifles and ammunition as well as a 60-millimetre mortar with bombs and detonators complete. By the evening he had his post established with six Lewis guns, two automatic rifles and the bomb thrower. With the *Arab*'s solitary 4-inch gun and Oerlikon he felt he was equipped to repel attack by sea, land or air.

When the *Carlisle* passed his post he reported the action he had taken, to receive a *Well done. Carry on*, which relieved his mind. For the first time since arrival the whole crew except for lookouts were able to sleep through the brief hours of darkness.

With daylight the *Angle* came by on her way to patrol outside the fiord, bearing the indomitable Congreve who was determined not to be driven from his station so long as one of his ships was undamaged. Soon afterwards the crippled *Aston Villa* arrived and made fast to the shore 100 yards from the *Arab*. It was not long before the three ships began to attract the attention of the enemy. In flights varying from six to twelve in number the Stukas swooped, bombing the immobilised ships but not escaping unscathed themselves as Stannard's machine-gun posts came into action.

The *Gaul* was the first to suffer, near misses being enough to split her in her damaged state. At 1.30 in the afternoon she sank and her crew came ashore. It was only a matter of time before the other two must be hit. Leaving only a few men aboard them to man the Oerlikon gun, the remainder came ashore to man the *Arab*'s machine-gun posts.

It was as well, for at 5 o'clock a direct hit smashed into the *Aston Villa* and set her on fire. An officer and three ratings were wounded. In makeshift stretchers made from fir saplings they were hoisted to the clifftop where a surgeon from a destroyer came to attend them.

So the day wore on with attack after attack hardly ceasing. By 8 o'clock the *Aston Villa* was blazing fiercely and might blow up at any moment. Stannard sought permission from Congreve, who had now returned, to go aboard to fight the fire but was sternly ordered to keep clear. Instead he took two volunteers from his crew, Sub-Lieutenants Lees and Nicholson, to try and save the *Arab*. Cutting her mooring lines they warped her along the shore, but had gone barely 100 yards when the *Aston Villa* blew up. The *Arab* was saved.

By now the evacuation of Namsos was under way. It was time to dismantle the *Arab*'s private stronghold. Embarking all three crews, Stannard steamed his rickety ship up to the harbour where he was able to find someone to take the men of the *Gaul* and *Aston Villa* and then turned thankfully seaward to make for home.

His adventures were not quite over, however. His initial speed of five knots was soon down to three as the accumulated damage to his engine began to have its effect. He had barely cleared the fiord at daylight. Fortunately no dive-bombers found him, but at noon a solitary Heinkel 115 appeared. The pilot, as Stannard reported later, 'seemed to be a novice'. Certainly he did not appreciate what a redoubtable opponent he was challenging when he signalled to the *Arab*, 'Go East or be sunk.' In Stannard's words, 'a suitable answer was sent in reply'.

The Heinkel then circled the *Arab*, getting gradually closer while keeping up a continuous but ineffective fire with its two guns. Stannard held his fire until, as the aircraft banked over at a range of 800 yards, he loosed every gun he had on to him. Oerlikon shells could be seen bursting on the fuselage. With a splash and a smother of foam the aircraft hit the sea. The *Arab*, her engine pounding and shaking, crept slowly and thankfully westward to safety, her crew grimly satisfied to have thus achieved some revenge for the long days of torment.

CHAPTER 13

The decision to withdraw the Allied expeditions from Central Norway reached Carton de Wiart on the evening of the 27th and General Paget the following morning. It was a bitter blow to General Ruge, the Norwegian Commander-in-Chief, who with the remnants of the Norwegian Army under him had been fighting loyally alongside Sickleforce based on Aandalsnes. Brigadier Clarke, bearer of a personal message from General Ironside, the British CIGS, has described the scene as General Paget broke the news to Ruge:

'There was a silence, and quietly he said, almost to himself: "So, Norway must go the way of Czechoslovakia and Poland." Then he looked up. "But why?" he asked. "Why withdraw when your troops are still unbeaten?" Once again he repeated how he had staked all his hopes upon British aid, and how it was from his advice alone that the Government had decided to fight on.... When next he spoke he was his old self once more. "But these things are not for us to decide, General," he said, "we are soldiers and we have to obey. Let us return to our plans. Please tell me what help I can give you to carry out your orders." The tension was over and we never heard another hint of bitterness.'

It was indeed hard to desert such a man, but though Ruge may have been right in describing Paget's force as still unbeaten, it could only, in the absence of air support, be a matter of time. Gallant rearguard actions and demolitions were for the moment holding up the German advance, but as soon as the road bridges were replaced the enemy tanks again rolled forward irresistibly and their heavy artillery came into action against the lightly-equipped infantry of the Allies.

The advance troops of the enemy were in fact about to make contact with outlying elements of their Trondheim occupation force at Storen, the railway junction 30 miles south of Trondheim. In the opinion of the Germans, 'the situation of the Allied troops south of Trondheim could be regarded as desperate'.

Evacuation was therefore inevitable, and if a debacle was to be avoided it must be done swiftly, before the enemy knew it had started and before he could bring up his heavy weapons to interfere. It was planned to take place from the Aandalsnes area on the nights of April 30th and May 1st, and from Namsos on the nights of May 1st and 2nd. Admiral Edward-Collins with his Second Cruiser Squadron, five destroyers and the two small troopships, *Ulster Prince* and *Ulster Monarch*, was entrusted with the first night's operations at Aandalsnes where the War Office estimated there were some 5500 troops to be lifted. Admiral Layton was to take two cruisers of the Eighteenth Cruiser Squadron and destroyers to bring off the rearguard the following night. For Namsos there was to be a force consisting of two ships of Admiral Cunningham's First Cruiser Squadron, the French cruiser *Montcalm* and three big French transports. The latter were to embark the first half of Mauriceforce while the cruisers would take the remainder on the second night, an estimated total of 6200.

Before Central Norway could be thus abandoned, however, there was yet another task to be performed, vital to the continuance of Norway in the war at the side of the Allies. King Haakon, Crown Prince Olav and the Norwegian Government, driven ever northward by the advance of the Germans since leaving Oslo, had reached Molde. Further retreat to the north was barred by the German occupation of Trondheim.

The cruiser *Glasgow* with an escort of two destroyers was therefore sent to Molde on the night of April 29th. Long before the coast was reached, Captain Pegram could see that the relentless bombing which had followed the King and Government wherever they went had found them again. Over the mouth of the Romsdal Fiord there hung a great pall of smoke from fires burning in Molde and Aalesund. As Molde came into sight it could be seen blazing fiercely. Soon after 10 pm the *Glasgow* nosed her way in to the wooden pier which was already on fire.

From the cruiser's forecastle, fire hoses played on the flames as she came alongside but only the fact that there was a light onshore wind made it possible for her to secure. The pier was deserted. A flashlamp winking gave a message from Captain Denny, the Naval Officer in Charge, that the main party for embarkation was cut off from the pier by the flames. He soon arrived on board by motor fishing boat to report that his Base Party was ready for embarkation. He had been under the impression — as was the Army base commander at Aandalsnes — that evacuation was planned for that night and that the *Glasgow* was the forerunner of other ships. Denny and his staff were very near the end of their tether after days of fierce air attack and nights of activity running the base. It had seemed like the end of a nightmare when, as he thought, his task was completed. It was a sharp disappointment to find that his ordeal was not yet over. Though it was agreed that the majority of his staff should leave in the *Glasgow*, he insisted on remaining himself with a skeleton staff to maintain communications and to assist in the evacuation plan. As Pegram reported, 'He was tired out but indomitable ... I hated to see him go. His courage and quiet composure under such an ordeal were grand to see.'

Meanwhile, the King and his Ministers had been brought aboard from a local tug together with the British, French and Danish Ministers and the staffs of the British and French Legations. There were 117 survivors from six sunken trawlers also, and twenty-three tons of gold bullion.

By the light of the flames from the burning town, German bombers had kept up their attacks while the ship lay at the jetty. As she cast off and drew away, her guns were in action against a last unsuccessful attempt to hit her. Then, as she slipped away into the darkness, there came respite and quiet.

Early the following morning the Norwegian Government went into session on board the *Glasgow* as she sped northwards, to decide where the King and his supporters should be landed. The majority were in favour of Mosjøen, 200 miles north of Trondheim. Pegram, however, was able to persuade them that they would not be able to establish themselves for long there and that Mosjøen was still within range of bombers working from Trondheim.

King Haakon agreed that Tromsø, north of Narvik, was the only possible place and there they were disembarked on the evening of May 1st. In their short stay aboard the *Glasgow*, the King and the Crown Prince had succeeded in making a 'tremendous impression' on Captain Pegram. 'His Majesty,' records Pegram, 'had undergone the severest ordeal and was feeling broken-hearted at the fate of his country..... His quiet composure and dignity, his kindliness and thought for others, his confident, even cheerful bearing when in public were an inspiration to all of us and unforgettable.'

Meanwhile, the operation had begun to evacuate General Paget's force from Aandalsnes. There the enemy's efforts to wipe out the base had gone on unabated and with considerable success — so much so that it had to be virtually abandoned during daylight hours by the base staff. By the glare from fires burning in the town, enemy bombers were now keeping up their attacks after dark.

The sloop *Fleetwood* which had taken the place of the damaged *Black Swan* on the evening of the 28th had expended all her ammunition by the end of the next day. The *Auckland*, after hastily replenishing at Scapa, was sent to replace her, and the anti-aircraft cruiser *Calcutta* was also ordered to the Romsdal Fiord.

Brigadier Hogg, commanding the Corps Headquarters and Base, almost completely out of touch with Paget and the forward troops, had assumed that the first night of the evacuation was to be on the night of the 29th. When no ships arrived he signalled that the situation was 'uncommonly grave'. He had hoped to embark 1000 men that night and had gathered them in for the purpose; 350 were taken aboard the *Fleetwood* which was sailing the next morning. The remainder were dispersed on the outskirts of the town.

The situation, though serious enough, was not in fact as grave as it seemed to Hogg under the full weight of the enemy air attack; for Paget's troops had fought a brilliant rearguard action to halt the Germans on the 28th, and had since been withdrawing in good order free for the first time of the attentions of the dive-bombers, who had been concentrating on Aandalsnes. They would arrive at the base according to schedule during the night of the 30th.

And now Admiral Edward-Collins' force was on its way. Entering the Romsdal Fiord at 9.45 pm, the *Ulster Prince* and the destroyer *Tartar* were detached to Molde. There by the weird light of the flickering flames from the burning wooden pier, they embarked the last of Captain Denny's base staff, of whom only some fifty remained after the *Glasgow*'s visit of the night before, and the staff of the Norwegian Commander-in-Chief. General Ruge himself had agreed to go too, on the assumption that one of the ships would take him north to Tromsø or Narvik. At the last minute he discovered that this was not so. With his foot already on the gangway, he drew back and refused to embark. As Commander-in-Chief he was adamant that only for direct passage to another port in Norway could he accept evacuation. Persuasions and promises of transhipment at Scapa or even at sea failed to shake his determination. Followed by his whole staff he turned resolutely back into the burning town to the wail of air raid sirens to await whatever fate might have in store. *Tartar* and *Ulster Prince* headed for the open sea.

In the meantime, the *Galatea* had berthed at the stone pier of Aandalsnes. At first there was not a soul in sight, but bodies of soldiers began to arrive from their dispersal points and quickly filed on board. Though dead-beat and ravenously hungry they went on board in a well-disciplined orderly manner, although many of them were without arms or equipment. Some 565 men were embarked in the *Galatea* before she cast off to allow the *Arethusa* to take her place and embark almost as many. At the same time the destroyers *Walker* and *Westcott* were ferrying others to the *Sheffield* anchored in the harbour. The *Ulster Monarch* had been awaiting her turn but it became evident that *Arethusa* would be able to take all that remained of the first night's quota. The troopship was therefore sent away empty soon after the *Sheffield* had sailed around midnight.

At 1 am the *Arethusa* had embarked the last man from the quay and she, too, sailed seawards. There were, however, two outlying bodies of men to be picked up. About 300 troops and sailors from the base party, many of them casualties, had been sent to the village of Alfames, six miles north of Aandalsnes, where there was a landing stage. The destroyers *Wanderer* and *Sikh* were sent there and ferried them off to the *Southampton*.

The other party was that of the Royal Marines under Colonel Simpson. Besides providing almost the only shore-based antiaircraft defence for Aandalsnes since being landed as part of Primrose force, they had fought with valour and efficiency alongside the soldiers. Now they were gathering at the village of Veblungsnes across the mouth of the Romsdal River and awaiting embarkation. Simpson himself had been wounded and taken aboard the destroyer *Mashona*. Admiral Edward-Collins detailed the *Walker* and *Westcott* to pick up the remainder. It was found that the rearguard could not arrive until 3 am by which time it would be daylight when the dive-bombers, against which the two old destroyers were almost unarmed, would be back.

The Marines were not to be left behind if it could possibly be helped. Sailing to follow the remainder of his force at 1.45 the Admiral instructed the destroyers that they were not to wait later than 3. The Marines were as good as their word. The last of their rearguard arrived at 3 am and a quarter of an hour later the *Walker* and *Westcott* were racing seawards. As Edward-Collins' force made its way down the fiord, the first of the enemy bombers arrived and attacked it, but in the face of cruiser fire they dropped their bombs mostly wide and without effect.

So, the first night of the evacuation had passed and the ships had escaped unscathed. Some 2200 men in all had been lifted but without guns or equipment. This was in accordance with the plan which stressed the paramount importance of speed if the troops were to be got safely away before daylight.

Signalling to his successor, Admiral Layton, who was already on his way to carry out the second night's evacuation, Edward-Collins estimated that there were probably some 1500 more troops to bring off, but this could only be a mere guess for, as he said, 'as a result of continuous bombing night and day all at Aandalsnes were shaken and no one knew the position at the front'.

May 1st dawned ominously fine and clear. In the bright sunshine the thawing snow sparkled; the waters of the fiord were a dazzling blue. It was a breathtaking vision of spring beauty, had there been anyone able to appreciate it. Instead, with daylight the Stukas were back to make all hideous as they snarled down out of the blue sky. The anti-aircraft ships *Calcutta* and *Auckland* were the centre of their attention as they lay off the town of Aandalsnes. With steadily increasing fury the attacks continued all day. By 4 in the afternoon, when a big formation of Stukas made a most determined effort to eliminate them in an attack lasting for an hour and a half, their ammunition was nearly exhausted. Though both ships were still whole at the end of it, prudence as well as peremptory orders from the Commander-in-Chief made a withdrawal necessary. The ships were to be preserved for the vital operation impending.

In company, therefore, the two ships headed seawards, still under attack, the faster *Calcutta* adjusting her speed in comradely fashion to bring support to her smaller and slower companion. As they reached the open sea to gain their first respite, the smoke-grimed, red-eyed, tired crews lined the rails to cheer one another again and again.

At 7 pm they met Admiral Layton's ships as they arrived, and in their company turned back. Having detached the *Somali* to Aalesund to pick up the detachment of Primrose Force there, the remainder hurried forward at 20 knots with bombers circling overhead and attacking at intervals but without effect, though the flagship had a narrow escape. The four surviving trawlers of the anti-submarine force — by now no doubt thinking they were forgotten men — were sighted and ordered to make for Scapa. As darkness fell the flames of burning Molde lit up the sky. The destroyer *Diana* was sent there to pick up the indomitable General Ruge and his staff and to take them, as they wished, to Tromsø in the north.

The remainder arrived off Aandalsnes at 10.45. Across the river, Veblungsnes was burning but fortunately intervening high ground left the quay in darkness. The *Manchester* and *Birmingham*, too big to use the quay, were anchored, while three destroyers went in to ferry the troops off to them. From the naval officer in charge ashore, Captain Champness, came the message that only 300 men had as yet arrived. The main body would arrive between 1 and 2 in the morning. Going ashore to get in touch with Champness and General Paget, Layton heard something of the situation, though information was scanty. A serious hitch in the withdrawal had occurred through an accident to the train which had been relied upon. It had fallen into a bomb crater, both engines overturning and the front coach telescoped. Casualties were heavy. While the uninjured set off on foot to march through the night the seventeen miles to where the last remaining train could be found, lorries were sent to bring back the injured. The troops arrived safely on the morning of May 1st at Verma, some twenty miles from Aandalsnes. There they spent the day in a tunnel where the train waited to take them on at dusk. One company of the Green Howards and some Royal Marines forming the last rearguard were to follow in lorries.

Embarkation could not begin at once, but soon the troops began to arrive and were ferried off to the cruisers. By midnight when some 1500 had been embarked, General Paget informed Layton that only the rearguard of 200 remained. Warnings of possible fog forming at daylight and penning the troop-laden ships in the narrow waters of the fiord made it imperative for them to get away in good time. Taking the General and his staff with him, the Admiral ordered the cruisers and destroyers to sail, while the *Calcutta* and *Auckland* would bring off the rearguard.

It was with considerable surprise therefore that the *Calcutta*'s crew viewed company after company of soldiers arriving on the quay, until over 750, as many as they could safely accommodate, were on board. With this number they sailed, leaving *Auckland* for the remainder. Fortunately this comprised the true rearguard of twenty-three officers and 218 men, and as the last weary soldier came aboard at 2 am the sloop cast off. Some 2200 men in all had been taken off: the gallant but fore-doomed fight of Sickleforce was ended.

In spite of the enemy appreciation that Sickleforce was being withdrawn, the evacuation had been completed without the loss of a single ship or a single soldier in them. The skill with which the disengagement of the troops had been conducted and the speed with which the embarkation had been completed achieved a measure of surprise and had prevented the enemy from interfering at that defenceless moment when the troops were being taken aboard.

The evacuation from Namsos, however, was timed to begin a day later than the other. Thus, there could hardly be any question of achieving surprise. The hours of darkness were even shorter than at Aandalsnes, and speed in embarkation was even more important. Consequently Admiral Cunningham, to whom the task had been entrusted, had been given three big French transports, the *El Kantara, El Mansour* and *El d'Jezair*, which he planned to fill and send home on the first night. Having brought them, under escort of his three cruisers as far as the Kya Light at the entrance to Namsen Fiord on the evening of May 1st, he intended to send them in with six destroyers to embark the first half of the troops, about 3000 men, and leave in time to be clear of the fiord before daylight. During the day they would be seen safely on their way by his warships who would then turn back in time to carry out the second night's operation.

Such was his original plan; but when he heard that one battalion of French troops had already been got away on April 29th, reducing the total remaining to some 5400 men, he signalled an alternative scheme whereby the whole force would be taken off on the night of May 1st. Rear-Admiral Vivian in his flagship *Carlisle* at Namsos as anti-aircraft guardship, passed this message to General de Wiart, to be told that from a military point of view it was not possible. The whole force, the General insisted, could not be fetched in and embarked in one night. It was not a question of shipping available, in his view, but of hours of darkness. This news was conveyed to Admiral Cunningham, and the General's decision would no doubt have prevailed had not weather, the ultimate arbiter of most naval operations, stepped in.

As his force approached the Norwegian coast on the afternoon of May 1st, thick fog came down to envelop it. Cunningham was forced to order a turn to seawards. One of his destroyer screen, the *Maori*, failing to take in the signal, continued on and was able to establish her position off the Kya Light. Thereupon Captain Lord Louis Mountbatten, whose ship the *Kelly* was also in the force, proposed that he should take two other destroyers, join the *Maori* and try to make their way into Namsos where they might be able to take off at least some of the scheduled first night load.

The proposal was approved. The *Kelly* duly made contact with the *Maori* and the four ships groped their way up the Namsen Fiord to break out into clear weather off Namsos. By then it was broad daylight. Already the first enemy aircraft were circling and seeking more worthwhile targets than the shattered town. There was no possibility of embarking troops under their threat, and Mountbatten led back into the fog. It was none too soon, for before the *Maori* was able to get into complete cover, and while her masts were still showing above the low-lying fog bank, a Stuka placed a bomb so close to her that she suffered twenty-three casualties from splinters.

When the first night of the evacuation was thus aborted, Admiral Cunningham reverted to his plan for completion in one night. He was confident it could be done, being influenced in his decision, as he says, 'by the gallant bearing of the French Admiral Cadart' — commanding the group of three troopships — 'and his confidence of being able to place two of his ships alongside the stone pier and subsequently the third'. Each of these could take 1700 men; the cruiser *York* and destroyers could take the remainder.

Rear-Admiral Vivian, who was to take charge of the details of the evacuation, had joined Cunningham at sea early on May 2nd in his flagship *Carlisle*. On the 30th, after the loss of the *Bittern*, he had consulted de Wiart as to whether the General felt that the presence of an AA ship in the harbour was vital during daylight hours. When the General replied that though the presence of the cruiser was undoubtedly of great moral value it was of little value for direct defence, Vivian decided that to ensure *Carlisle* being still available during the evacuation he should take her to sea during the day — a decision which was supported by an order from the Commander-in-Chief.

Once at sea he had been caught in the same fog which had turned Cunningham away and, throughout May 1st, he had remained at sea. Now he was given Cunningham's intentions, but could only reply that he knew that de Wiart did not consider them possible. Meanwhile, they had reached the General who signalled for Vivian to return to discuss their implications and help him complete his plans.

By 7.30 pm the *Carlisle* was once again off Namsos. The last two serviceable trawlers of Commander Sherwood's group were told to embark 500 French soldiers at once, ready to ferry them to the *York* and the third French troopship. The Admiral then went ashore to confer with de Wiart and Audet, commanding the French troops. There he stressed the importance of speed which meant that a minimum of equipment must be taken by the men and that no stores or guns could be embarked. Audet promised that all his troops would be in the vicinity of the pier by 9.15, while de Wiart expected that the last British soldier would arrive not later than 1 am.

Meanwhile, Admiral Cunningham's force, except his flagship *Devonshire*, the *Montcalm*, flagship of Admiral Derrien, and three destroyers who were to remain at sea, were coming up the fiord. Led by Captain Vian in the *Afridi*, followed by the *York*, *Nubian* and the three transports, they were joined in the fiord by Lord Mountbatten's four destroyers. The first ship to get alongside the stone pier was the *Kelly* where 270 French soldiers were quickly aboard. Admiral Cadart was then as good as his word, berthing the *El d'Jezair* there at 11.30 pm and the *El Kantara* outside her. The *El Mansour* remained under way off the town, and to her and the *York*, further out, there was soon a stream of destroyers and trawlers ferrying troops from the wooden pier, miraculously still usable amidst the ruins around it.

By 1 am the *El Kantara* had a full load of 1700 men and, in company with the *Kelly*, she sailed down the fiord, soon followed by the *York* and *Nubian*. Then Admiral Vivian, ashore to superintend the operation, was told that 780 men of the York and Lancaster Regiment were still some way from the town. He thereupon called for volunteers from any who could drive a car to take any available lorry to fetch them. By this means they were all brought to the pier by 2.20.

All were now embarked except the final rearguard. To bring them off, the *Afridi* was to remain behind. Carton de Wiart, anxious for the safety of these last troops, had wished to stay with the *Afridi*, but had been persuaded that the *York* was prepared for him. He knew that it was going to be touch and go for the rearguard as the last bridge had not been blown until after midnight, leaving them ten miles of atrocious, snowbound road to cover. Already the hilltops were in view against the morning twilight when he left. Daylight was not far off.

In the *Afridi* they waited and scanned the skies anxiously. At last, at 3.15, the lorries clattered on to the pier. The rearguard — the Colonel and thirty-three men of the York and Lancaster Regiment — piled out and were quickly aboard. As the *Afridi* cast off from the pier she turned her guns briefly on to the massed transport before turning and gathering speed down the fiord. The campaign in Central Norway was at an end, sixteen days after it had opened. Not a man had been left behind. General de Wiart, who had said it was impossible, gracefully acknowledged — 'I found that the Navy do not know the word.'

Admiral Cunningham's force was not to get away scatheless. Finding that Mauriceforce had escaped them, the Luftwaffe turned their full fury on the ships at sea. Attacks started at 8.45 that morning when high-bombers and JU88 dive-bombers arrived and concentrated on the *Devonshire* and the *Montcalm*. For nearly two hours the attacks continued without achieving anything better than a near miss. But then the French destroyer *Bison* was hit, disabled and set on fire. As flames spread through the ship, it was decided to abandon her. A number of her crew were able to get aboard the British destroyer *Grenade* which had gone alongside. Others took to the water to swim to the *Afridi* and *Imperial* lying close by. When fire spread to the oil fuel gushing on to the surface of the water from ruptured tanks, many were engulfed by the flames and horribly burnt before being rescued, while bombs continued to burst around the rescue ships.

A further calamity was to befall before the ships drew out of range of the enemy aircraft. As the *Afridi* was rejoining, she was set upon by three Stukas. One bomb hit her squarely at the foot of her foremast and plunged on down to burst between decks, causing heavy casualties, and starting a furious blaze. Another fell close alongside her forecastle and blew a hole in her hull. The combination was too much for the ship. An effort was made to take her in tow by the stern, but had to be abandoned when it was clear she was foundering. Survivors of her crew and passengers were taken aboard the destroyers *Griffin* and *Imperial*. It was particularly poignant that among the hundred dead were thirteen men of the rearguard and thirty of the *Bison*'s crew, who had already endured so much.

CHAPTER 14

The dissolution of the operations in Central Norway, aimed at the recapture of Trondheim, permitted all Allied effort to be concentrated on Narvik. Indeed the main centre of interest had begun to shift northwards as early as April 23rd when General Carton de Wiart's clear-sighted appreciation of the futility of the Namsos expedition had led to the French 27th Demi-Brigade of Chasseurs-Alpins, which had been held in reserve to go to him, being re-allocated to Narvik.

There, a situation in some ways similar to that in the Trondheim region had developed since the battle on April 13th had eliminated the last German naval forces in the area. There were two schools of thought, one advocating an immediate seaborne frontal assault on the town of Narvik, the other an investment by sea while sufficient troops were gathered for a two-or three-pronged attack overland. Unlike Trondheim, however, the supporters of the two opposing conceptions were the naval and military commanders entrusted with the control of operations, a situation not uncommon in the history of combined operations and usually fatal to success.

The military commander, Major-General P. J. Mackesy, as has been previously related, had sailed from Scapa on April 12th in the cruiser *Southampton* with half a battalion of the 1st Scots Guards. Following, and due to arrive two days after him, was a convoy with the remainder of the 24th (Guards) Brigade and the 146th Infantry Brigade. When the battle of April 13th led to sanguine beliefs that Narvik would no longer require so large a force for its capture, the 146th Brigade had been diverted to Namsos.

The selected army base in the Narvik region was at Harstad. This little port, serving only the coastal traffic of this part of Norway and having correspondingly limited wharfage facilities, was on the eastern shore of the island of Hinndy, the largest of the chain of the Lofoten Islands which formed the western shore of the Vestfiord. Between Harstad and the mainland was Vaagsfiord to which the convoy was directed, approaching it from the sea through Andfiord. Narvik was some thirty miles to the south-eastward as the crow flies, but the shortest sea route, south from Harstad, through the narrow channel known as Tjeldsund, past the little village of Skaanland on the mainland and into Ofotfiord, was seventy-five miles. Alternative routes by road and water were available. Landing at Skaanland, forty-five miles by road which skirted the Ofotfiord and the Herjangsfiord would bring the traveller to Oyjord, at the entrance to the Rombaks Fiord, whence a ferry would take him to Narvik. Other landing places from which Narvik could be approached by road from the north were Gratangen and Salan-gen at the head of two side fiords of the same names, leading off Vaagsfiord. From them the road also ran north to Bardufoss and on towards Tromsø. Norwegian troops under General Fleischer were astride this road at Fossbakken some fifteen miles inland from Salangen.

Harstad was the only town of any size besides Narvik in the area, so it was perhaps unavoidable that it should have been selected as the base for a military force organised as was this one in such haste and confusion that not until the stores and equipment in the troopships had been landed and sorted out were the troops in any state to go into action. The inconvenience of an island situation which entailed water transport for every move of troops and their supplies from base to forward area was in fact little greater than would have been experienced from a base on the mainland; troops would still have had to go by water to the various landing places selected as starting points for movements against Narvik.

Owing to the topography of the countryside, snow-covered mountains and steep valleys along which the few roads ran and the whole coastline indented with fiords, any regularly mounted military operation against Narvik was bound to be a long drawn-out affair requiring an extensive base organisation and careful preparation. It is not surprising therefore that both in London and at the scene of operations there should have been a body of opinion prepared to accept heavy risks to find a short cut by taking Narvik by direct assault before the enemy had established himself too strongly.

The naval force commander. Admiral of the Fleet the Earl of Cork and Orrery, had sailed from Rosyth in the *Aurora* at about the same time that General Mackesy had left Scapa. Outranking the Commander-in-Chief, Home Fleet, though wearing his flag in a ship belonging to that fleet, his appointment, sponsored by Winston Churchill himself as First Lord of the Admiralty, was peculiar to say the least of it — equivalent to a Field Marshal being given command of one brigade of an Army Corps. It was certainly to produce its embarrassing moments.

Lord Cork had at first steered for Harstad, where he would meet for the first time the soldier associated with him in the enterprise, and the two commanders would now be able to reveal to each other the nature of the orders given them by their respective Ministries. Such was the uncoordinated nature of the higher direction of the war at this time.

On the morning of the 14th, Admiral Whitworth's encouraging signal, in which he stated his conviction that Narvik could be taken by direct assault without fear of meeting serious opposition on landing, was handed to Lord Cork. He at once ordered a change of course for the Vestfiord and called for the *Southampton* to meet him there, bringing the General and the two companies of Scots Guards so that they might concert, with the aid of a landing party of some 200 sailors and marines, a landing at daylight on the 15th.

For better or for worse according to opinion, this signal failed to reach the *Southampton*, owing to the radio blackouts common in that region, until the afternoon of the 14th, by which time not only had the Scots Guards already been landed at Salangen to join the Norwegian troops in that area, but it was too late for the *Southampton* to reach Vestfiord that day.

Disappointed in this first proposal for vigorous and speedy action, Lord Cork left the Vestfiord and, during the night, the *Aurora* took him to Harstad to meet General Mackesy. Meanwhile, Mackesy had been acting strictly in accordance with written instructions in which it was laid down that 'your initial task will be to establish your force at Harstad, ensure co-operation of Norwegian forces that may be there and obtain the information necessary to plan your further operations'. Here in one sentence can surely be seen the fundamental obstacle to the rapid reduction of Narvik for which the Government, and particularly its mainspring, the First Lord of the Admiralty, was looking. There was not enough information in the hands of the War Office for any plan to be made; so, first a base was to be established, then information sought on which a plan could be formed.

On the other hand, Lord Cork, who had received no written instructions but had been verbally briefed by Mr Churchill while driving with him to the House of Commons, was quite clear that 'it was the desire of HM Government to turn the enemy out of Narvik at the earliest possible moment and that he was to act with all promptitude in order to attain this result'. The two sets of instructions were perhaps not entirely incompatible, but the operational atmosphere and tempo called up by them were certainly poles apart.

Any inclination the Admiral may have had to try a purely naval solution to the problem was dispelled by a signal which reached him during the night of the 14th: *We think it imperative that you and the General should be together and act together and no attempt at landing should be made except in concert.*

General Mackesy, on arrival of the *Southampton* off Harstad, had gone ashore to sound out the reactions of the Norwegians to the arrival of a British force. He was cordially received and made preliminary arrangements for the establishment of his base there. Learning that there were no enemy troops in the immediate vicinity and that Norwegian forces were opposing the German advance northward from Narvik, he had himself and the two companies of Scots Guards carried across the Vaagsfiord to Salangen where his troops landed and were at once in contact with the Norwegian forces.

The bearing and discipline of the Guardsmen made a good impression and brought encouragement to the Norwegians; but this was tempered by the obvious unfamiliarity of the British soldiers with the arctic conditions under which they were going to have to fight and the lack of equipment or training necessary to make them mobile in deep snow.

The *Southampton* returned to Harstad in time to meet the *Aurora* early on the 15th when Mackesy went on board Lord Cork's flagship to meet him. Behind the *Aurora* came the troop convoy, consisting of the liners *Batory*, *Reina del Pacifico* and *Monarch of Bermuda* carrying the remainder of the 24th (Guards) Brigade — 1st Irish Guards, 2nd South Wales Borderers and the other two companies of the 1st Scots Guards. With them came also an equal number of troops of the Divisional and Base staff, lines-of-communication troops and a railway construction company.

As the ships steamed in from the sea through Andfiord, a message reached the escort from a Norwegian military lookout post that a submarine had been sighted lying in wait in the approaches. Two destroyers of the escort, *Fearless* and *Brazen*, streaked away ahead to sweep the area with their asdics. Almost at once they were in contact. A single well-placed salvo of depth charges, and the *U49* came frothing to the surface, the crew abandoning ship at once before their craft went to the bottom again. In the freezing water, they screamed frantically for rescue. This was undertaken so smartly by the destroyers that forty out of the forty-two comprising the U-boat's crew were saved. While thus engaged, the *Brazen*'s boat's crew picked up a bundle of documents in one of which was set out the U-boat dispositions for the whole of Norway.

The harbour of Harstad could not accommodate the large troopships, which were sent to an anchorage at Bygden, some twelve miles away on the other side of Vaagsfiord, whence they and their supplies were ferried to Harstad in destroyers. Enemy aircraft had already arrived overhead and flying high in the cloudless blue sky, made leisurely practice against the ships. Fortunately there were no dive-bombers among them, Narvik being still outside their range. High bombing proved ineffective; but it could not be ignored and inevitably it interfered with the disembarkation.

While this was going on, Lord Cork and General Mackesy were having their first meeting. In the Admiral's hands was a report from Captain de Salis who, in his destroyer, the *Faulknor*, and accompanied by the *Zulu*, had been sent to reconnoitre the shoreward approach to Narvik. It said that a landing north of the town on the Rombaks Fiord would not be opposed by any fixed defences and might be covered by warships' guns.

With this information Lord Cork opened the meeting with a proposal for an assault on the following day, the troops to be landed in ship's boats. To his astonishment he learnt for the first time that Mackesy's orders categorically forbade any landing in the face of opposition. Thus it was at once apparent, as he read the situation, that his instructions and the General's were diametrically opposed.

It was, of course, true that a hastily scribbled message from the Chief of the Imperial General Staff, General Ironside, which had accompanied General Mackesy's orders, contained the exhortation, 'You may have a chance of taking advantage of naval action and you should do so if you can. Boldness is required.' But against this Mackesy had balanced the fact that his force had arrived in ships which had been loaded on the assumption that only an unopposed landing was to be undertaken. Indeed, so hasty and confused had been the preparation that there was little visible planning of any sort. The Scots Guards, for example, had been embarked with no mortar ammunition and had to share that of a battalion of the 146th Brigade, which in the event went to Namsos. Furthermore, some gear for one brigade was stowed in the ships carrying the other so that men and their equipment were parted when the convoy divided. When Captain Maund, Lord Cork's Chief of Staff, who had accompanied General Mackesy in the *Southampton*, went on board one of the troopships on its arrival, the first person he met was Brigadier Phillips, Commander of the 146th Brigade which was on its way to Namsos.

All this was enough by itself to daunt a military commander invited to consider an immediate assault from ship to shore by a force which had no landing craft, no artillery, no tanks, against a garrison which, in spite of naval opinion, showed no evidence of any real demoralisation. Furthermore, the configuration of the landscape around Narvik, running up steeply from the shore line to low ridges, told Mackesy, with his specialised military knowledge, that the enemy would be able to cover the landing beaches and approaches to the town by machine guns from positions which were secure from naval guns with their flat trajectory. Struggling forward in snow up to three feet deep, the troops would be mercilessly mown down and, as Mackesy put it, a landing could only result in the 'snow of Narvik being turned into another version of the mud of Passchendaele'. Instead, Mackesy proposed that operations should be set on foot to eject the Germans from the north shore of Rombaksfiord, and from the Ankenes peninsula on the other side of Narvik. Further progress would have to await the thaw which was expected to set in within a few weeks.

The General's firm refusal to contemplate an immediate assault was a considerable shock to Lord Cork; but he could do no other than accept it. He signalled to the Admiralty that the attack proposed for the 16th had had to be abandoned. There the news was equally unwelcome. As the First Lord put it in a Minute to the Military Co-ordination Committee, 'This information is at once unexpected and disagreeable.' He proposed that a signal should be sent to Lord Cork and General Mackesy urging consideration of an assault under cover of the guns of the *Warspite* and destroyers and demanding their reasons why this was not possible. The message contained a warning that the *Warspite* would only be available for two or three days more and that certain military reinforcements on which the General was counting would not be coming.

The fact was, however, that the chance of taking Narvik by a frontal assault, if it had ever existed, had by now evaporated. The collapse of German morale as a result of the naval action on the 13th, which has been quoted from the book of memoirs by Theodor Broch, the Mayor of Narvik, was of brief duration. No doubt British troops, had they been available then, or even a landing party of seamen and marines, could have occupied the waterfront without difficulty that evening, but to have retained their hold against the 2000 trained German soldiers under General Dietl, they would have required support by the guns of warships which would have been committed to firing into the houses of the Norwegian inhabitants.

It is probable that, even later, warships could have landed troops at the quays, but again destructive covering fire, perhaps at the expense of many Norwegian lives, would have been necessary. Winston Churchill appears to have accepted the risk. In his volume *The Gathering Storm* he writes: (an assault) 'involved no marches through the snow, but on the other hand, landings from open boats both in Narvik Harbour and in Rombaks Fiord, under machine-gun fire. I counted upon the effect of close-range bombardment by the tremendous ship batteries which would blast the waterfronts and cover with smoke and clouds of snow and earth the whole of the German machine-gun posts.'

In this matter, instructions by the Cabinet, of which Churchill was of course a member, and the passionately expressed convictions of General Mackesy combined to make such action out of the question. The Government instructions with regard to bombardment were explicit and binding.

'Bombardment must be carried out in such a way that there is a reasonable expectation that damage will be confined to the objective and that civilian populations in the neighbourhood are not bombarded through negligence.

'Thus it is clearly illegal to bombard a populated area in the hope of hitting a legitimate target which is known to be in the area, but which cannot be precisely located and identified ......

'Thus an anti-aircraft or coast defence gun situated in the centre of a populous area could not be bombarded with reasonable expectation that damage would be confined to it.'

The alternative, a landing on the shores of Rombaks Fiord, did, in spite of Churchill's contention, involve an advance through snow. In the face of unanimous military opinion that this was impossible, Lord Cork felt bound to agree to wait at least until the thaw had set in.

Churchill has written of this episode, 'Moreover the orders sent to the Commanders were of such a clear and imperative character, and so evidently contemplated heavy losses, that they should have been obeyed. The responsibility for a bloody repulse would fall exclusively on the home authorities, and very directly upon me. I was content that this should be so.'

The evident impatience of the Government and a message from the Admiralty and the War Office pressing the two commanders to make an immediate assault failed to move General Mackesy in his determination not to act without careful, unhurried preparation and re-organisation of his troops.

Lord Cork's reaction was to call a meeting with the General at which once again an assault after a preliminary bombardment was proposed.

The two commanders were utterly at variance, the Admiral vigorously pressing for action, the General as doggedly objecting. In justification Mackesy quoted the verbal instructions he had received from the War Office before sailing, in which he was informed that the War Office realised that it might take him *some weeks* to make a plan, whereas in fact he had made his plan within twenty-four hours and it was already being carried out. Agreement was finally reached that a bombardment by the *Warspite*, cruisers and destroyers should be carried out and that troops should be embarked ready to be thrown ashore if the result warranted it. They would then land in ships' boats under cover of a further bombardment.

Even this reluctant concurrence by the General was modified following a personal reconnaissance made by him in the *Aurora* on the 19th. As a result of this, he informed the Chief of the Imperial General Staff: 'Owing to the nature of the ground, flat trajectory of naval guns, and the impossibility of locating the concealed machine guns, I am convinced that the naval bombardment cannot be militarily effective, and that a landing from open boats in the above conditions must be ruled out absolutely. Any attempt of the sort would involve *not* the neutralisation but the destruction of the 24th (Guards) Brigade.'

Thus Mackesy returned to his insistence that an opposed landing was out of the question. Only if the bombardment itself induced the enemy to surrender would he countenance his troops going ashore. To attain this the ships' guns would have to be turned on the enemy positions in the town, a proceeding to which he was adamantly opposed and which he was able to point out was forbidden by his instructions.

In a letter to Lord Cork, Mackesy said, 'Before the proposed action against Narvik commences, I feel it is my duty to represent to you that there is not one officer or man under my command who would not feel ashamed for himself and his country if the thousands of Norwegian men, women and children in Narvik are subjected to the bombardment proposed.'

This was passed on to the Government and, though in reply the First Lord of the Admiralty suggested that Mackesy's objections might be met by issuing a warning to the inhabitants 'by every means, including, if possible, leaflets'. Lord Cork felt unable to override his colleague's views.

On the following day the weather came to support them. Snow, continuous and heavy, began to fall and persisted for the next three days. Testing conditions for himself with a section of Marines, Lord Cork found it 'easy to sink to one's waist, and to make any progress was exhausting'. Thus even when on the 21st the Government's decision reached him, placing him in supreme command of the expedition, the Admiral felt unable to insist on any attempt at an opposed landing.

Orders were given for a bombardment to be carried out on the 24th by the *Warspite*, the cruisers *Effingham* and *Enterprise* and the destroyer *Zulu*, supported by aircraft from the *Furious*. Only if this induced the enemy to surrender would the Irish Guards, embarked on the fleet repair ship *Vindictive* from Bogen on the north shore at Ofotfiord, be sent on shore to take over. In deference to Mackesy's objections, however, the bombardment was so hedged about with restrictions that it was very doubtful if such a result would be attained.

The Admiral felt bound to try it, nevertheless. Once again the fiord reverberated to the sound of the 15-inch guns of the *Warspite*, the 8-inch of the *Effingham* and the 6-inch of the *Enterprise* and *Aurora*. For three hours the thunder echoed and re-echoed among the tumbled mountains and the houses of the little town shook at the blast and concussion. But little else resulted. Under their mantle of snow, few military targets could be distinguished nor could the result of the shell bursts be seen. Recurrent snowstorms frequently reduced visibility to a few hundred yards. Conditions made any reconnaissance impossible, and there was no way of judging what moral effect had been produced on the defenders. A wireless station was destroyed as well as a few sheds and railway rolling stock, and a ferry steamer was sunk. The machine-gun nests could not be located, while the strongpoints guarding the harbour waterfront were in any case forbidden targets.

Narvik lay quiescent under the cannonade but showed no sign of any willingness to surrender. The Irish Guards were disembarked again from the *Vindictive* at Bogen. The ships returned to Harstad with the disappointed commanders. From now onwards, though Lord Cork continued to urge the Army commander to more vigorous action and the Government continued to press querulously for an assault to be made, all efforts were directed firstly towards a close investment of the Narvik peninsula and then to the preparation of airfields from which fighters could counter the steadily mounting weight of German air attack which soon became the limiting factor in Allied operations as it had at Namsos and Aandalsnes.

In pursuit of the first objective, the Irish Guards had already been brought round by sea to Bogen whence a road and ferry, held by the enemy, led to Narvik. On the 26th the South Wales Borderers were landed on the other side of Ofotfiord at Ballangen whence they hoped to advance to and capture the Ankenes peninsula, across the harbour from Narvik. On the next day three battalions of Chasseurs-Alpins arrived and Mackesy was now in a position to assist the Norwegians under General Fleischer, who was attempting a thrust behind Narvik towards the railway which, if successful, would complete the investment.

Each of these drives, however, made little progress while the snow lasted and the long-awaited thaw held off. Even the French mountain troops found conditions more severe than anything to which they were accustomed. Frost-bite and snow-blindness took a heavy toll of them, and in ten days they succeeded in advancing only five miles.

During the last days of April, however, the thaw had begun to set in at sea level. Lord Cork's thoughts turned at once to reconsideration of the project of a direct assault. In the stout-hearted French General Béthouart, who had come from Namsos to command the Chasseurs-Alpins, soon to be joined by two battalions of the Foreign Legion, he found a military commander more in accord with his own ideas. For the time being, however, it was upon the British General and the troops under him that he was forced to depend, for, as Mackesy was quick to point out, he had been appointed in command of all British and French troops in the area, and Béthouart was but one of his subordinate commanders. Béthouart's proposal to land on the Oyjord Peninsula and attack Narvik from across the Rombaks Fiord was therefore rejected.

While the military commander was thus deploying his forces with cautious deliberation and waiting for the thaw to bring mobility to his troops, the passage of time was maturing a threat which might lead to casualties at least as great as those which a frontal assault on Narvik would have incurred. On May 2nd, as we have recounted earlier, the last allied soldier had been withdrawn from Central Norway. The German Army was free to press on up the road to the north. The Luftwaffe was not only enabled to turn its full attention to Narvik, but as the Army went forward it was able, from airfields nearer the scene of action, to deliver a heavier and more continuous attack and eventually to reinforce the less dangerous high bombers with the deadly dive-bombers.

Foreseeing this, the Admiral had issued a Memorandum setting forth his ideas which he hoped might spur the soldiers to greater effort. 'I consider speed in preparation is essential. It is our duty to comply with the Government's wishes and occupy Narvik within the next fortnight. This may involve taking greater risks and involve greater loss of life than if time were of no consideration. It is, however, an important consideration and to save time we must be prepared to face losses and take risks — in fact to fight hard.... Our turn for air attack will come shortly and any gain we may make by delay will be more than offset by air attacks such as Namsos is undergoing..... The primary object being the capture of Narvik, too much attention is liable to be given to outlying detachments which, if Narvik is once captured, will soon fall into our hands. The conditions which will allow of us doing this may be with us in the next few days. Equally within a very short time a great part of the German Air Force may be free to turn their attention on to us, thus adding enormously to our difficulties. We have been warned.'

Point was to be given to the Admiral's warning when, a few days later, on May 5th, the Polish destroyer *Grom*, hit by a bomb on her torpedo tubes which detonated the torpedo warheads, was blown asunder to sink within a few minutes with the loss of sixty-five lives. Two days after this the cruiser *Aurora* was also hit and had two of her 6-inch turrets knocked out of action.

By May 3rd the thaw had clearly set in and Lord Cork gave orders for an assault to be prepared either directly on to the Narvik peninsula or from across Rombaksfiord, as judged best, for the 8th, but agreed to a postponement until the 10th as the General said he could not be ready before then. On the 5th, however, the Supreme Commander was faced by what amounted almost to a revolt by the senior military officers of the British expedition. In a written memorandum it was represented that in their opinion there were a number of military objections to the proposed operation. There were only four landing craft instead of the necessary fourteen; the rate at which troops could be landed was too slow to come in good time to the support of the first assault troops; there could be no surprise; the available beaches were too restricted, and little faith was reposed in naval bombardment sufficiently smothering the enemy machine-gun posts covering the beaches.

Faced by what amounted to unanimous military objections, while being simultaneously goaded into action by the First Lord of the Admiralty, the Admiral could only, 'with great reluctance', submit them to the Government. The War Cabinet, unwilling to interfere in a matter of tactics, called for his personal opinions and at the same time informed him that a new military commander would shortly be arriving — General Auchinleck. Lord Cork gave his opinion that the soldiers were exaggerating the difficulties. 'I do not consider success certain,' he signalled, 'whereas it is quite certain that by not trying, no success can be gained.' Though in reply the First Lord told him that 'HM Government will support you in taking any risk which you consider necessary to accept', the Admiral not unreasonably shrank from insisting on the assault when his military commanders were so unwilling to go ahead with it. From this moment he gave up all hope of the operation being carried out by the British Brigade, and determined to pin his hopes on the French.

In this he was aided by two factors. Firstly, the steadily increasing threat by the German army coming up the coast from Namsos was calling for more and more British troops to be sent to repel it until it was finally to be necessary to divert the whole of the British Brigade to that object, leaving the French troops and four battalions of a Polish Brigade, who had arrived on May 9th, to proceed with the capture of Narvik.

Secondly, General Béthouart, who since his arrival on April 28th had never ceased to advocate a landing in the Herjangs Fiord and an occupation of the Oyjord Peninsula whence the final assault on Narvik could be mounted across the narrow Rombaksfiord, now had sufficient French troops with which to achieve this, since the arrival of the Foreign Legion on May 6th. Though General Mackesy was still in overall command of Allied troops in the area, he could not continue to stand out against the Frenchman's enthusiasm. On May 7th he gave his approval, and plans were made for an assault during the night of May 11th/12th combined with a simultaneous attack by the Chasseurs-Alpins from Gratangen towards Bjerkvik at the head of the Herjangs Fiord and by the Norwegian 6th Brigade on their left over the mountains.

Before following the events which at last led to the capture of Narvik, we should turn to examine the situation on the approaches from the south up which the German Army was pressing from Trondheim.

CHAPTER 15

The need to try to prevent German aid reaching General Dietl's isolated force by the road running up the coast from Namsos had been foreseen as early as April 30th when a party of a hundred Chasseurs-Alpins was sent in the destroyer *Janus* from Namsos to Mosjøen, a hundred miles further north and at the terminus of the railway. They were landed there on May 2nd.

At the same time Lord Cork had been instructed to send a small force to Bodo, the port near the entrance of the Vestfiord and also on the main road to the north, to guard against its occupation by parachute troops. A company of the Scots Guards was therefore landed there.

Meanwhile, the question of cutting the road to the north had been actively pursued at home and a group to be known appropriately as 'Scissorsforce' had been assembled under Lieutenant-Colonel C. McV. Gubbins. Appreciating from experience at Namsos that a regularly based force could not be maintained in the face of the enemy's supremacy in the air, Scissorsforce was made up of five Independent Companies, each with some twenty officers and 270 other ranks in strength, and self-contained; it was hoped they would be able, with the co-operation of the local population and of Norwegian troops in the area, to harass and delay the enemy advance up the solitary road to the north.

No 1 Independent Company was the first to arrive in Norway, going on May 4th to the little port of Mo at the head of Ranfiord, fifty-four miles north of Mosjøen by road. Nos 2 and 3 Independent Companies went to Bodo and established themselves in the village of Hopen eleven miles eastward of that town. Colonel Gubbins himself took the remaining two companies to Mosjøen on May 8th to replace the French troops. There he left No 4 Company to protect Mosjøen from the sea and moved south down the road with No 5 to join the Norwegians twenty-five miles south of the town. There were only 400 of these and it was not long before German forces streaming up the road had forced British and Norwegians to retreat to Mosjøen and beyond.

The Independent Companies were neither trained nor equipped to withstand a direct assault by a determined and well-armed enemy, but it had been expected that by guerilla methods and demolitions they would be able to harass and delay the German advance. Now, however, they were outflanked by a brilliant seaborne coup. A crew from the German destroyers at Trondheim had manned the Norwegian coasting steamer *Nord-Norge*, and embarking 300 German troops had set off up the coast through The Leads. Though she was reported to British Naval Headquarters at Harstad, delay in dispatching the only ships available, the *Carlisle* escorting a convoy fifty miles to seaward and the *Zulu* at Skelfiord, resulted in her entering Ranfiord without being intercepted. By the time the two warships came up with her, the troops had been put ashore at Hemnesberget on the Hemnes peninsula. Two Dornier seaplanes had first bombed the little town and then landed to disembark about forty men with mortars and machine guns.

The *Nord-Norge* was sunk before her stores could be landed, but the Germans were in sufficient strength to drive out the platoon from No 1 Independent Company which had been on guard there. By the next day seaplanes were landing to bring replacements for the lost stores. With his line of retreat thus cut, Colonel Gubbins was forced to abandon Mosjøen and embark his men in local craft to retire northwards. He took them down the Vefsenfiord at the head of which Mosjøen lay and on to Sandnessjoen, a hamlet on the seaward side of the large island at the mouth of the fiord.

Four days earlier, on May 7th, Lord Cork, whose official title was Flag Officer, Narvik, had been given command of all these outlying forces, so that his already fully occupied naval force was further burdened with the task of supporting another forlorn military operation.

Furthermore, it was already apparent that Scissorsforce was quite inadequate to hold the German northward advance. Their reinforcement by detachments of the Guards Brigade from Narvik had begun with the company of Scots Guards sent to Bodo. It was soon after this that Lord Cork had decided to rely on the French contingent to carry out the long delayed assault on Narvik, and to employ the whole of the British Brigade to try to hold the southern approaches. Now the remainder of the Scots Guards battalion was on its way to Mo in the cruiser *Enterprise*, the anti-aircraft ships *Cairo* and *Fleetwood*, and the destroyer *Hesperus*, with four field guns and a light anti-aircraft battery in a small storeship, the *Margot*.

The chances of such a force holding up the advance of the German Army, by now swollen to a complete mountain division, with plenty of artillery, may have looked promising from a study of maps of the difficult terrain, but the arrival of the Stukas of the Luftwaffe, opposed only by the occasional patrols of Fleet Air Arm Skuas from the *Ark Royal* operating to seaward, soon changed the picture.

As the ships steamed up the forty miles of the narrow mountain-girt Ranfiord in the early hours of Alay 12th, they were mercifully unmolested until their arrival off Mo, when the

Stukas appeared in force. The experiences of Namsos and Aandalsnes were now repeated as the warships were harried up and down the fiord while working parties strove desperately to get the storeship unloaded. There was no darkness in this latitude during which unloading could be done free of attack. It was evening before the *Margot* was finally ready to sail, still miraculously undamaged, and the ships set off on their return journey. Though for long stretches the fiord was too narrow to allow of any manoeuvring, the guns of the *Cairo* and *Fleetwood* successfully kept the bombers at arm's length and all ships reached the open sea without serious damage.

But the Stukas could now give their full attention to the town and to the troops; and it was not to be long before Mo had to be abandoned while the Guards, the men of No 1 Independent Company, and their Norwegian allies fell back northwards.

Meanwhile, the destroyers *Janus* and *Javelin* had been sent to Colonel Gubbins' aid. They found him at Sandnessjoen where some 350 of his men were already embarked in a coasting steamer. He himself with the remaining 100 went aboard the *Janus* and, under escort of the two destroyers, his force was taken to Bodo. This little port on the Saltfiord near the entrance of the Vestfiord was to be held at all costs as an outpost of the operations round Narvik. It was for Bodo, therefore, that the Irish Guards, together with the Brigade Headquarters, antiaircraft guns and a troop of the 3rd Hussars with their tanks, were embarked in the troopship *Chrobry* and sailed on the 14th.

Escorted by the A/A Sloop *Stork* and the destroyer *Wolverine*, she had rounded the Lofoten Islands and under the midnight sun was crossing the Vestfiord towards Bodo when dive-bombers arrived. The great ship was an easy target. At the third attack a salvo of bombs hit her, setting her ablaze and lulling all officers of the Irish Guards above the rank of Captain. As the stacked ammunition blazed up, the fire spread uncontrollably. With the ship becoming uninhabitable and many of the boats destroyed, the *Wolverine* was put alongside. With discipline and cool courage reminiscent of the historic loss of the *Birkenhead*, the Irish Guards formed up on deck with their arms and waited their turn to go aboard the destroyer; 694 men embarked in sixteen minutes, after which the *Wolverine*, loaded beyond safe capacity, drew off and headed for Harstad. After driving off further attacks, the *Stork* embarked the remainder of the passengers and crew and followed suit, leaving the burning hulk to be eventually sunk by aircraft from the *Ark Royal*.

Thus again, as in Central Norway, British sea power was now to be hamstrung by the lack of an adequate air component of the Fleet. The ability to transport military expeditions to strike at her own time and place is one of the principal advantages of a naval power. But now, even though the enemy fleet had been largely eliminated or put out of action, the British Fleet was reduced to hasty, perilous destroyer dashes to land and supply troops on a friendly shore, while the troops themselves were left unprotected from the enemy's air attacks.

Perhaps the oddest naval vessel used in support of the military operations along the Norwegian coast was HMS *Raven*. This was the quite unofficial name given to the Norwegian coastal steamer *Ranen* which was taken over by Commander Sir Geoffrey Congreve whom we last met with a group of trawlers at Namsos. Manned by a mixed and somewhat piratical crew of sailors, Irish Guardsmen and South Wales Borderers and with a hidden armament of an army Bofors gun and an Oerlikon, it roamed The Leads acting as a decoy ship, delivering surprise attacks on enemy positions and generally harassing the Germans as opportunity offered.

Another calamity was now to befall the ill-starred British Brigade. With the final decision to divert the whole of the British force to the Bodo area, the South Wales Borderers, who had been replaced by the Polish battalions on the Ankenes peninsula near Narvik, were embarked in the cruiser *Effingham*. An unfortunate attempt at a short cut ran the cruiser aground at twenty knots, causing her to become a total loss. The troops were rescued but valuable military equipment, including Bren gun carriers, was lost. The troops themselves had to return to Harstad to reform and re-equip, as had the Irish Guards, so that it was not until the 20th that the first sections of these two battalions began to arrive at Bodo in destroyers and the ubiquitous local fishing craft which, from the lazy cough of their one-cylinder diesel engines, were known as 'Puffers'.

Meanwhile, the Scots Guards and Norwegians had been steadily driven north from Mo, outnumbered, outflanked and 'Stuka-ed' at every attempt at a defensive stand. The road, after swinging inland and crossing desolate plateaux high up where the snow is perpetual, drops down to the head of the Saltfiord at Rognan where a ferry normally carries the traveller across the water to where the road begins again at Langset. At Rognan the defeated British and Norwegians arrived on May 26th, the enemy hot on their heels, and hoped for the Navy to come to their rescue.

It came in the shape of a flotilla of 'puffers' under Lieutenant-Commander W. R. Fell which had already taken to itself the name of 'The Gubbins Flotilla'. Its story is one of typical naval resource and self-reliance and at the same time exemplifies the untidy, ill-prepared nature of the whole of the Norwegian campaign.

Fell had been sent out with a group of deep-sea trawlers to operate as required in The Leads and up the fiords. He had not been long in the area before he realised that they were quite unsuitable craft for the purpose, being too large and unwieldy and drawing too much water. He therefore laid them up and set about gathering a force of ten puffers in the Harstad area. The Norwegian crews were retained and a seaman guard drawn from the trawlers and the crew of the *Effingham* sent to each boat.

The first task given to the Gubbins Flotilla was to transport the South Wales Borderers to Bodo. Embarking them at Borkenes, across the island of Hinnöy from Harstad, Fell delivered them safely, 1000 strong. Then, when the first air attack arrived as the troops were being disembarked, his troubles started. The Norwegian crews saw no future in running their craft and risking their lives for the British. If they were left unguarded for a moment they took flight or sabotaged their engines. Before long the Gubbins Flotilla had been reduced to three.

Undismayed, Fell, assisted by Lieutenant-Commander Nicholls and Lieutenant Riley, RNVR, the self-appointed Sea Transport Officers as he called them, gathered in a fresh force of eight local puffers to replace those from Harstad. They were urgently needed, for at a conference with Gubbins at 2 am on the 20th, he learnt of the predicament of the Scots Guards and Norwegians at Rognan. Embarking crews and guards he set out, reaching Rognan that evening to find the retreat in full swing in every available craft.

As the soldiers arrived they were taken aboard the puffers and the local ferry boat lying at the pier. Towards midnight most of the main body and their Bofors guns had been embarked but the rearguard was still to come. The sound of battle drew nearer, and the last lorries rumbled down the road. As the men tumbled out of them, the first of the enemy came into view. Snipers' bullets were beginning to crack and whine as the fuses of demolition charges were lighted and Fell's puffer, the last, cast off and sheered out into the fiord to make way for the ferry boat.

The engine of the ferry refused to start. One of the demolition charges had been laid under the pier at which she lay. Her crowded decks would have become a shambles had not a Sapper sergeant leapt ashore and cut the fuse in the nick of time. The other two demolitions exploded, covering the ferry and Fell's puffer in falling debris. The ferry was set alight, but having slipped her berthing ropes she had drifted off and grounded some twenty yards from the pier. Getting his puffer alongside her, Fell towed her clear and finally her engine coughed and started and she was safely on her way. As Fell was about to follow her, three stragglers were seen wading out from the shore and appealing to be taken aboard. A midshipman and a subaltern volunteered to man the dinghy and managed to rescue all three, and the puffer flotilla set off down the fiord and landed the soldiers on the far side at Finneid where the road came down to the shore.

This task completed, the puffers of Gubbins Flotilla made their way back to Bodo where incessant air raids made it clear they would soon be required again. A makeshift airstrip had been laid outside Bodo, the runway being made of wire-covered grass sods. Three Gladiators from the airfield at Bardufoss, north of Narvik, which had at last come into use on May 25th, had landed there. Though one had crashed on trying to take off, the other two had kept up a patrol for two days, one at a time, and had had an astonishing success in keeping the enemy aircraft at bay, unused as the German pilots were to meeting any opposition in the air.

On the morning of the 27th, however, the two surviving Gladiators were caught on the ground, both pilots were wounded and the aircraft destroyed. The following day the bombers arrived in force, evidently determined to wipe Bodo out of existence. Coming down as low as 200 feet they first destroyed the airstrip and then turned on the hospital and the town. Fell, from a point midway between the aerodrome and the hospital, watched with horror and disgust as the Stuka pilots swooped down to machine gun patients being carried out of the hospital. When fire engines approached to save the hospital, they too were ruthlessly machine gunned. For two hours the raid continued without ceasing. At the end of it the town lay in a heap of ruins under a pall of black smoke. The wooden quay was burning but was saved from destruction by the effort of a Major Harrison, a factor which was to be of the greatest importance when the inevitable evacuation began.

Once again Fell's little flotilla had disintegrated, several vessels having been destroyed or put out of action and others dispersed. Orders now arrived to prepare for a complete evacuation. Destroyers would be coming to Bodo for the purpose but Gubbins' headquarters and most of his men were at the village of Hopen, ten miles up the fiord. With the enemy close at their heels, their evacuation would become a desperate affair unless disengagement could be achieved by the use of sea transport from Hopen and the denial of it to the Germans.

A fresh fleet of puffers was gathered in and, throughout May 29th and 30th, a ferry service ran, taking men and materials from Hopen to Bodo in the intervals between bombing attacks during which the defenceless craft could only hide as best they could. To augment the puffers a local coasting steamer, the ss

Bodin, which had been bombed and damaged, was commandeered by Fell's men. Under Petty Officer Skeene as captain and engineer, she was put into service until, running aground under fire while embarking Norwegian troops, she had to be abandoned, the soldiers being taken off in puffers.

By the evening of the 30th, Hopen had been completely evacuated. The destroyers had in the meantime been doing their share; 1000 men were taken off to the *Vindictive* lying in the offing on the 29th and were moved directly to Scapa in that ship; 1500 more were embarked on each of the next two days in destroyers which took them to Harstad to join the main evacuation which had by now been ordered. By the end of the 31st Bodo was cleared of all Allied troops. The Gubbins Flotilla had been paid off — all but Fell's own craft which remained behind until the early hours of June 1st to collect any stragglers, while the indefatigable Lieutenant Riley with Captain Croft of the Royal Engineers carried out demolitions and destruction of petrol stocks ashore.

Operation Scissors had gone the way of Maurice and Sickle at the very moment when the factor which had done most to bring about the Allied defeat, the enemy's air supremacy, seemed about to be countered. For on May 21st the first RAF fighter aircraft, Gladiators of the same squadron, No 263, which had been destroyed on Lake Lesjaskog, had landed at Bardufoss airfield, at long last cleared of its winter snow. As already related, three of these made a brief but notable intervention in the operations round Bodo. On May 26th, Hurricanes of No 46 Squadron, flown off from the *Glorious*, also arrived and at once began to make their presence painfully felt by the Luftwaffe.

Had there been no other overriding pre-occupation for the Allies the situation in the North, at least, could probably have been stabilised and the Norwegian coast north of Mo denied to the enemy with important consequences to the future prosecution of the war at sea. But this was very far from the case. On May 10th the great German offensive in the west had been launched. As the panzers streamed irresistibly across Belgium and France and the British and French main armies began to learn the meaning of armour and tactical air power as their detached forces in Norway had been doing, every man, every weapon and every aircraft was needed to try to stem the advance.

When that failed, the fear of invasion called for every British warship, too. None could be spared for what had become a very minor theatre. That the fear of invasion was in fact exaggerated, not least because of the heavy naval losses the German Navy had suffered in the Norwegian campaign, is perhaps irrelevant. The fact remained that on May 20th Mr Churchill, by then Prime Minister, who had up to then never ceased to urge the importance of seizing and holding Narvik, first broached to the Defence Committee the argument that even when captured it should subsequently be abandoned. The mainspring of the effort being thus broken, it was not long before the Chiefs of Staff fell into line. On May 24th the decision was taken. That night the order to evacuate the whole of his forces reached Lord Cork whose plans for the final assault on Narvik were about to reach fruition.

The effect on the British and Norwegian forces unsuccessfully attempting to hold up the German advance from the south, we have seen. It is to the Narvik area we must now go to witness the last act of this northern saga.

CHAPTER 16

When we left the Narvik area to examine the course of events further south, Lord Cork had just finally despaired of getting vigorous action out of the British Brigade and had decided to pin his hopes on the French under General Béthouart. On May 7th General Mackesy had given his approval for an assault on Bjerkvik at the head of Herjangsfiord by two battalions of the French Foreign Legion from the sea on the night of May 11th/12th. Simultaneously the Chasseurs-Alpins were to attack down the road from Gratangen and the Norwegian 6th Brigade were to advance over the mountains on their left.

The test was about to be put to the rival theories of the Supreme Commander, Lord Cork, on one hand, and his senior British Army Officers on the other. Perpetual daylight would make surprise impossible; there were but four assault landing craft (ALCs), and naval gunfire was to be relied upon to silence the opposition. There were, however, five small tanks to support the infantrymen once they had landed. It was to be the first experiment in delivering an opposed amphibious landing, the first of a long series in all parts of the world which was to bring final victory to the Allies.

The assault was postponed twenty-four hours at the last minute but on May 12th the operation began in accordance with the plan. In this the Legionnaires were to be embarked at Ballangen, twenty miles from Bjerkvik, the leading company of infantry making the passage in the ALCs while the remainder of the 1500 troops were to go in the cruisers *Effingham* and *Aurora*, transferring to ships' boats for the landing. Four of the tanks were embarked in the battleship *Resolution* together with two motor-landing craft (MLC) in which they would go ashore. The fifth tank was to go in a more modern type of MLC which was relied upon to make the twenty-mile passage under its own power. Five destroyers under Captain E. B. K. Stevens of the *Havelock* would give gunfire support, the *Havelock* in addition mounting a French mortar battery on her forecastle.

By 9 pm all were embarked and the armada set off slowly across the fiord, the cruisers towing the boats which would land the troops. In the *Effingham*, Lord Cork's flag was flying, and accompanying him were General Béthouart and the newly arrived Lieutenant-General C. J. E. Auchinleck, though the latter had not yet taken over the overall military command from Major-General Mackesy. At midnight, in broad daylight, the guns bellowed forth as the preliminary bombardment sent echoes slamming back and forth between the hills. The houses in which German troops were sheltering were set ablaze and ammunition dumps blown up. For an hour everything on the foreshore was blasted before the barrage lifted as the first landing craft approached the beaches. The first battalion was scheduled to land on a beach half a mile to the west of the village of Bjerkvik, while the second were to land on beaches to the south-eastward of Bjerkvik whence they would go on to capture Elvegaard, the former Norwegian regimental depot a mile inland, which was strongly held by the enemy.

The first to arrive should have been the MLCs, each carrying a tank, but delays in hoisting out from the *Resolution* were such that the single more modern MLC went in on its own to the first battalion's landing place and was at once followed by the ALCs. By the time the remaining MLCs reached the beaches the main waves of troops in ships' boats were already piling ashore.

The warships' bombardment had by no means silenced the German machine-gun posts but it had subdued them sufficiently to allow the troops to land with very light casualties. With the aid of their three tanks the first battalion had soon overrun the village of Bjerkvik and were moving up the road towards Gratangen to meet the Chasseurs coming south.

On the beach to the south-eastward allocated to the second battalion, too many machine-gun nests had survived the bombardment and the assault troops were forced to land further north, near to Bjerkvik. There the bombardment had been more concentrated and effective and they were soon ashore and heading for Elvegaard, their tanks clearing a path for them through the enemy defences. Elvegaard was stormed and the Germans evicted after a house to house fight. By midday Legionnaires were in possession of Oyjord. Victory had been achieved at the cost of only thirty-six casualties.

The success of the assault, contrary to all the predictions of the senior British military officers, was most heartening, but the main task, the final assault on Narvik itself, still remained. By now the delays which had been imposed were beginning to exact their toll in the increased weight and vigour of the German air attacks, as Lord Cork had foretold. Every day now the enemy aircraft were over, harrying the warships and transports. The day after the success at Bjerkvik the *Chrobry* was crippled in the Vestfiord and the Irish Guards fortunate to escape with no more than a few casualties though these included all their senior officers. Between May 11th and 27th the *Cairo* was to record that she engaged enemy aircraft every day but two and expended 5700 rounds of 4-inch ammunition, wearing her guns to such an extent that she had to put more than half of them out of action on account of dangerous premature shellbursts from the barrels whose rifling had been worn almost smooth.

Thus Lord Cork and General Auchinleck, who had now relieved General Mackesy, were agreed that an assault must wait until either they could rely upon weather which would keep the enemy bombers from attacking or on airfields from which fighters could operate. All efforts were to be concentrated upon clearing the aerodrome at Bardufoss and constructing the landing ground at Skaanland.

Thus when messages from home continued to express deep disappointment at the stagnation which seemed to follow the success at Bjerkvik, it was Lord Cork who now insisted that the delay was unavoidable.

'I fully understand that occupation of the town of Narvik is desired,' he signalled on May 20th, 'and am anxious to report its capture. The most important work at the moment, however, is the completion and protection of the aerodromes and for these all MLCs are required. If we are to maintain our position here it is of paramount importance that we can operate aircraft as quickly as possible.... It might be described as the essential preliminary to any combined operations on whatever scale. It would be folly under existing conditions to switch from essential preparation of aerodromes to an assault on Narvik. A delay with aerodromes has become dangerous.'

The following day the first 'RAF fighters, Gladiators of No 263 Squadron, brought over in the *Furious*, landed on Bardufoss airfield. Hurricanes were coming in the *Glorious*. While waiting for an assurance that an airfield would be ready to take them, day to day postponements of the assault were imposed. When it was known on the 26th that the Hurricane squadron had landed, orders were at last finalised for the operation to begin during the night May 27th/28th.

Meanwhile, on the 25th had come the disheartening news that the Allied Governments had decided to evacuate the whole of Norway. The message containing the order stressed the desirability of first capturing Narvik and destroying all facilities for the loading of iron ore. For General Béthouart the disastrous news from France — Dunkirk was only two days away — posed a bitter problem. His troops were urgently needed at home, and to continue with the plan for the assault might delay their return. But he proved a loyal ally. In agreeing to go through with the capture of Narvik he took into consideration the crying need for an Allied victory to boost morale in that dark hour, though he also concurred in the British contention that defeat or destruction of the German forces would facilitate a safe and speedy evacuation when the time came.

The most painful aspect of the decision to evacuate was the abandonment of the Norwegians who had been fighting loyally and gallantly alongside the Allied troops in the Narvik area. For reasons of security it seemed essential to keep the decision from them until the last moment. Béthouart protested that for reasons of national honour he could not leave the Norwegian troops, with whom he had been working, in the lurch on the field of battle. Only by completing the rout of the enemy after the occupation of Narvik could it be made possible for the Norwegians to disengage in good time to enable their troops to reach back areas. There they could be demobilised before the Germans could overrun them and take them prisoner.

So it was arranged. Under an elaborate smokescreen of inspired rumours of an additional base to be established at Tromsø, arrangements for evacuation went secretly ahead. The first transports left for the United Kingdom before the end of May carrying a quantity of equipment and stores, including some French tanks and guns. Meanwhile, preparations for the assault were completed. General Auchinleck, recognising Béthouart's great qualities, had placed him in command of all troops in the Narvik area and the Norwegians had added a battalion of infantry — men recruited from the area — to his force.

By this time the French and Norwegians were in control of the north shore of the Rombaks Fiord as far as the narrows. On the other side of Narvik three Polish battalions were in occupation of the ridge looking down on the Beisfiord and had cleared the enemy from part of the hamlet of Ankenes. The plan for the assault, therefore, was for the Poles to launch a double thrust to capture the whole of Ankenes and to drive the enemy eastwards to the head of Beisfiord, while the two battalions of the Foreign Legion and the Norwegian battalion would be landed on the south shore of Rombaksfiord some three miles from the town of Narvik.

The landing would perforce be on a dangerously narrow front as only at one beach was the terrain of such a nature that enemy machine-gun posts could for certain be dominated by ships' gunfire. Furthermore, the continued shortage of landing craft — there were by now only three ALCs available — meant that the small initial assault wave could not be reinforced for some time. If naval gunfire did not provide the support expected of it, the first flight might suffer a bloody repulse and be driven back into the sea. This was what General Mackesy and his Brigade Commanders had foretold in their doubts as to the effectiveness of naval bombardment. Béthouart had no such doubts.

At the same time the ability of the ships to maintain their support depended upon the newly arrived Hurricanes giving them cover from the dive-bombers; for if the bombarding ships were attacked by the bombers they would be forced to concentrate on their own defence at the expense of their other duties. Only the day before the assault, the anti-aircraft cruiser *Curlew*, under way off Skaanland to provide air defence, had at last, after three days of incessant attack, been caught by a salvo of bombs and sunk.

Thus the interdependence of the three arms which was to be the main feature of every operation in the long years of war stretching ahead was to be first displayed. The lack of one arm, the air force, had led to defeat elsewhere in Norway. Now that the lack had been made good, success would surely follow.

At last, on May 27th, six weeks after his sanguine arrival, during which the British and French military force under his supreme command had swollen to more than 24,000 men without the capture of Narvik being attempted, the sorely tried, frustrated Lord Cork hoisted his flag in the *Cairo* and gave orders for the operation to go ahead. At his side were the gallant Béthouart, supremely confident in the ability of his troops to carry the day under cover of naval bombardment, and General Auchinleck, in no doubt as to the considerable risks entailed by the bold plan but yet ready to accept them.

The first battalion of the Foreign Legion, battle-tried veterans, were assembling. There would be no darkness to shroud their movements, so embarkation was to take place inside Herjangsfiord out of sight of enemy eyes in the hope of attaining some measure of surprise. As soon as the ALCs rounded the point of Oyjord, however, their purpose would at once be betrayed.

Towards midnight the ships of the bombardment force began to take up their positions and, at twenty minutes to twelve, the guns blazed out together. Four destroyers operated in the Rombaksfiord while the *Cairo*, *Coventry* (flagship of Rear-

Admiral Vivian) and another destroyer were stationed in the Ofotfiord. Further out, the cruiser *Southampton* lay where her 6-inch guns could bring support to the Poles on the Ankenes Peninsula. Anxious eyes, red-rimmed from day after day of scanning the skies for enemy aircraft, saw with incredulous relief the patrol of Hurricanes circling overhead. Cheers, not unmixed with ribaldry, rose from ships' companies which had prayed so long, so fervently and so vainly for such a sight.

While the guns slammed and echoed and the Poles went in to the attack, the little ALCs rounded Oyjord Point and headed across Rombaksfiord, their blunt bows pushing a tumbling froth of water in front of them. Punctually at midnight they beached and the Foreign Legionaries leapt ashore to find that the ships' guns had so blasted the hillside in front of them that opposition was negligible and not a man was hit. The solitary small tank landed nearby from an MLC in support became bogged down and played no further part in the battle; but in spite of this the first wave of assault troops were able to advance up the hillside and secure the summit.

An anxious time followed while the landing craft returned to fetch the next flight during which only naval gunfire could prevent an enemy counter-attack in greatly superior strength. The next Company had been ordered to Oyjord to embark, but as the troops arrived on the pier, mortar shells from German positions across the fiord began to fall around and among them. By the time the first landing craft was loaded there had been a number of casualties including the Royal Marine Embarkation Officer. As the precious, irreplaceable craft were in danger of being sunk, Lieutenant Francklin, the naval officer in charge, divided them up, sending two to beaches on either side of the pier. Oyjord had then to be abandoned as an embarkation point for some time and the longer sea passage from Herjangsfiord reverted to. This also delayed the addition of puffers to the landing force as there was insufficient water for them except at the pier of Oyjord.

In spite of this the first troops ashore held their ground and by 4 am one battalion of the Foreign Legion and the Norwegian battalion were ashore and advancing over the hill against fight opposition. But now, at the most critical moment, when the final advance was about to be made, there occurred the misfortune which had been feared. The British aircraft were withdrawn. At Bardufoss, the only available landing ground, a sea fog was rolling in. Landing just in time, the Hurricanes were thereafter fog-bound until it cleared.

Had this occurred during the landings it would have been disastrous, for with their departure, the German dive-bombers arrived and swooped on the warships. The familiar scene repeated itself of circling, swerving ships in the fiord desperately fighting off the aircraft and being steadily driven from their bombarding positions in the process. Lord Cork's flagship, *Cairo*, was hit by two bombs and suffered thirty casualties. Others had narrow escapes and many near misses.

The previously cowed German troops, freed from the threat of naval gunfire following their every move, took heart and counter-attacked the French and Norwegians, driving them steadily back down the hill and on to the beaches. Casualties were becoming heavy and the situation critical. Lieutenant-Commander S. H. Balfour, who had landed with the French as liaison officer to signal for gunfire support as required, had lost his signal lamps in the sudden retreat. He therefore boarded a landing craft and set off down the fiord to get in touch with the ships and call for help in this emergency. After a considerable chase he came up with and boarded the *Coventry*, flagship of Rear-Admiral Vivian, who at once sent the destroyer *Beagle* back to Rombaksfiord. As her 4.7-inch guns opened on the enemy positions the Germans turned and ran for the shelter of the skyline. With a great cheer, the French troops swept forward after them and restored the situation.

By now the fog at Bardufoss had cleared and as the first section of three fighters appeared the bombers fled. Though they returned to make two attacks on the troops later in the forenoon, they were not seriously to affect the situation again. By 11 am the second French battalion had been landed and the Germans, by now greatly outnumbered, were driven steadily back. The Poles, too, had successfully secured the Ankenes peninsula. Threatened from two sides, the last of the German garrison of Narvik escaped eastwards down the road to Beisfiord. At 5 pm the Norwegian battalion, to whom the French had gracefully conceded the right of first entry, occupied the town. At 10 o'clock that evening, the capture of Narvik and the peninsula on which it stands was officially announced by General Béthouart. Casualties to the French 1st Battalion and the Norwegians amounted to some 150, the French suffering thirty-four killed and fifty wounded. Such losses could only be considered light considering the importance of the prize and the nature of the operation. But for the unfortunate interval of two hours in the air cover at a critical moment of the assault when the supporting ships were driven from their stations by dive-bombers, they would have been lighter. It is difficult to disagree with Lord Cork's final comment on the operation.

'Nothing that I witnessed at Bjerkvik on May 13th and 14th or at Narvik on the 27th and 28th caused me in any way to alter my conviction that had the landing taken place at Narvik on May 10th as intended, it would have had complete success, always supposing that the leadership and resolution would have been equal on all occasions.'

Once the opportunity had been missed for a *coup de main*, immediately after the destruction of the German destroyer flotilla, it was obviously necessary for British troops, unfamiliar and ill-equipped to deal with conditions of deep snow, to await the thaw, and this was agreed to by Lord Cork; but the factors on which the objections to the assault on May 10th were based still prevailed on May 27th.

The fundamental cause of doubt on the part of the British military leaders was a lack of faith in the power of naval gunfire to silence the enemy's opposition during the assault landings. From a purely material point of view, this may seem justified, but it overlooked the moral effect of heavy shelling on troops who had not previously experienced it. General Mackesy and his Colonels thought back to the stoical endurance of troops in the Kaiser's War under far heavier bombardments. At the final assault on Narvik, the weight of the bombardment had been greatly reduced from that available at Bjerkvik and earlier. There was no capital ship to bring the monstrous blast of 15-inch guns into play, for the *Resolution*, damaged by bombs, had been sent home. There was only one ship with 6-inch guns, *Southampton*, since the loss of the *Effingham* and the return of the *Aurora* for repairs. Yet Lieutenant-Commander Balfour, after his experience as liaison officer with the Foreign Legion, commented on the 'terrific moral effect on troops, far in excess of actual material damage done to them'.

The eighteen days' delay in the capture of Narvik had incalculable results for the future shape of the war. By June 1st, when the Norwegian Government was told of the decision to evacuate, General Dietl and the remnants of his force were penned in the mountains with retreat into Sweden, where trains were held ready for them, their only hope of escape. Before the final attack planned by the Norwegians could be mounted, which would have completed Dietl's discomfiture, General Ruge's troops found themselves abandoned by their Allies.

Had the Germans been driven across the border, it might have meant the retention of the north of Norway in Allied hands. Voices were not lacking in high places in England to give their opinion that the evacuation was not necessary. The sound of guns from across the English Channel was to stifle them.

So, for better or for worse, the decision was taken. The Norwegian Government, bowing to the inevitable, agreed to follow their King into exile, the cruiser *Devonshire* being placed at their disposal at Tromsø. Now it remained for Lord Cork and General Auchinleck to organise the withdrawal of the Allied force, by now numbering 24,500 and spread over a wide area of territory, with sufficient secrecy and speed to avoid what could easily become a disaster.

CHAPTER 17

Rejoicing over the long-delayed capture of Narvik was held down to a sober level by the grim news from France, where the routed British Army was undergoing the ordeal of Dunkirk, and by the knowledge, slowly filtering down from the senior officers, that the conquest was shortly to be abandoned. Secrecy could not be maintained much longer, for already merchantmen were being loaded with guns and equipment, though their destination was given out as Tromsø where a new base was ostensibly being prepared.

Beyond these preliminary steps, which were taken with the transports already available to Lord Cork, a plan was prepared which would involve a considerable fleet of troopships and transports, units of which were sailed from England singly or in small groups to arrive off the coast during the first week of June. The storeships came mostly directly to Harstad, with a few going to Tromsø to load. The latter sailed as soon as they were ready on June 7th, with an escort of trawlers.

The convoy of storeships from Harstad put to sea on the same day, eight merchantmen with an escort of ten trawlers, to be augmented by a sloop and a destroyer as soon as they could be spared from the duty of ferrying troops to the troopships and giving anti-aircraft defence to the anchorages. This was referred to as the slow convoy.

These escort forces were proof only against U-boat attack and quite inadequate in the face of air attack or in the event of an encounter with enemy surface forces. But the risk was accepted and was perhaps unavoidable. Though the impunity with which transports had been shuttling back and forth between England and northern Norway had bred a certain complacency, the possibility of interception by units of the German fleet had not by any means been overlooked by Lord Cork. His request for fifteen destroyers, however, had remained unsatisfied owing to the losses at Dunkirk and the many commitments for such craft in the period following it. Other than the three allocated to the *Ark Royal* and two to the *Glorious* for screening duties, he had but six, all of which were required for embarkation and for protection of the anchorages until the last soldier had been evacuated.

Meanwhile, each of the fifteen troopships had gone to one of two rendezvous allotted some 180 miles from the coast, thus forming into two Groups. There they were met by Rear-Admiral Vivian in his flagship, *Coventry*, and given their instructions. Group One, comprising the large passenger liners *Monarch of Bermuda*, *Batory*, *Sobieski*, *Franconia*, *Lancastria* and *Georgic*, was sent in first. Berthing in various inlets and minor fiords off Andfiord, their troops were brought to them in destroyers which themselves had been loaded from the ubiquitous 'puffers'. Embarkation was carried out chiefly at night when, although it was daylight all round the clock, the enemy aircraft less frequently put in an appearance. Overhead patrolled the RAF fighters from Bardufoss and Skuas from *Ark Royal*. *Ark Royal* and *Glorious* had arrived in the area on June 2nd, the latter with a reduced complement of aircraft so that she could embark the surviving Gladiators of No 263 Squadron.

Unmolested by the enemy, who were quite unaware that an evacuation was taking place, the ships of the 1st Group completed loading on June 6th, 15,000 men having been embarked in three successive nights. The following day they left the distant rendezvous, where they had reassembled, and under escort of the fleet repair ship *Vindictive*, set course for home.

It had been Lord Cork's intention not to sail this group from the rendezvous until the 2nd Group had completed embarkation, when four destroyers could be sent to augment the *Vindictive*'s largely token strength. But an appeal had come from the Admiralty for the return of the troopships as soon as possible to fit in with other movements for which they were being called upon to provide.

It thus comprised a rich, defenceless target for any enemy squadron which might fall in with it. The risk to this convoy and to the 2nd Group, which would be following it two days later, as well as the slow convoy, had been foreseen. Lord Cork, his own force quite inadequate in strength and numbers to provide reasonable defence to the several separate convoys, had addressed himself to the Commander-in-Chief, Home Fleet, when formulating his original plan. He signalled that he would 'much appreciate if some covering protection could be given'. Now, with the six great liners steaming virtually unprotected, he asked again: 'could covering force be provided and convoy met, where you consider necessary. All destroyers in area required for rapid embarkation of the last flight'.

Sir Charles Forbes, on whom the responsibility fell as soon as the convoy had cleared the Norwegian coast, had at once appreciated the need to comply with this request and had earmarked the battle-cruisers *Renown* and *Repulse* with a screen of four destroyers and a further flotilla of five destroyers as close escort for the convoy. Once again moves were being planned which seemed fated to bring about a clash between major units of the two fleets so narrowly missed two months earlier. Early on June 4th a force comprising *Scharnhorst*, *Gneisenau*, *Hipper* and four destroyers under the Commander-in-Chief of the German fleet, Admiral Marschall, had sailed from Kiel and, rounding the Skaw during that night, had headed out into the North Sea. By the evening of the 5th, undetected by the aerial reconnaissance maintained by the RAF, they were speeding north.

Two factors were to intervene to prevent the full flowering of the situation which was thus in bud on June 5th. On the British side a report reaching Sir Charles Forbes on the 5th of two unidentified warships sighted hull down by the Q-ship, *Prunella*, in a position 200 miles north-east of The Faeroes and heading for the Iceland-Faeroes passage, raised the same anxieties about a possible breakout into the Atlantic which had so adversely affected our strategy on April 8th. The true explanation of this false report seems never to have been discovered. Its result was to cause the Commander-in-Chief to send a powerful force consisting of the *Renown* and *Repulse*, the cruisers *Newcastle* and *Sussex* and five destroyers pounding after the will-of-the-wisp, leaving the sprawling mass of the Narvik expedition wide open to attack.

It was a move which might have proved calamitous. Left with the battleship *Valiant* as the only other capital ship at Scapa besides his flagship *Rodney*, at a time when fears of invasion demanded a reserve of capital ships available to go south, he had only the *Valiant* to send to cover the great sweep of ocean over which the returning Narvik expedition was spread. The best she could do was to meet Group 1 at 1 am on the morning of the 8th, stay with it until safely past The Faeroes, and then return to meet Group 2 on the evening of the 10th. Thus Group 1 was without any effective protection for the first twenty-four hours of its passage, during which its course was taking it within a hundred miles of Admiral Marschall's squadron.

Operation Juno, on which this force had set out, had not envisaged any such possible encounter. The German Naval staff and Group West, under whose directions Marschall was operating, had no inkling as yet that an evacuation of north Norway was in progress. In spite of their ability to decipher many British naval messages at this time, from which they had learnt of Lord Cork's convoy rendezvous, and in spite of aerial reconnaissance reporting the British Group 1 early on June 7th, they and Admiral Marschall linked these two pieces of information to an increased effort in the Narvik area which they believed to be taking place.

The object of Operation Juno — an attack on Allied shipping at Harstad — seemed only the more desirable, therefore. During the night of June 6th/7th the German squadron reached the latitude of Harstad and made rendezvous with the tanker *Dithmarschen* from which the *Hipper* and the destroyers refuelled. All was now in train for the projected attack on Harstad, and Admiral Marschall informed his commanding officers that it would take place on the night of the 9th. When, early on the 7th, reports of the British Group 1 came in from a scouting plane, describing it as composed of four large ships and three escorts, in a position some 150 miles south-east of him, steering southerly, it did nothing to deflect him from his purpose. He looked on them as probably empty transports on their way home and not big enough game to make worthwhile an attack which would betray his presence.

As the day wore on, Marschall fretted at the absence of reconnaissance reports from the Harstad area. Writing in his diary that evening he noted with waspish irritation, 'Air reconnaissance in northern area is, as previously, not available.' In fact, he was less than just to the Luftwaffe. Around midday a German aircraft had sighted and reported some of Group 2 in the entrance to Andfiord making for the ocean rendezvous after completing loading, under escort of the *Coventry* and two destroyers. Another report gave the position of *Ark Royal* and *Glorious* as they manoeuvred to operate their aircraft some forty-five miles further north.

These reports did not reach the German Commander-in-Chief until 8 pm at which time he was holding a conference of commanding officers aboard his flagship, the *Gneisenau*. Unlike his superior officer, General-Admiral Saalwaechter of Group West or Grand-Admiral Raeder himself, Marschall at once suspected that these reports might indicate a British evacuation of Norway and that the previously despised, presumed empty ships might after all constitute a worthwhile target. According to the German official account, he therefore steered south in pursuit of them. It would seem that he must have greatly underestimated the speed of Group 1, composed of fast liners, for they were by now far out of his reach.

His southerly cast was to bring a reward, nevertheless. Before following his movements further, however, we must turn back to study the progress of the evacuation operations.

Lord Cork's evacuation plan had been going very smoothly. It was a highly intricate operation involving smooth coordination of 'puffers' and other small craft picking up troops and equipment from dozens of minor embarkation points, and destroyers to ferry the men and material to the liners in their dispersed berths. Skilful disengagement operations by the French and Polish troops had not only enabled the Norwegians to withdraw to back areas prior to negotiations for an armistice being opened by General Ruge, but had concealed from the enemy the scope of the evacuation until the 8th when General Dietl re-entered Narvik. Similarly, the Gladiators and

Hurricanes from Bardufoss, by keeping in action until the last possible moment, had succeeded in disguising the nature of the operation as well as protecting the troopships from serious molestation. Other aircraft from the *Ark Royal*, bombing German troops and communications, kept the enemy at arms' length during the evacuation.

The critical days were June 7th and 8th. On the 7th, as we have seen, Group 1 had left the ocean rendezvous on its way home, while Group 2, the large liners *Oronsay*, *Ormonde*, *Arandora Star* and *Duchess of York* with three Irish Channel packet-boats, *Royal Ulsterman*, *Ulster Prince* and *Ulster Monarch*, had begun to load. Two other ships had arrived at the ocean rendezvous with this Group, the liner *Orama* and the armed boarding vessel *Vandyck*. There was sufficient accommodation in the other seven ships, however, and Rear-Admiral Vivian, finding that the 20,000-ton liner *Orama* was short of 500 tons of oil fuel and 300 tons of fresh water, neither of which were readily procurable, ordered her to return home. Accordingly she left without escort, in company with the hospital ship *Atlantis*. The *Vandyck* was to remain at sea in the vicinity of the rendezvous, in case she was required.

On the 7th there had been another important departure. From Tromsø the cruiser *Devonshire*, flagship of Vice-Admiral John Cunningham, had sailed with the King of Norway and his Government and the Allied Legations.

On the following morning, the 8th, General Ruge was to open negotiations with the Germans for an armistice. It was vital that, before this opened the enemy's eyes to what was going on, the last Allied soldier should have left the shore, the demolition of abandoned equipment finally accomplished. For some days operations had been under way to deny to the enemy the use of anything of value left behind. The ore-loading capacity of Narvik had been destroyed to such an extent that, together with the cluttering of the harbour with more than twenty wrecks, the port would be unusable for the next seven months. The Mobile Naval Base ship *Mashobra*, which had been bombed on May 25th and beached, was blown up. The 700-ton tanker *Oleander*, disabled by a near miss, was sunk, as were a number of disabled trawlers.

Sir Geoffrey Congreve's irregular command, the self-styled HMS *Raven*, was given the task of destroying the oil tanks at Solfolia, north of Bodo. Having duly set them ablaze, she encountered an enemy corvette considerably more heavily armed than herself, but boldly went after it in company with a trawler. A strange game of hide-and-seek followed among the narrow channels between the islands; but unable to come to grips with the faster enemy vessel, his solitary long range gun, an Army Bofors, having only time-fused self-destroying ammunition, Congreve was forced to abandon the pursuit and continue his interrupted journey to Scapa Flow.

Throughout the 7th, under the umbrella of Gladiators and Hurricanes, destroyers and 'puffers' scurried to and fro. The military rearguard of Harstad was composed of Chasseurs-Alpins. The final party of Military Police and Royal Engineers in charge of the piers embarked and left, the evacuation of the army being completed in the early hours of the 8th.

The last men to leave the shore, however, were the ground staff from the airfield at Bardufoss. Shortly before midnight on the 7th the last fighters had taken off, whereupon the demolition of the runway had begun. The aircraft were to land on the deck of the *Glorious*. For the Gladiators, with their low landing speed, this was quite reasonable, even though their aircraft were not fitted with the arrester hooks which, catching in the wires stretched across the deck, were designed to bring them to a halt in the limited space available. By steaming the ship at her maximum speed a wind could be produced down the deck sufficiently to reduce the landing run. None of the pilots had landed before on a carrier's deck, a hazard they cheerfully accepted and relied upon their flying skill to overcome.

It was a different matter for the Hurricanes. Those racy monoplanes had a considerably higher landing speed than the biplane Gladiators; their sleek, streamlined shape gave them a longer run after touching down. It had been intended that after their last patrol they should be destroyed on the ground; but when the time drew near, the pilots of No 46 Squadron approached the senior RAF officer of the expedition, Group-Captain M. M. Moore, and begged to be allowed to take the risk of attempting a landing on the *Glorious*. The gesture was a gallant one, in tune with the valour that the pilots of Nos 263 and 46 Squadron had already displayed in combat. It was perhaps an even more courageous act on the part of Group-Captain Moore to take responsibility for permitting it.

Led out to sea by a naval Swordfish, the ten surviving Gladiators and eight Hurricanes were all skilfully and safely landed on the carrier's deck — a notable feat and, at a time when every British fighter aircraft was a priceless asset, a most valuable one. But the gallantry of the airmen was soon to be squandered in one of the bitterest calamities of the war.

By the morning of June 8th, a number of groups of ships had accordingly left or were leaving the Norwegian coast and heading south-westward en route to the United Kingdom. The *Devonshire* with her royal and most important political passengers; the slow convoy with its valuable cargo of war material escorted only by trawlers; the storeships which had loaded at Tromsø; the unescorted liner *Orama* and the hospital ship *Atlantis*, Group 2, carrying 10,000 troops; all were steering towards the area where, unknown to them, the German Commander-in-Chief's powerful squadron was lying in wait.

Though Group 2 included in its escort the *Ark Royal* whose torpedo-carrying aircraft might hope to strike a blow if the German squadron were encountered, the only surface ship in the area which could be expected to stand up to the modern German capital ships was the twenty-four-year-old *Valiant* — and she was far to the south-west, soon to join Group 1, the only British formation which had already slipped from Marschall's grasp.

The scene was set for tragedy on a grand scale. Tragedy indeed there was to be, but the deathless valour of the captain and crew of one little destroyer was to reduce its scope.

Through the grey twilight of the northern night, in calm summer seas, the German squadron had been steering south since the previous evening in vain pursuit of Group 1. At 3 am the Commander-in-Chief had reported his intentions to the High Command. Both Group West and the German Naval Staff, still unenlightened as to the meaning of the British naval moves reported to them, intervened at 4.30 to direct Marschall to concentrate on the task given him, 'the destruction of the naval forces in the Harstad-Narvik area'. Only the *Hipper* and destroyers should be sent after the 'empty' convoy. The battle-cruisers must be kept for the main objective.

Before action could be taken on this — and it appears that Admiral Marschall, confident of the correctness of his view of the situation, had decided to ignore the message — a ship was reported to the southward. Hoping that this might be a straggler from the convoy, speed was increased and the squadron swept down on her. It proved to be the tanker *Oil*

Pioneer with its escort of one little trawler *Juniper*, which had sailed the day before from Tromsø. The defenceless ships were shattered by an overwhelming blast of fire in a few moments before either had been able to get a radio report away; twenty-five survivors from the tanker and four from the trawler were picked up before continuing with the search for the reported convoy.

Scharnhorst and *Hipper* each launched scouting planes, the former searching to the north, the latter to the south. The *Hipper*'s airman, with wishful thinking for which no explanation has been offered, soon reported a non-existent cruiser and a merchant ship to the southward. In the opposite direction the other aircraft sighted a large liner and a hospital ship. Sending *Hipper* to sink the ship to the northward, the Commander-in-Chief took the remainder of his ships in fruitless search to the south.

Hipper's prey was the *Orama*, still in company with the *Atlantis*. The radio operator of the liner, as soon as the approaching menace was identified, sent out urgent SOS signals; but the Germans were ready for this and successfully jammed them until, at n o'clock, the *Hipper*'s 8-inch shells smashed home, sending the *Orama* to the bottom.

The *Atlantis*, obeying the rules of war, made no signal and so obtained the immunity which those same rules gave to a hospital ship. She was allowed to go unmolested on her way, but Marschall knew that the presence of his squadron could not be hidden much longer from the British. Ships and aircraft would soon be scouring the sea for him. His powerful, speedy battle-cruisers had little to fear, but the *Hipper* and the destroyers, with their low endurance, could hardly expect again to be able to refuel peacefully at sea. He would continue the operation with his two capital ships only. *Hipper* and the destroyers were ordered back to Trondheim.

He had no intention, however, of proceeding with Operation Juno as originally envisaged. No reports had come in as to the situation round Harstad and Narvik, and shrewdly he suspected that there was little there to report. Meanwhile, the two aircraft-carriers to the northward, Britain's most valuable warships, were a prize which could not be ignored.

Giving up the vain search for the convoy to the southward, he turned back on a northerly course. At 4 o'clock in the afternoon, had he still had a scouting aircraft aloft, there would have been sighted a bare eighty miles to the north-west of him a solitary cruiser, the *Devonshire*. Her destruction, which must have followed, resulting in the death or capture of the King of Norway and his entire Government, would have had political consequences difficult to over-estimate, doubtless inflicting a crippling blow to Britain's naval reputation in the eyes of all the world.

But it was not to be. The fates had decreed another encounter equally tragic but of less far-reaching consequences. Group 2, the last of Lord Cork's evacuation fleet, had cleared the Norwegian coast during the day, escorted by the *Ark Royal*, whose reconnaissance aircraft were scouting ahead and fighters giving protection above, the *Southampton*, carrying Lord Cork and Generals Auchinleck and Béthouart, the *Coventry* and five destroyers. The *Glorious*, having embarked the Gladiators and Hurricanes, was largely ineffective for flying operations. Her hangars were cluttered with the Hurricanes and Gladiators, whose wings, unlike those of the Fleet Air Arm aircraft, did not fold. Movement of her own reduced complement of aircraft — one squadron of Skuas and half a squadron of Swordfish — was thus greatly hampered. When, furthermore, her captain reported that she was too short of fuel for the high-speed steaming required for flying aircraft, on and off, it was decided to detach her to make her way home independently, escorted by the destroyers *Ardent* and *Acasta*.

Thus, at 3.45 on the afternoon of that day, June 8th, a masthead came into sight to the eastward from the German battlecruisers which turned at once towards it at full speed. The unmistakable silhouette of an aircraft carrier came quickly up over the horizon, and at 4.30 the 11-inch guns opened fire at a range of nearly fourteen miles — far beyond the range of the 4.7-inch guns of the British ships. The *Glorious* turned away at her best speed, but full speed was not immediately available, and she could not outdistance her pursuers. Her signals reporting the enemy were at once jammed by the watchful radio operators in the *Gneisenau*.

Making undisturbed target practice, it was not long before the Germans scored their first hit as a shell plunged into the carrier's thin-skinned, unarmoured hull, burst in the forward upper hangar and set ablaze the Hurricanes stowed there. The fire spreading through the hangar made it impossible for the Swordfish aircraft or their torpedoes — the carrier's only defence — to be got ready. For a time the smokescreens laid by the two destroyers gave her a respite, but at 5 o'clock a shell hit square on the bridge putting her out of control. When a further devastating hit was scored aft, the *Glorious* was doomed. The order was given to abandon ship, and at 5.40 she sank.

Meanwhile, the *Ardent* and *Acasta*, while continuing to screen the carrier with their smoke, had been boldly trying to reduce the odds in this one-sided fight by attacking with their torpedoes. The *Ardent* had been the first to turn back through the smoke to fire, but though her torpedoes had caused the enemy to sheer off to avoid them and so gave *Glorious* a brief respite, she had been met by an overwhelming blast of accurate gunfire which tore her apart, capsized her and sent her to the bottom.

By now the *Glorious* was seen to be sinking. Commander C. E. Glasfurd, captain of the *Acasta*, would have been justified in making good his escape, but he decided otherwise. Against all the wildest probabilities, his heroism was to achieve a result which may well have saved the British fleet from an even more resounding calamity. The story has been told by the sole survivor of the *Acasta*, Leading Seaman C. Carter:

'On board our ship, what a deathly calm, hardly a word spoken, the ship was now steaming full speed away from the enemy. Then came a host of orders, prepare all smoke floats, hose-pipes connected up, various other jobs were prepared. We were still steaming away from the enemy, and making smoke, and all our smoke floats had been set going. The Captain then had this message passed to all positions: "You may think we are running away from the enemy, we are not, our chummy ship has sunk, the *Glorious* is sinking, the least we can do is make a show, good luck to you all." We then altered course into our own smokescreen. I had the order stand by to fire tubes 6 and 7. We then came out of the smokescreen, altered course to starboard firing our torpedoes from the port side. It was then I had my first glimpse of the enemy, to be honest it appeared to me to be a large one and a small one, and we were very close. I fired my two torpedoes from my tubes, the foremost tubes fired theirs, we were all watching results. I'll never forget that cheer that went up; on the port bow of one of the ships a yellow flash and a great column of smoke and water shot up from her. We knew we had hit, personally I could not see how we could have missed so close as we were. The enemy never fired a shot at us, I feel they must have been very surprised. After we had fired our torpedoes we went back into our own smokescreen, altered course again to starboard. "Stand by to fire remaining torpedoes"; and this time as soon as we poked our nose out of the smokescreen, the enemy let us have it. A shell hit the engine-room, killed my tubes' crew, I was blown to the after end of the tubes, I must have been knocked out for a while, because when I came to, my arm hurt me; the ship had stopped with a list to port. Here is something believe it or believe it not. I climbed back into the control seat, I see those two ships, I fired the remaining torpedoes, no one told me to, I guess I was raving mad. God alone knows why I fired them but I did. The *Acasta*'s guns were firing the whole time, even firing with a list on the ship. The enemy then hit us several times, but one big explosion took place right aft. I have often wondered whether the enemy hit us with a torpedo, in any case it seemed to lift the ship out of the water. At last the Captain gave orders to abandon ship. I will always remember the Surgeon-Lieutenant (H. J. Stammer, RNVR), his first ship, his first action. Before I jumped over the side, I saw him still attending to the wounded, a hopeless task, and when I was in the water I saw the Captain leaning over the bridge, take a cigarette from a case and light it. We shouted to him to come on our raft, he waved Goodbye and good luck — the end of a gallant man.'

Seldom can a more gallant action have been fought than that of C. E. Glasfurd; seldom can such desperate valour in a forlorn hope have had such important consequences. The torpedo which struck the *Scharnhorst* aft (not on her bow as Leading Seaman Carter described) killed two officers and forty-six ratings, flooded her centre and starboard engine rooms, reducing her speed to twenty knots and put her after turret out of action. The German Commander-in-Chief shaped course at once for Trondheim to get the *Scharnhorst* to safety. The way home was cleared for the immensely valuable convoys — Group 2 and the slow convoy — to make their way unscathed to England, an outcome which could hardly have emerged if the *Acasta*'s torpedo had not found its mark.

The jamming of the *Glorious*' radio had been so successfully accomplished that nowhere in the British Fleet was it yet appreciated that a German squadron was at sea. Only in the *Devonshire* 100 miles to the westward was a garbled, incomplete reference received to 'two pocket battleships'. Vice-Admiral Cunningham, thinking of his so important passengers, decided that this was insufficient cause to break wireless silence and perhaps betray his position to the enemy.

Not until the hospital *Atlantis* met the *Valiant* early on June 9th, as the battleship was steaming northwards to meet Group 2, did any hint of the enemy activities reach the Commander-in-Chief. Only then, when the threat had in fact evaporated, were the capital ships of the Home Fleet directed to cover the returning convoys. Sir Charles Forbes in his flagship *Rodney* with the *Renown*, which had been recalled from its wild-goose chase by the Admiralty on the day before, left Scapa and headed north, while the *Repulse* still in Icelandic waters with two cruisers and three destroyers was similarly ordered to join the convoys.

But the danger was already over. Marschall's squadron were all at Trondheim during the 9th where at last he received firm news of the British evacuation. In spite of this he was ordered to sea again on the 10th with *Gneisenau* and *Hipper* to continue the operations. Having a clearer picture of the situation than the Naval Staff and guessing that all targets were by now out of his reach, the Commander-in-Chief persevered only until the night of the 10th when he turned back for Trondheim.

The loss of one of the few carriers available to the British Fleet in those, the darkest days of the war, was calamitous indeed. In addition there had been an appalling loss of life from the three ships. The German Admiral, anxious to get his damaged ship to port, had not tarried to rescue survivors. A number had succeeded in reaching life floats but as hour followed hour the cold of the northern waters took a steady toll. One float which twenty-two officers and men had managed to board had only four remaining by the next morning.

During the 9th, hopes were roused in the survivors when a British cruiser was sighted five miles away, and again when two aircraft from the *Ark Royal* passed overhead. Both ship and aircraft failed to see them. Not until 3 o'clock on the morning of the 11th did a Norwegian steamer, the *Borgund*, find and rescue three officers and thirty-five ratings from the *Glorious*, and the solitary survivor, Leading Seaman Carter, from the *Acasta*. They were landed in The Faeroes. Another Norwegian ship picked up five from the *Glorious*, landing them in Norway where, together with two men from the *Ardent*, picked up by a German seaplane, they were made prisoners of war; 1474 naval officers and ratings and forty-one RAF personnel, including nearly all the pilots of the Gladiators and Hurricanes who had made such valiant efforts to get their aircraft aboard the carrier, had lost their lives.

The disaster to British arms from the loss of the *Glorious* did not by any means satisfy Grand-Admiral Raeder. Admiral Marschall had failed to carry out his orders to penetrate the fiords and attack the Allied shipping thought to be assembled there. The Naval Staff disagreed with his (correct) appreciation that he would have found the Vaagsfiord and Ofotfiord empty. The Commander-in-Chief's disregard of his operation orders and of the signal disapproving of his change of plan was unreasonably held against him. The Naval Staff were on surer ground, however, in criticising the Commander-in-Chief's tactical handling of his ships during the action which permitted a single destroyer, in broad daylight, to get a torpedo home into the *Scharnhorst*. With this undoubted tactical blunder as an excuse, the Chief of the Naval Staff felt justified in removing Admiral Marschall from his command, relieving him by the ill-fated Vice-Admiral Lütjens.

Operation Juno was to cost the Germans still more. The submarine *Clyde* was waiting for Lütjens on June 29th when he took the *Gneisenau* and *Hipper* to sea from Trondheim for a foray towards Iceland to distract British attention from the damaged *Scharnhorst*, which started her journey home at the same time. A torpedo struck the *Gneisenau*, so damaging her that she was, like her sister battle-cruiser, to be out of action for many months to come.

On the British side, there were also criticisms and recriminations directed at the organisation which allowed the *Glorious* to sail alone and inadequately protected in a condition in which she was incapable of providing for her own defence. Complacency, bred from the long immunity from attack of ships running to and from Norway during the campaign, had undoubtedly grown to dangerous proportions. But the situation of divided authority arising out of the appointment of an officer, greatly senior to the Commander-in-Chief, Home Fleet, to command an operation inside the area of the Home Fleet Command was partly responsible. For this the Admiralty could not escape blame. It is difficult to imagine the Commander-in-Chief dissipating his scanty force of capital ships on a wild-goose chase based on such flimsy evidence as the *Prunella*'s report if he had felt directly responsible for the safety of the Narvik expedition throughout its return passage. Lord Cork's flag continued to fly in the *Southampton* until midnight June 9th/10th. Until it was struck, the responsibility was his. The ships he needed were under the command of an officer junior to him who was being constrained by the Admiralty to give his prior attention to the danger of a possible invasion of the British Isles.

With perhaps a more realistic acceptance of the part which chance must always play in naval operations, blame was not directly brought home to any of the authorities concerned in the British Fleet.

CHAPTER 18

As the Union Flag of Admiral of the Fleet, the Earl of Cork and Orrery, fluttered down from the masthead of the *Southampton*, the untidy, sprawling combined operation known as the Norwegian Campaign came to its unsatisfactory conclusion. It was possible to estimate the profit and loss resulting from it.

A defeat it had been, most certainly. Being on perhaps too small a scale to merit description as a disaster, it was not transformed in the eyes of the British public into a heroic episode as was the catastrophe of Dunkirk. Like Dunkirk, however, British sea power had succeeded in blunting the edge of military defeat — defeat which history seems to show as inevitable in the first clash between a democracy and a dictatorship. The Royal and Merchant Navies had successfully withdrawn the outclassed and ill-equipped armies, albeit almost weaponless, behind the barrier of sea to reform, re-equip and above all to train so that they might, in the fullness of time, return to face the armies of Germany on equal terms.

It was no disgrace that British troops, many of them half trained Territorial regiments and all of them hopelessly deficient in the weapons of modern war, ill-equipped and unprepared for operations in Arctic conditions and subjected to complete enemy air superiority, were defeated by the specially trained mountain troops of Germany, many of whom had been sent to study the terrain before the war as 'tourists'.

That the Guards Brigade appeared deficient in leadership and resolution in comparison with the French troops at Narvik cannot be denied but it must be said in their defence that the

French troops were Chasseurs-Alpins, presumably inured to some extent to bitter weather conditions such as were found in Norway, or Foreign Legionnaires, perhaps the toughest trained soldiers in the world and permanently on active service.

So much for the military aspect of the campaign on which this book has touched but briefly. From the naval angle there is much to deplore; the misreading of the intelligence available, which permitted the German naval units, wide open to attack by greatly superior forces, to throw the assault troops ashore unmolested at every key position on the coast; and the unfortunate intervention by the Admiralty to alter or forestall dispositions by their sea commanders.

The German Navy, displaying the skill, resolution and ruthlessness demanded of it, secured for Hitler a strategic success of immense significance in the prosecution of the naval war, one which was to cost the Allies dear when the business of supplying Russia by the Arctic route came into being. But in doing so they had been made to pay heavily. The total loss of one heavy cruiser, two light cruisers and ten destroyers and the disabling for many months of both their battle-cruisers and a pocket battleship, left them with but one heavy cruiser, two light cruisers and four destroyers fit for action. The German Navy was thus left in no position to dispute control of the Narrow Seas, an essential preliminary to Hitler's grandiose schemes for the invasion of England.

On the British side even the destruction of the *Glorious* did not lift the total losses beyond the safe margin which the Allies required at that time, though in addition two old cruisers, one sloop and nine destroyers had been sunk and six cruisers, two sloops and eight destroyers damaged.

The majority of these casualties had been caused by air attack and it was this which gave the Royal Navy its first insight into an aspect of naval warfare which should have been clear much earlier. No longer could the ships of even a greatly superior naval power operate off the coasts of an enemy without fighter cover or at least suitable gun armament with which to drive off dive-bombers. That the Navy was taken by surprise arose from a number of causes. Some of them stemmed from an inherent conservatism among the senior officers of the naval hierarchy who, brought up to believe in the big gun as the queen of battles, could not be persuaded that aircraft could not be mastered by it. All, however, were the result, direct or indirect, of the disastrous political decision which in 1918 handed over the Navy's own Air Service, lock, stock and barrel to the newly-formed Royal Air Force.

The consequences were most unfortunate. As all air pilots for some years afterwards belonged to another service, there were no senior naval officers who knew anything about flying or the characteristics and capabilities of aircraft. Similarly there were no airmen with up-to-date knowledge of the defensive capabilities of modern warships. Thus a generation of senior naval officers grew up who looked on aeroplanes as flimsy, unreliable machines and the men who flew them as lightheaded, if daring, fools. High flying bombers would rarely hit a ship particularly if she were free to manoeuvre, they believed, while the noisily impressive 2-pounder pom-pom would take care of the dive-bomber.

The senior Royal Air Force officers, on the other hand, pinned their faith in attack on the high bomber, being encouraged in this belief by the demonstrations in America of the famous General Mitchell. In defence they correctly trusted in fighter aircraft, but failed to develop a high performance fighter for the fleet.

Each side was right in one particular but neither could convince the other. Consequently when war came, the Royal Air Force, called upon to strike at enemy squadrons discovered at sea or in harbour, invariably failed to hit them, while the Royal Navy, possessing no efficient fighter aircraft or close-range automatic weapons, lay open to the dive-bombers of the Luftwaffe.

This brief digression into a very controversial subject only touches the fringes of it. Nevertheless, it focuses upon the main reason why the campaign in Norway was a failure — the absence of defence against air attack.

Later in the war, the Bofors and Oerlikon automatic guns mounted in warships were to drive the Stuka from over the seas even before the construction of aircraft carriers in large numbers and the provision of high-performance fleet fighters won back air superiority from the Luftwaffe. In North Africa, at Salerno, in the South of France, it was the presence of fighter aircraft taking off from the decks of carriers that gave air defence to ships and troops alike until shore-based fighters of the Allied Air Forces could establish themselves. In Norway it was their absence which made victory impossible. The knowledge that every aircraft seen or heard is an enemy, seeking whom he may devour, takes the heart out of the sailor or soldier weary with ceaseless hours on watch, sore-eyed with sleepless scanning of the skies and ill-equipped to hit back. Even the occasional Skua, cross-bred fighter-dive-bomber, from the handful in the carriers working off shore, brought a lift to the heart and new hope as it zoomed overhead. It was sufficient to show what a difference regular patrols of proper fighters would have made.

Finally, when Allied deficiencies on land, sea and air have been thus very briefly assessed, there remains the almost total absence of any provision or training for a combined operation such as the Norwegian Campaign. After two months of combined operations up and down the coast, when every form of local craft had to be pressed into service for landings and sea transport, only three assault landing craft had reached the scene of operations. The dismal story of the Gladiator squadron at Lesjaskog indicated a total lack of preparation for rapid transfer overseas. The lack of a Supreme Commander in the early stages of the campaign in the north and the contradictory orders given to the naval and military commanders were blunders which should have been avoided.

These are but a few of the grievous shortcomings which betrayed themselves during the Norwegian Campaign.

When all is said and done, even if the thoroughness and foresight shown by the Germans had been matched by the Allies, and the German advance northward had been held south of Trondheim, it must remain uncertain whether, with France overrun and German soldiers lining the southern shore of the English Channel, forces could have been spared to hold northern Norway. It is known now, and the belief was expressed at the time by Sir Charles Forbes and others, that in the absence of control of the sea by the enemy, an invasion of this country was never feasible. But to many the threat seemed very real at the time and it would have taken bold war leaders to have maintained an army in Norway with its necessary naval and air support when every man, ship and aircraft might have been needed to defend the home country.

For the rest of the war Norway was to lie under the conqueror's heel. It was not an unalloyed advantage to Hitler.

Ever fearful that Britain was planning to invade Norway again, he was forced to maintain a considerable and inactive army there. For the same reason his warships, which were to be conserved against the day when invasion was attempted, were so barred from taking any risks in other encounters with British ships that they allowed themselves to be defeated again and again by greatly inferior forces. Nevertheless, it cannot be disguised that German possession of the whole Norwegian coastline for the rest of the war greatly increased the burden on the over-extended forces of the Royal Navy. Its loss to the Allies was a grievous blow.

There were, however, certain very valuable invisible gains to the British. The sloth and complacency engendered by the 'phoney war' were swept away and, at a moderate cost in casualties, the inefficiencies and defects of the fighting Services were starkly revealed and lessons in the facts of modern war thrust home.

In the final assessment, perhaps the individual acts of heroism which won three naval Victoria Crosses in the two months of the campaign, and the cheerful endurance and courage against great odds of countless other sailors, soldiers and airmen, made the most valuable collective contribution.

ACKNOWLEDGMENTS

No account of the Norwegian campaign from the naval angle, such as this book sets out to be, could have been attempted without the general assistance so willingly given to the author by the Historical Section of the Admiralty headed by Lieutenant-Commander Peter Kemp, to whom the author tenders his most sincere thanks.

Besides the reports and dispatches made available to him, the author has taken advantage of the excellent *Official History of the Campaign in Norway* by Professor T. K. Derry (HM Stationery Office), to paint the broad picture, and is grateful to the Controller of HM Stationery Office for permission to use the seven maps reproduced. Two other books have helped to fill in certain details.

In *Seven Assignments* by Brigadier Dudley Clarke (Jonathan Cape), the conditions under which our soldiers had to fight are vividly portrayed. The situation in Narvik during the long fight for its capture is also well described by Theodor Broch who was its Mayor, in his book *The Mountains Wait* (Michael Joseph).

A NOTE TO THE READER

If you have enjoyed this book enough to leave a review on **Amazon** and **Goodreads**, then we would be truly grateful.

Sapere Books

Sapere Books is an exciting new publisher of brilliant fiction and popular history.

To find out more about our latest releases and our monthly bargain books visit our website:
saperebooks.com

Printed in Great Britain
by Amazon